THE SOUL OF THE PERSON

THE SOUL OF THE PERSON

A Contemporary Philosophical Psychology

ADRIAN J. REIMERS

The Catholic University of America Press
Washington, D.C.

LIBRARY OF CONGRESS CATALOGING-IN-PUBLICATION DATA
Reimers, Adrian J.
    The soul of the person: a contemporary philosophical psychology /
Adrian J. Reimers.
        p. cm.
Includes bibliographical references (p.   ) and index.
ISBN-13: 978-0-8132-2719-1 (pbk : alk. paper)
ISBN-10:   0-8132-2719-4 (pbk : alk. paper)
1. Soul—Christianity.   2. Christianity—Psychology.   I. Title.
BT741.3.R45 2006
128´.1—dc22
                                                    2005021902

Contents

Acknowledgments

As is the case with any scholarly piece of writing, this author owes an intellectual debt to colleagues, students, and friends who have inspired, corrected, and suggested thoughts that eventually find expression in the finished work. Among these friends are certainly Thomas Aquinas, Charles Peirce, and Pope John Paul II—as well as Plato, Aristotle, Augustine, and others. Though no longer alive, these have left enough of themselves in their writings that we can turn to them still for help as we think through the hard questions. Among living thinkers who have contributed to my development of this work, I specifically thank two colleagues here at Notre Dame: David Burrell, C.S.C., who patiently read through the earlier drafts and offered invaluable advice, and Paul Weithman, who alerted me especially to my earlier lack of clarity in my expression of the relationships among habits, signs, and mental events. I thank also the reviewers from the Catholic University of America Press, whose keen analyses and critiques resulted in my significantly improving several key arguments and in the sharpening of important conceptual distinctions. Their comments have contributed to this being a much better book than the original manuscript was.

More than anyone else, however, this book has been made possible by the contributions and sacrifices of my wife, Marie Reimers. First, to share a life, build a home, bring children into the world, and converse every day founds a rich experience of what it means to be human—and in addressing the question of the soul we address what it means to be human. Second, she has been supportive of my efforts to complete this work, carrying the larger share of our financial burden and putting up with my moments of abstraction and absent-mindedness. But third—and especially important—she has served as a kind of philosophical conscience for me, not only in her sharing in my life and in our common project of building a home and raising a family, but especially in her professional work. Marie founded and runs a company to provide case management services to the developmentally disabled. She has even invited me to share in her work (as her part-time financial officer and clerical helper). Her company serves those whose bodies and brains do not work right—those whose IQ may measure as low as 9 or 10, or those with autism whose sense perception is so distorted that an ordinary (to normal people) sound may be acutely painful and send them into paroxysms of anger, or those retarded persons whose naivete leaves them vulnerable to exploitation by financial or sexual predators. In working with such persons, she and her close colleagues must also confront the fact that many—perhaps most—normal people, including many who control resources that her clients need access to, do not want the developmentally disabled in their world and treat them as problems, which is to say, as objects, rather than as persons. I say that Marie has been a philosophical conscience to me, because whatever I may want to say philosophically about the human being, about the human soul and the manifestations of human rationality, must apply to these people, whom nature or misfortune has deprived of properly functioning brains or nervous systems. Her work keeps me real.

Therefore, in gratitude and with great respect, I dedicate this present work to Marie Reimers, Qualified Mental Retardation Professional, my wife, mother of our four children, and true friend.

Preface

The Christian scholar lives in two different worlds. These are not simply separate spheres that we treat at different times, compartmentalizing our thoughts and reactions according to the needs of the hour. The worlds we live in are incompatible, founded on principles that are mutually contradictory. The "conflict between religion and science" has become a common shorthand for this contradiction, although the true contradiction does not lie in the respective natures of faith in God and disciplined inquiry into the natures of things around us. Rather the conflict goes much deeper. What we have seen since the Enlightenment is the development of a set of concepts, a model of understanding that is fundamentally incompatible with those underlying Christian belief (and, indeed, most other traditional religions). These new concepts and models have profoundly affected not only the way we think, but also the way we live. In his personal reflections, Pope John Paul II wrote:

How else can we explain the increasing gap between the rich North and the ever poorer South? Who is responsible for this? Man is responsible—man, ideologies, and philosophical systems. I would say that *responsibility lies with the struggle against God, the systematic elimination of all that is Christian.* This struggle has to a large degree dominated thought and life in the West for three centuries.[1] [emphasis in original]

1. John Paul II [Karol Wojtyła], *Crossing the Threshold of Hope* (New York: Alfred Knopf, 1994), 133.

The difference between these intellectual worlds is sharply illustrated by how each understands human nature. The one is the world of mechanistic materialism, the world of scientific reductionism, in which the human is nothing more than a variant on the animal, in which life arose from the chance interactions of carbon-based molecules, and human life from the chance variations in the genes of less-complex species. The thinking, desiring, imagining, willing human being is nothing more than a complex biological mechanism, whose inner life reflects (or perhaps simply is) a state of the brain and nervous system. The notion that there is something special about human beings, something distinctive that makes us different from all other beings on earth, is rejected as unscientific, a subjectively useful belief, perhaps, but one without objective foundation in established fact. The philosophical literature (especially in mind-brain theory), the scientific literature, and the semi-popular media for the educated—such as *Scientific American* and the documentaries of PBS—express a vision of the human being as simply an evolutionary development, no more and no less than so much matter in motion, albeit motion interesting to us.

The other world is that which we enter on Sunday or the Sabbath, and when our humanity is affirmed or challenged by marriage, a birth, or death. It is a world in which each of us stands before God, as sinners no doubt, but also as objects of his mercy and love, a world in which God himself commands us to love him and each other. In this other world, our actions have eternal significance and eternal consequences. Religious faiths teach that there is a something about us, a soul or spiritual aspect, by means of which we can approach God. In this conception, God created the world with human beings in mind. Christians affirm that the human being is worth infinitely more than the largest galaxy, is of greater weight than any black hole—of such great value that God himself became one of them to redeem them. This religious conception is based on the biblical statement that human beings are created in the image of God. "So God created man in his own image, in the image of God he created him; male and female he created them" (Gen. 1:27 RSV). In his writings and speeches on the human person, Pope John Paul II, formerly professor of ethics at the Catholic University of Lublin, Poland, appealed regularly—indeed, thematically—to this conception of the human being as the "image of God": Repeatedly this philosopher and pope emphasized that to understand human beings and the human condition aright, we must start with the notion that the human being reflects not just the nature of which he is part but also the God who brought him to being.

It is this idea that we want to explore in this present work. The text from Genesis is divine revelation and, to be understood properly, must be taken as such; that is, it expresses something beyond what we are capable of knowing through unaided human powers of rational investigation. To examine biblical revelation is the theologian's job. But as a philosopher, one may ask: Is this even reasonable? In the light of what we know about the physical world and our own biological and physical nature, does it even make sense to talk in terms of "image of God"? Philosophers of earlier ages situate this image in a spiritual soul. Is there such a thing? Or is this only so much wishful thinking, a comforting metaphor for the lonely denizens of a meaningless universe? For if scientific materialism's worldview is right, then it is impossible to regard human being as the image of God in any way but as metaphor.

While the Christian who practices science may reconcile his or her presence in both worlds, taking with a grain of salt the anti-religious sentiments of his more famous colleagues and keeping discreetly silent during discussions in the church basement, the conceptions of the world themselves cannot be reconciled. As the writings of Peter Singer, Robert Edwards, and Francis Crick,[2] among others, make clear, how we relate to those on the fringes of human society and activity—the unborn and newborn, the very aged and the mentally infirm—depends decisively on what kind of beings these persons are, on whether they even count as human persons. Inspired by the conception of the inherent dignity of every human being, the United Nations and increasing numbers of countries around the world affirm fundamental human rights. By the same token, however, it is argued—precisely on the ground of a scientifically inspired metaphysics—that in the name of those rights, unborn human beings may be aborted, the infirm elderly killed by medical professionals, and

2. See, for example, Peter Singer, *Practical Ethics,* 2nd ed. (New York: Cambridge University Press, 1993); Robert Edwards, *Life Before Birth: Reflections on the Embryo Debate* (New York: Basic Books, 1989); Francis Crick, *The Astonishing Hypothesis: The Scientific Search for the Soul* (New York: Charles Scribner & Sons, 1994); and Daniel Voll, "Soul Searching with Francis Crick," *Omni* 16, no. 5 (February 1994): 46–82.

the poor submit to government sponsored sterilization or contraception. Whether such programs are acceptable or not depends on what a human being is, what its nature is. Religious believers and thinkers appeal to the existence of a *soul* in virtue of which the human is superior to other entities in the material world, including the animals. It is the status of this soul that I investigate in this work.

This book has been brewing for about five years; that is the period during which I have been actively writing text for it. In another way, it is also the product of a life of thinking. As a youngster I announced to my parents that "when I grow up" I would be a priest and a scientist, and after graduating from the University of Notre Dame with my B.S. in mathematics, I entered a Roman Catholic seminary . . . and left after three months. In my scientific studies I experienced first-hand with delight that the oscillation of a spring can be described by integrating a simple function, and with amazement that $e^{\pi i} + 1 = 0$.[3] I was able to share the scientists' wonder, to see how complex physical phenomena can be reduced to and explained in terms of relatively few mathematically expressed principles. And I was also devout, to the point of taking serious steps toward a life in service to the Church as a priest. From these two serious interests sprung an inner dialogue. The loyal churchman within is embarrassed by the Galileo affair and would, did honesty not prevent, make excuses for the cardinals and the pope. But even more troubling are the implications of the sciences, for if Newton was right then how could it be that my religion—or any belief at all—be possible? If the world of science is governed by strict mathematical laws, where is there room for human freedom, for grace or love? It was long a puzzle to me. And eventually came the truly troubling, indeed, dismaying discovery that many in the scientific community rejoice in this, taking pride in having overcome religious and folk "superstitions." For while my professors and friends in the sciences may have been believers, it became clear that the leaders of the scientific community, the best and the brightest, those whose views set the agenda, are often hostile to

3. For the nonmathematicians: This simple equation elegantly combines the fundamental values in mathematics: 0 and 1, the identity values under addition and multiplication, respectively; e, which is the base of the natural logarithms; π, the ratio of the diameter of a circle to its circumference, and i, the square root of -1. That this equation actually holds true is a wonderful mathematical fact.

religious faith, and not only that, but to the notion that we human beings are anything other than so much matter in motion, governed only by the same laws that spin the galaxies and fuel its stars. In the end, it is not the believer but the scientist within that is embarrassed.

The book is the fruit of a conviction that science and the notion of a transcendent human nature are compatible, in other words, that the idea of a spiritual soul is reasonable and defensible, that within this scientifically knowable universe there can be—indeed are—beings that may admit of the expression "image of God." Indeed, without such a conception we cannot account for some obvious and important truths about ourselves and those we share our social lives with. The casual reader will recognize that this work is an effort to rethink St. Thomas Aquinas's account of the human soul as form of the human being. Aquinas lived about three centuries before the scientific revolution, and, although I am convinced his Aristotelianism fits better with contemporary science than is usually thought, a restatement in more contemporary terms of some fundamental physical and metaphysical principles is called for. The reader will also notice, therefore, a reliance on Charles Sanders Peirce's theory of habits as signs. Indeed, even where not explicit, the framework of Peirce's thought is present.

Finally, the work is significantly inspired by the thought of Pope John Paul II, whose conception of what it means to be human deserves much closer attention than has been given it to date. In his pre-papal philosophical work and especially in his speeches and writings as Pope, this scholar and churchman has sketched out what he calls an "adequate anthropology," one characterized by an affirmation of the meaningfulness of the human body itself and the ability of the human person to transcend temporal goods precisely through the body. A Thomist, John Paul II took personal human experience as his "indispensable" starting point.[4] This present work takes up his challenge and governing principle, seeking the roots of science and religious faith—as well as the full richness of human life and experience as a whole—in human experience.

The governing conception of this work is that to be human is to be rational, by which should be understood that everything about the human

---

4. Karol Wojtyła [John Paul II], *Person and Community: Selected Essays* (New York, San Francisco: Peter Lang, 1993), 193.

being is—or can be—an expression of reason. We are not souls inside irrational or non-rational bodies. The entire human being is a rational being. It is this rationality that constitutes the distinctiveness of the human person. In arguing this, I follow John Paul II in rejecting consciousness as the foundation of the ontological supremacy and distinctiveness of human beings vis-à-vis the natural order. The human being is rational animal. Or, as Peirce has put it: "The mind is a sign, developing according to the laws of inference."[5]

5. Charles Sanders Peirce, *Collected Papers* (Cambridge: Harvard University Press, 1965), 5.313.

PART ONE THE CENTRAL ISSUE

CHAPTER 1

The Status of the Question

To ask about human nature is to ask about the soul. Or one might say it is to ask about the status of this term *soul*. We speak of the soul. But what does *soul* mean? Generally, this term has to do with what makes us distinctive as humans. We speak of the most intimate, most human aspect of ourselves as being expressed by this term, *soul*. The science of psychology, which investigates how humans act, comes from the Greek *psyche*—or soul. Psychology is, hence, the science of the soul. At issue then is the status, the meaning of this term *soul*. Is it a "folk expression," as some have suggested, a metaphor? Or does it refer to something real?

The thesis of this work is that because the human being is a rational being, the soul is real, that this term *soul* refers to the spiritual basis of human nature, a basis that can be reduced neither to the material constitution of the body nor to mechanisms governing its behavior. Although the human being is an integral whole, the soul can be distinguished conceptually from the body and its functioning. To put it more explicitly, the human being cannot be reduced to its physical or biological components, for beyond the laws discoverable by the natural sciences, the human body is structured and governed by a rational principle, called the soul. Further, we shall maintain that after death the soul can be separated from the body and continue to exist.

A NATURE DIVIDED

To be human is to have an inner life. While living in the physical world of things, the human being lives also in a world of imaginations, thought, wishes, dreams, and projects. The adolescent in poverty dreams of a future secure home. The defeated candidate plans for his comeback. We understand this inner life to be free from the constraints of the physical world. The German song has it: "Denn meine Gedanken zerreißen die Schranken. . . . Die Gedanken sind frei."[1] The resentful subject or employee or slave may have to yield his body and property, but not his consent. Indeed, St. Augustine made precisely this point with regard to the Christian women who were raped during the sack of Rome. The violation of their bodies need not have implicated their souls.[2] In this freedom of our thoughts we find a reflection, if not the source, of the freedom of our will.

On the other hand, we experience the constraints of our bodies even on our minds. Certainly the experience of addiction, whether to nicotine, alcohol, or drugs, calls seriously into question the extent of our freedom. "Tomorrow I'm going to stop" is rightly dismissed by the chain smoker's friends as so much wishful thinking—good intentions paving an unintended road. In recent years the mental health community has taught us all that our moods and even thoughts are profoundly affected by the chemical interactions within our brains. The experience of falling in love has recently been attributed to increased endorphins in the brain.[3] Perhaps our deepest emotions are nothing more than the effects of biochemical interactions of which we are not directly aware. If I am who I feel myself to be—if the human person's innermost self is identified with his consciousness—then this self seems to dissolve under the microscope of biochemistry.

With his dialectical materialism, Marx raises a further concern. For Marx, the imaginations of the mind are but the outgrowth of the sensuous, physical being in the world, specifically in the nexus of production.[4]

1. "For my thoughts tear down the [prison] walls . . . Thoughts are free."

2. Augustine, *The City of God*. In *Great Books of the Western World*, 18. (Chicago, Toronto, London: Encyclopedia Britannica, 1952), Book I, chap. 16–18.

3. Janet Shibley Hyde and John D. DeLamater, *Understanding Human Sexuality*, 7th ed. (Boston, New York, San Francisco: McGraw Hill, 2000), 352.

4. Karl Marx, *Thesen über Feuerbach*. In Marx und Engels, *Werke*, Bd. 3, (Berlin 1978,

Human consciousness is class consciousness. In one obvious respect, Marx has been discredited: Free-market economies have prospered and Marxist regimes have collapsed. In another respect, however, his insight lives on. The capitalist tools of advertising and democracy's use of propaganda techniques attempt to replace thinking with response to images—the protestations of their practitioners, that these media provide information for decision making, notwithstanding. The truth we too often hate to face is that what we think is, in fact, what we are expected to think or feel or believe. What we value is often what we are conditioned to value.

In short, we human beings experience ourselves, individually and communally, as divided, disintegrated—free in our thoughts and dreams, but constrained by the biological, chemical, and social structures we find ourselves in. The challenge before us is to determine where the truth lies, to integrate the freedom and the determinations of our being, to reconcile (if possible) the bodily with the spiritual—to determine, in short, whether the human person is some *one thing* and what kind of thing that is.

Scientific materialism

Scientific understanding, which has given rise to fresh discoveries and important therapies for illnesses mental and physical, puts common understanding of our nature into serious question and directly challenges many philosophical conceptions of human nature. Since the program of empirical science is to determine the properties of things according to their interactions with their environments, human intelligence *must* be accounted for in terms of such interactions. These properties can be stated in terms of general laws, which ideally—and indeed ultimately—are to be expressed in mathematical terms. Therefore, to determine what are the characteristics of the human being, the scientist must study both the interactions of the human being with other things in his environment and the components by which he is constituted. As a consequence, two important general trends within the sciences have exercised especially strong influence on our conception of human nature.

Marxists' Internet Archive), S. 533–5. http://www.marxists.org/deutsch/archiv/marx-engels/1845/thesen/thesfeue.htm. See especially Theses 1–3.

Evolutionary theories: the human as continuous with the animal.   In his *Descent of Man*, Charles Darwin proposes that human beings are the result of an evolutionary process driven by chance variations and the preservation of some variations by the mechanism of natural selection. This vision persists to the present day, even if Darwin's own account has long been superseded.[5] Biology understands the evolution of human beings to have resulted from a nondirected process of genetic modifications preserved (when advantageous) by natural selection. Two aspects of this process are worth noting here. First, the process is mechanical, not teleological. Even if one might say that the infant is directed or ordered toward becoming an adult, one cannot say that the existence of the trilobite or even the early hominid was ordered toward the appearance of human beings. Adulthood is the capstone and goal of the child's growth; human beings are not, however, nature's goal. Stephen Jay Gould writes, "Our impression that life evolves toward greater complexity is probably only a bias inspired by a parochial focus on ourselves."[6] Rather, chance genetic variations in particular kinds of environments resulted in erect, large-brained animals that could learn speech, tool-making, and the like. Second, as the outcome of the evolutionary mechanism, the human being is not radically different from or discontinuous with his animal cousins. Darwin was quite explicit on this,[7] and his successors agree. The human DNA differs from that of the chimpanzee by about 1 percent. The difference between human beings and the other animals is of degree, not of kind. Elephants are stronger than mice, and people are smarter than cats. Human beings do not occupy a higher position on the evolutionary ladder. Indeed, Dawkins[8] argues that this honor should go to the ubiquitous bacterium. Human beings are not special.

No scientist or philosopher can deny, of course, that the human intelligence differs dramatically from the animal. Indeed, socio-biologists ar-

5. See, for example, Colin Patterson, *Evolution* (Ithaca: Cornell University Press, 1978); Craig Stanford, *Significant Others: The Ape-Human Continuum and the Quest for Human Nature* (New York: Basic Books, 2001); and John R. Searle, *The Rediscovery of the Mind* (Cambridge, Mass., London: MIT Press, 1992), 24.

6. Stephen Jay Gould, "The Evolution of Life on Earth," *Scientific American*, (October 1994): 87. See also Richard Dawkins, "God's Utility Function," *Scientific American*, (Nov. 1995): 81.

7. Charles Darwin, *The Descent of Man*, vol.49 in *Great Books of the Western World*, Robert Hutchins and Mortimer Adler, eds. (Chicago: Encyclopedia Britannica, Inc., 1952), chap. 21.

8. Dawkins, "God's Utility Function."

gue that the capacity for language, which follows upon the superior intelligence, gave early human beings a crucial survival advantage—an advantage so great that they (we) have come to dominate all other species.[9] This intelligence has yielded the further happy fruit of artistic and cultural flourishing among humans. Shakespeare, DaVinci, and Mozart notwithstanding, however, the decisive point about intelligence and language is the survival advantage. Hannay sums this position up:

> Collectivities, institutions, languages, works of art, values, even such apparently abstract entities as numbers, may one day be construed as properties or relations of physical things. And as far as mind itself is concerned, the well-supported belief that human mentality has its origins in natural selection, and therefore must be grasped in terms of behavioural adaptation, supports an equation of the mind with some set of causal powers relevant for the control of the environment.[10]

So intelligence is in essence a tool to enable us to get around in the world. Just as the giraffe can see farther than the gerbil and the jay hawk than the giraffe, so the human being can "see" farther than the chimpanzee or the Neanderthal in that he can reason and infer, communicate, and accept communications. Intelligence is therefore on a par with perception and does not confer an ontological supremacy on one who has it.

To sum, from the perspective of evolutionary biology, to be human is to be nothing more than a particularly sophisticated kind of animal. *Soul*, if it means anything, has to do only with what one might think of himself, not with his essential constitution (a point to which we shall return later in this chapter).

Mind and brain: the human as a complex functioning system.   Complementary to evolutionary biology are the discoveries of neuroscience concerning the human brain and nervous system. Although to summarize the achievements of brain sciences would be impossible here, the significance of these studies for our present undertaking is relatively simple. Neuroscience suggests that the distinctively human can be accounted for in terms of

9. See John Horgan, "The New Social Darwinists," *Scientific American*, (October 1995), 174–181.

10. Alastair Hannay, *Human Consciousness* (London, New York: Routledge, 1990), 6.

the functioning of the brain and nervous system, that no "spiritual"agency is required if one understands how the brain is constructed and the neurons wired. The human being is a biological structure or organism of a particular kind whose properties, characteristics, and behavior are determined only by physical factors. Given the states of both the human organism and its environment, one can know how it will behave. To be sure, the human being is an extremely complex organism, its brain surpassing even the most sophisticated computers in complexity and adaptability, if not in speed. Likewise, the human environment is varied and complex, impinging upon the organism in a bewildering variety of ways. Given the variations among the structures of different human beings and the different ways their sensory apparatuses can receive and process information, it is not surprising that human behavior is so notoriously hard to predict. Furthermore, because human behavior results from the interplay of the organism and its environment, a commitment to scientific materialism is not ipso facto a commitment to one side of the nature-nurture debate. We may keep in mind that to determine the behavior of even so simple a physical system as the solar system, the scientist must rely on approximations and ignore minor influences from within and without the system.

According to the scientific model, human nature and behavior can be described and accounted for entirely according to physical factors. According to John Searle, we can find the roots of human behavior in the neuron firings within the brain and nervous system: "These variable rates of neuron firing in different neuronal circuits and different local conditions in the brain produce all of the variety of our mental life. The smell of a rose, the experience of the blue of the sky, the taste of onions, the thought of a mathematical formula: all of these are produced by variable rates of neuron firing."[11] Weinberg writes, "In principle, no obstacle stands in the way of explaining the *behavior*, of other people in terms of neurology and physiology and, ultimately, in terms of physics and history."[12] To know the state of the organism is to know what it is. To know this and the salient factors within its environment is to know what it will do. According to scientific materialism, there is no need to posit any spiritual, nonphysical, or immaterial entity to account for human existence and behavior. In par-

11. Searle, *Minds, Brains, and Science* (Cambridge: Harvard University Press, 1984), 9.
12. Stephen Weinberg, "Life in the Universe," *Scientific American*, (Oct. 1994), 47.

ticular, such "spiritual" activities and states as thought, desire, consciousness, and religious experience can eventually be accounted for in terms of the physical state of the organism in relation to its environment. The chief problem for the materialistic theory of mind, then, is to account for the apparent causal influence of mental events on overt bodily behavior. If an account of the operation of the brain and nervous system adequately explains human behavior, then what role does "mind" play? How can our conscious experience of trying or intending to act be said to determine what we will do? Why are some stimuli pleasant and others disgusting, some lovely and others ugly?

The strength of the materialist approach is that it rests upon a nexus of highly successful sciences, which are daily expanding our knowledge of the human brain and nervous system. We know now with great precision which parts of the brain govern vision, hearing, limb movement, imagination, and so on. Indeed, scientists can even identify which groups of cells control perception of shape, which of motion, and which of color.[13] Given its extremely high number of diversified cells with differing functions, the brain has an astonishingly complex structure. Although science is far from understanding this operation in full, even the present knowledge of brain structure suggests the following hypothesis: *The brain is a physical system different from other physical systems only in its degree of complexity, and what we call mind is simply the operation of this system.*[14]

If this hypothesis is true, then the very role of consciousness becomes acutely problematic. We each tend to identify our consciousness with our own causality: "It was no accident; I did it consciously." But such an identification seems to fly in the face of the scientific evidence. Sperry writes:

The common, naïve impression that we use the mind to initiate and control our physical actions has long been rejected almost universally in science, following the doctrine of scientific materialism, which predicates that a full account of brain behavior and reality is possible in terms purely physical.[15]

13. See, for example, Floyd E. Bloom, Arlyne Lazerson, and Laura Hofstadter, *Brain, Mind, and Behavior* (New York: W. H. Freeman & Co., 1985), chap. 3.

14. See Joseph LeDoux, *Synaptic Self: How Our Brains Become Who We Are* (New York: Viking, 2002).

15. Roger Wolcoll Sperry, "Consciousness and Causality," in *The Oxford Companion to the Mind,* ed. R. L. Gregory, (Oxford, New York: Oxford University Press, 1987), 164.

By its very nature, science disregards nonphysical entities and factors, even while allowing for significant rethinking of what a physical being might be. Thus, scientists will allow for the existence of such ghostly entities as quarks and neutrinos, extreme phenomena such as black holes and relativistic contraction of space, and counterintuitive things such as twenty-four-dimensional strings. Such entities can be allowed for by science because the behavior of other kinds of things seems to require them, and because physical tests can be constructed to detect them. Indeed, even such a pseudoscience as parapsychology could be accepted as a serious science if its methods and experiments can turn up the appropriate regularities of behavior that can justify the positing of the psychic entities it purports to investigate. That is, parapsychology needs to be able reliably to detect ghosts, to measure mental telepathy, and similar things before it can be accepted as a science. Let us also note, however, that any such entities that a science of parapsychology discovers will count as physical.[16]

A physical entity must behave according to physical laws. The scientific point is not only that a full scientific description of the human being will be complete and adequate to its subject, but also that any spiritual soul would be either ineffectual or redundant and therefore irrelevant. As commonly understood, the soul is what makes the human being think, choose, love, hate, fear, and desire. And it is what puts the body into motion according to those mental states. The farmer observes an eerie stillness on the prairie and then hears a distant roar. Calling to his wife, he throws open the storm cellar and exerts all his strength to gather children and dog into the shelter. What moved his arms and legs and voice? If we say it was the soul, then where did the soul get the energy it adds to the organic system that is his body?[17] How does it move the arms? Or, if we seat the soul in the brain, then how does the soul fire the neurons? If the soul has physical effects on the body, then it must have physical properties. This is not a new objection. Thomas Aquinas recognizes the same problem in considering whether the human soul is a physical body: "Further, between the mover and the moved there must be contact. But contact is only between bodies. Since,

---

16. D. M. Armstrong, *A Materialist Theory of the Mind* (New York: Routledge & Kegan Paul, 1968), 53.

17. Daniel Dennett, *Consciousness Explained* (Boston, Toronto, London: Little, Brown & Co., 1991), 33.

therefore, the soul moves the body, it seems that the soul must be a body."[18] D. M. Armstrong puts the issue starkly in his argument against nonmaterialist theories of mind in general:

It seems increasingly likely that all chemical and biological happenings are explicable in principle as particular applications of the laws of physics that govern nonchemical and nonbiological phenomena. Consider what this means for a non-Materialist theory of the mind. It means that the whole world studied by science contains nothing but physical things operating according to the laws of physics *with the exception of the mind*. [emphasis in original][19]

From a scientific point of view, the soul appears to be superfluous. Francis Crick writes, "A modern neurobiologist sees no need for the religious concept of a soul to explain the behavior of humans and other animals."[20] It is a folk expression, like "the setting of the sun," by which we express experiences that we cannot yet fully explain. Such notions as free will and consciousness become epiphenomenal and misleading. What we call the "mind" is really the brain and nervous system. Damasio writes: "I contend that the biological processes now presumed to correspond to mind processes in fact *are* mind processes." [emphasis in original][21] Patricia Smith Churchland summarizes the scientific position: "I am predicting that explanatory power, coherence and economy will favor the hypothesis that awareness *is* some pattern of activity in the neurons." [emphasis in original][22]

Philosophies of consciousness

If the scientific account is correct, then human beings have lost much that is important to us. Religion, unless reduced to myth and morals, is false. The notion of freedom is lost. A mother's tender, self-sacrificial love

---

18. Thomas Aquinas, *Summa Theologiae*, Ia, 75, 1, Obj. 3. Vols. 19–20 in *Great Books of the Western World* (Chicago, London, Toronto: Encyclopedia Britannica, 1952).

19. D. M. Armstrong, *A Materialist Theory of the Mind*, 49.

20. Francis Crick, *The Astonishing Hypothesis*, 6.

21. Antonio Damasio, "How the Brain Creates the Mind," *Scientific American*, (December 1999), 115.

22. Patricia Smith Churchland, "Can Neurobiology Teach Us Anything about Consciousness?" *Proceedings and Addresses of the American Philosophical Association* 67, no. 4 (January 1994), 31.

is reduced to a sophisticated development of the queen bee's instinct to protect her hive. Indeed, the evolutionary mechanisms that brought the species into being dictate that mother and child are locked in a mutual codependent struggle. The child is as much a parasite to resist as a treasure to protect.[23] Art and literature become a happy accident of our power to communicate, truly valuable and comprehensible only insofar as they serve the needs of the human organism. It is not surprising then to see many philosophers take a quite different tack concerning the human essence. If the modern era has been the age of science, it has also been the era whose philosophies of human nature have focused most persistently and sharply on consciousness and freedom. One finds almost a note of protest: "I am *not* only so much matter in motion!"

As the technologies arising from the sciences spread, so did the concern that the human is becoming lost in the technological. From the dehumanizing mines and factories of the nineteenth century to the computer HAL's murder of the astronauts in *2001: A Space Odyssey*, we have seen persistent resentment of and resistance to the threat that human beings will be subordinated to the machines we have created. The early assembly line, efficient as it was, reduced the worker to a part of the machine; today, precisely those workers are being replaced increasingly by robots. Freedom and humanity, our consciousness of ourselves as distinct from the material world around us are important to us. We cherish our human uniqueness, rebelling against what would deny us our humanity. This resistance to the scientific vision of human nature has occasioned important philosophical developments.

Freedom and the denial of human "nature."   The impulse to defend the distinctively human, to preserve human freedom, has led to the denial that there is any such thing as human nature. Frithjof Bergmann writes, "We do not accept the notion that man is endowed with an inner, let alone eternal essence, and we deny this even for the individual."[24] While Bergmann's position seems at first to support materialist claims, his denial of an inner essence amounts to a rejection of *any* definitive claims of what the human

23. Craig Stanford, "Natal Attractions," in *Significant Others: The Ape-Human Continuum and the Quest for Human Nature*. Basic Books, 2001, chap. 6.

24. Frithjof Bergmann, *On Being Free* (Notre Dame, London: University of Notre Dame Press, 1977), 91.

being is. If I am to be truly free, then I cannot be reduced to my body and its dynamisms. This principle underlies the feminist objection that biology is not destiny. For the sake of protecting human freedom, Rorty wants to dispense with the idea that the self has an intrinsic nature.[25] This does not mean, of course, that one would deny that human beings are bipedal, almost naked of hair, seldom taller than seven feet, and so on. The point, rather, is that *nature* implies *determination*. If it is possible to affirm that human beings have a specific nature, then it follows that one may say what is best for any human being whatever, to proscribe what is bad for everyone, and to restrict the individual's freedom and autonomy according to what is "natural" and "unnatural." While arguing against this rejection of a specific human nature, Cardinal Jean Danielou notes sympathetically: "It is perfectly true that a false notion of nature has often been the mask for laziness and the fear of innovation. . . . It is certain that one has sometimes considered the inequality of wealth, the subordination of slaves, and the inferior condition of women to be expressions of natural law."[26] It is argued that to the extent that there is something distinctively human, it is to be found in the subjectivity of freedom. The abstract concepts of the philosopher and scientist cannot capture the existence of the free individual. The roots of such a rejection of human nature might well be found in the thought of Immanuel Kant, who sharply distinguished between the objective world of phenomena and the subjective moral world of freedom.[27] The human subject is a free and autonomous lawgiver, constrained only by the requirements of reason.[28] Kant's point was that human dignity—the dignity of the rational being—lies precisely in its not being subject to heteronomous laws. The human being is more than what any human nature would prescribe.

25. Richard Rorty, *Contingency, Irony, and Solidarity* (Cambridge, New York: Cambridge University Press, 1989), 8.

26. Jean Danielou, "Y a-t-il une nature humaine?" in *De Homine: Studia hodiernae anthropologiae,* vol. 2, (Rome, 1972), 6.

27. David Burrell, C.S.C. "Freedom and Creation in the Abrahamic Tradition," *International Philosophical Quarterly* 40, no. 2 (2000): 161–172. Burrell traces this conception of human autonomy back further, all the way to Duns Scotus.

28. Immanuel Kant, *Grounding for the Metaphysics of Morals,* James W. Ellington, trans. (Indianapolis, Cambridge: Hackett Publishing Co., Inc., 1993), Third Section.

The vanishing self of pure consciousness.   When Descartes penned his famous *"Cogito, ergo sum,"* he located the human precisely in consciousness.
Attempting to find certain bases for his knowledge, he defined himself in
terms of his own thought: "I am a thinking substance."[29] This radical identification of self with consciousness leads to an irreconcilable dualism, to
an unbridgeable gulf between the thinking substance of his consciousness
and the extended substance that was his body. The "real" Descartes was in
danger of being lost. Though opposed in many respects to Descartes, the
empiricism of Locke and especially Hume further develops this focus on
consciousness. If what we know are ideas (which for Locke and Hume are
copies or memories of sense impressions), how do we know how things really stand in the world? What is the human self that knows things? What
we know, and for all practical purposes, what there is, is constituted in
memory and perceptual awareness. Twentieth-century phenomenology
attempted to resolve these questions systematically by putting the human
subject, and not the separately existing realm of things, at the center. The
world with all its relationships and laws is constituted in and by consciousness.[30] Human subjectivity is, therefore, the starting point; epistemology
replaces metaphysics. In the phenomenological perspective, science is put
in its place as it were, for science and all that it investigates depend for its
very being as world and understanding on human consciousness.

The phenomenological turn does save the human. Whether Cartesian
or Husserlian, such a conception restores the sense of uniqueness that the
sciences have taken away. The cost, however, is significant. The consciousness solution does not overcome Descartes's dualism. There remains the
question of what kind of thing this is—the thinking, conscious subject. It
is impossible to deny the intimate connection between consciousness and
the body. If it is not the body that is conscious, then what is? If we strip
the conscious self of its body, its relationships with things about it, its history—of every physical, empirical thing—then the self vanishes.[31]

29. René Descartes, *Meditations on First Philosophy,* 3rd ed., trans. from the Latin by Donald A. Cress (Indianapolis, Cambridge: Hackett Publishing Company, 1993), Meditation II.

30. See James M. Edie, *Edmund Husserl's Phenomenology: A Critical Commentary* (Indianapolis-Bloomington: Indiana University Press, 1987), 13 ff.

31. Karol Wojtyła [John Paul II], "Person: Subject and Community," in *Person and Community* (New York and San Francisco: Peter Lang, 1993), 219.

The functional unity of materialism and absolute freedom

Both materialism and the philosophy of pure consciousness effectively deny human nature, the one in the name of the continuity of science and the other in the name of freedom. Their different bases notwithstanding, on the practical level they tend to the same result. If, as materialists suggest, what we call human nature is simply the result of natural evolutionary processes, if the human being is simply a primate whose brain and other biological characteristics give him certain advantages, then that species can admit of further change. With our growing understanding of genetics and biological engineering, what nature has hitherto wrought, we can now direct. Thanks to electronically assisted prosthetics, the blind can see (although not yet too well) and the lame walk. Researchers actively pursue ways to correct genetic defects *in utero*, so that no one may be born defective. In short, contemporary scientific and technological developments suggest strongly that we do have the capability to remake human beings, to control our own evolution, so that human beings are what we choose them to be. If to some this scientific promise is uncomfortably reminiscent of Huxley's *Brave New World*, others see a positive humanist advantage. We need no longer be children, but humanity can now come to full maturity, in control of our own destiny. Thanks to artificial methods of contraception and increasingly sophisticated reproductive technologies, the connection between sexual activity and procreation is being severed. Indeed, ordinary Americans and Europeans regard the connection between sex and reproduction entirely as a matter of choice, not of nature. It seems that what we will be is not what we inherit by nature, but what we make by our own art.

Underlying presumptions and the failure to understand spirit

Underlying both the scientific vision and the philosophies of consciousness are presumptions about matter and the material realm, presumptions that make any reconciliation of mind and body, consciousness and the physical realm very difficult. On the one hand, matter is conceived as dead "stuff," governed by unvarying laws of nature. Insofar as something is material it is not teleological. Whatever is made of matter is constituted by its material parts and their interrelationships and interactions. Another way to put it is that we conceive the material to admit adequately of characterization by mathematical expressions. The simplest entities are defined in terms of mass, charge, spin, location, and velocity—all of which can be expressed mathematically. The material thing always behaves the same way in the same situation. Theo Belmans calls this "physicism," "the temptation to understand by *object* a perfectly neutral *thing*, an *en soi* of the impersonal order, receiving its significance from the *pour soi*, which is the subject."[32] Another way to express this is that material things have no teleology. There is no good or evil in the material realm. Material things do not behave in such a way as to fulfill some plan or realize some goal.

Complementary to this understanding of matter are contemporary understandings of *spirit*. For the most part, we discuss spirit in one of two different ways. On the one hand—let me add, the philosophical hand—we understand the spiritual as the mental, the conscious. Spirit has to do with how we represent our lives and experiences to ourselves. On the other hand, it often commonly represents a kind of entity that is somewhat like a physical thing, but not physical. Angels and ghosts are spirits. They perceive things, know, love, and attend to matters rather as we living humans do, but without physical bodies. Clarence (the angel in *It's a Wonderful Life*) disappears when the policeman jumps on him. I am being deliberately simplistic here. Yet, as we examine how people, including philosophers, speak of body, soul, and spirit, we find that the presuppositions are quite close to these images.

THE HEART OF THE QUESTION: THE REALITY OF THE SPIRITUAL

Is the spiritual real? And if it is, how does it relate to the physical? The drama of Plato's *Republic* arises from Thrasymachus's challenge to the human spirit. When Socrates and his interlocutors attempt to define justice, Thrasymachus challenges the foundations of their enterprise: "I affirm

---

32. Theo G. Belmans, *Le sens objectif de l'agir humain: Pour relire l'amour conjugale de saint Thomas* (Vatican City: Libreria Editrice Vaticana, 1980), 6.

that the just is nothing else than the advantage of the strong."[33] In the real world, which has to do with giving and getting goods, honors, and power, justice is an ideal for naive simpletons.[34] Against a stronger adversary one whose only claim is to justice is lost. To get what one wants or needs, material advantage—not an immaterial quality or moral virtue—is needed. In his way, Thrasymachus is arguing the evolutionist point, that human beings are creatures of nature and their environments. The virtue of *justice*, if one insists on speaking in those terms, is the advantage of the stronger simply because only the strong survive. Only those who can impose their will on others can attain what they need and desire, and whosoever would deny this is a "simpleton." His are the ethics of marketplace competition and democratic politics of power, when these are conceived only in terms of the manipulation of regulations and structures.

Although Socrates out-argues Thrasymachus in Book I of *The Republic*, neither Thrasymachus, nor Glaucon, nor we are convinced. At the beginning of Book II Glaucon poses the question again, challenging Socrates to show that even when all else is lost—comfort, wealth, honor, freedom, and reputation—justice is nevertheless worth having. To meet this challenge, Socrates shifts the ground away from Thrasymachus and shows how injustice harms the soul—and in such a way that even the tyrant's surfeit of goods and honors cannot alleviate his misery. As if to punctuate this point, while in his cell awaiting execution, Socrates remarks that, were it up to his limbs and their natural desires, he would have run away long ago.[35] The drama of the *Republic* (and, indeed, of the *Phaedo*) is that of the human spirit in relation to matter, of the soul in relation to the body.

If there is no spirit, then Thrasymachus is right. We can live only for material advantage and are subject to the "slings and arrows of outrageous fortune." The question, then, of the nature of the human being becomes decisive. If the biological evolutionary vision is correct, and our power to reason is nothing other than a sophisticated and flexible means of adapting to the physical environment, then we are none other than physical or-

33. Plato, *The Republic*, in *The Collected Dialogues of Plato*, Edith Hamilton and Huntington Cairns, eds. (Princeton: Princeton University Press, 1961), Book I, 338c.

34. Ibid., 348c.

35. Plato, *The Phaedo*, in *The Collected Dialogues of Plato*, Edith Hamilton and Huntington Cairns, eds. (Princeton: Princeton University Press, 1961), 99a.

ganisms and Thrasymachus is right. Just as sharks and biting dogs are not wicked, but only dangerous, so too are felons, plotters, and betrayers of trust. If religion, broadly conceived, is the effort to orient one's life and self to a being or realm that is higher, then religion is false and foolish—at best a psychological aid or metaphor for getting through the thickets of daily life on an even emotional keel. The willingness to die for an idea, to sacrifice one's goods for a principle becomes foolish.

The question of human nature impinges directly, of course, on contemporary discussions of life issues—abortion, euthanasia, assisted suicide, cloning, and fetal research. Peter Singer's conclusions are ultimately compelling if one accepts his premise that, as a species, human beings are neither ontologically superior to, nor fundamentally different in kind from, other animals. We do shoot horses when they are old, useless, or in unrelieved pain. If the human being does not, as Socrates puts it, owe his life to the gods,[36] it is perfectly reasonable to allow the terminally ill and those with an irreversibly deteriorating quality of life to end their lives on their own initiative. On the other hand, if the human being is in some sense a spiritual entity that can meaningfully transcend its life in the physical world, a being with responsibility to something higher than itself, then the taking of human life becomes a distinctive moral issue. If the embryo in the Petri dish has an immortal soul, then to destroy or experiment on it is not equivalent to performing a biopsy on a tumor. The life issues, which today are in the forefront of public discussion, depend for their answers on how we conceive human nature. They are not, however, the only issues so affected.

The nature, structure, and goals of education also hinge on our concept of the human. In everyday discussions in our homes, schools, and public forums, we speak frequently of the economic importance of education. Our young people need good educations to compete in the workforce. The economy, especially the post-industrial information economy, needs educated people to continue to grow. Education is an *investment* for both the young person and society. Important though these considerations are, we note a different accent in earlier eras. The ideal of the liberal arts has long been the formation of the mind. To have an educated mind, one able to

36. Ibid., 62b–c.

judge the merits of things with equanimity, to consider things as a whole, to reflect within oneself, and to find the best recreation in things of the mind, has long been the aim of the liberal education.[37] Aristotle regarded the speculative sciences as superior to the practical precisely because they had no end beyond themselves. "All men desire to know,"[38] and in contemplating truth one reaches the highest state attainable in this life.[39] The best life, the happiest life is one marked by contemplation.[40] Such ideals are false however, suitable only for commencement speakers, if the essential nature of thought is to be a biological adaptation of the nervous system to ensure survival. If the mind is not something to be improved, save in the sense of increasing its practical scope and adaptability, then education is the same as vocational training. If this is so, then Socrates is indeed a corrupter of the young and Meletus their true guardian.[41] We are all servants to businessmen and engineers. At the family level, the task of parents is not so much to develop the character and personalities of their children as to equip them with the information and savvy to make their ways through the world successfully.

Other persons: human community

The ordering of public life—our communities and political structures—also depends on our conception of human nature. What is one human person to another? Are communion and community possible? Democratic political institutions have shown themselves remarkably effective for building peaceful, reasonably well-ordered societies. The historical evidence is that true democracies do not go to war against each other. According to Amartya Sen (winner of the 1998 Nobel Prize in Economics), where there are functioning democratic institutions and open information exchange—

37. John Henry Newman, "Knowledge Its Own End," in *The Idea of a University* (Notre Dame: University of Notre Dame Press, 1982), Discourse V.

38. Aristotle, *Metaphysics*, vol. 8 in *Great Books of the Western World*, W. D. Ross, ed. (Chicago, London, Toronto: Encyclopedia Britannica, 1952), I, i, 980a 1.

39. Aristotle, *Nicomachean Ethics*, David Ross, trans., introd. (Oxford: Oxford University Press, 1998), Book X.

40. Josef Pieper, *Glück und Kontemplation* (Munich, 1979), 9–10.

41. See Plato, *The Apology* in *The Collected Dialogues of Plato*, Edith Hamilton and Huntington Cairns, eds. (Princeton: Princeton University Press, 1961).

especially through a free press—famine does not occur.[42] Where citizens, adequately educated and reasonably well-informed, have an effective voice in the government of their own lives, they can sort out their differences and compromise so that everyone gets something. Similarly, free-market economies have proven to be reliably prosperous. If people have access to resources (even modest ones) and can reap the rewards of their initiative and hard work, then they and their neighbors tend to prosper. Limited democratic government and regulated free markets have proven to be effective solutions to the ancient problems of attaining relatively high levels of peace and prosperity. The success of such institutions, especially in a huge and diverse country such as the United States, can blind us, however, to fundamental underlying questions that such successes do not address.

The genius of both democratic institutions and free-market economic mechanisms is that they recognize the individual as competent to care for his or her own interests and to work with others to realize them. While the Soviet Union devised elaborate state plans for manufacture and distribution—often with disastrous results—the people of New York City daily bring in tons of food and goods to meet their needs, with no one person or agency to plan or oversee this distribution. Individuals and freely chosen groupings of common interest enable people to meet their common needs with remarkable efficiency. Effective as this conception is in some respects, we may ask, nevertheless, whether this adequately represents all that the human person is. Two aspects of contemporary American life illustrate how this conception may be deficient.

In 1865, after 200 years as slaves, blacks in the United States were freed and recognized as citizens. For another century they were second-class citizens, laboring under harsh segregation laws in some states and informal but real discrimination in most areas. The 1964 Civil Rights Act and the 1965 Voting Rights Act finally broke down those legal and administrative obstacles to full participation in American political and economic life. At the end of the twentieth century, American blacks were fully enfranchised, enjoying legal status and protection comparable to those of white people. Neverthe-

---

42. Amartya Sen, "Human Rights and Asian Values: What Lee Kuan Yew and Le Peng Don't Understand about Asia," http://www.brainsnchips.org/hr/sen.htm. Article extracted from *The New Republic*, 217, no. 2-3 (July 14, 1997).

less, serious racial problems remain in the United States. Despite the great political and economic success enjoyed by many black Americans and the dramatic improvement in standing enjoyed by all, a profound sense of racial unease permeates the society. Why? The problem has not so much to do with economic and political opportunity as with the spirit. Do black people really belong? Can they be *real* Americans? Or is the United States a "white" country? These are questions of culture and community, of the spirit.

An even clearer and more dramatic example is the ongoing debate over legal abortion. Despite many attempts to work out compromise understandings ("agree to disagree") and even the U.S. Supreme Court's insistence (in the *obiter dictum* of the *Planned Parenthood v. Casey* decision) that it is time to end the debate for the sake of our common political life, there is still no compromise, and the reason for this is fairly clear. At issue in the abortion debate is a practice that many citizens believe to be absolutely, always, and everywhere wrong. In a debate over tax structures, passions may run high as interested parties protect significant amounts of their own money. Nevertheless, compromise is possible, because although different parties may disagree about what constitutes a corporation's fair share vis-à-vis a homeowner's, they agree that taxation is necessary and that all should contribute. By contrast, opponents to legal abortion recognize no middle ground. The life of the unborn child cannot be balanced against a sum of money or a greater share of political power. Pope John Paul II puts the issue starkly in his encyclical *Evangelium Vitae:*

Thus society becomes a mass of individuals placed side by side, but without any mutual bonds. Each one . . . intends to make his own interests prevail. Still, in the face of other people's analogous interests, some kind of compromise must be found, if one wants a society in which the maximum possible freedom is guaranteed to each individual. In this way, any reference to common values and to a truth absolutely binding on everyone is lost, and social life ventures on to the shifting sands of complete relativism. At that point, *everything is negotiable, everything is open to bargaining:* even the first of the fundamental rights, the right to life. [emphasis in original][43]

43. John Paul II [Karol Wojtyła], *Evangelium Vitae,* in John Paul II, *The Theology of the Body: Human Love in the Divine Plan* (1995, repr., Boston: Pauline Books and Media, 1997), §20.

John Paul II's point is that democracy, understood only as a set of procedures and mechanisms without reference to the truth about human nature, undermines the principles on which democracy is founded, especially the recognition of the fundamental dignity that attaches to each human
person. Rather every decision is the result of a balance among interested
powers, and the truly powerless have no rights. Right and wrong, good
and evil are nothing more than the results of parliamentary votes or ju-
dicial decisions. Analogously, if the free market becomes the sole arbiter
of worth, then the price of everything and everyone becomes its true and
only value. If human nature does have an inviolable essence, if humanity
consists in one's having an immortal soul, then political and economic institutions of themselves are insufficient for full human development and
life, as John Paul II argues.

AN INTEGRATED VISION

Aristotle and Aquinas

The peculiar status of the human person is that he is both material and
spiritual. The trends that we have reviewed thus far represent efforts to account for the reality of the human in terms that fail to reconcile these two
aspects. The materialist seeks to subsume the spiritual under the material,
so that whatever it is that we call *spiritual* or *mental* is really another name
for some physical process or interaction. The philosophies of consciousness, on the other hand, posit a kind of epistemological supremacy of the
knowing subject, effectively reducing the physical order to the constitution
of conscious intentions. Both approaches share this in common, that they
are dualist insofar as they deny the possibility of reconciling the material
and the spiritual. There is, however, a middle way, one pointed out by Aristotle.

In his *On the Soul*, Aristotle argues that the soul is nothing other than
the form (or formal cause) of the living being,[44] by which this physical
thing is a man. In other words, if the form is taken away, then there is no

44. Aristotle, *On the Soul*, J. A. Smith, trans. Book II, ii, 414a 28, accessed at http://clas-
sics.mit.edu/Aristotle/soul.html.

man—organic matter in the shape of a man, perhaps, but no man. Aquinas accepts this definition and follows Aristotle in applying it to the human being. "The soul is the primary actuality of a physical bodily organism."[45] This means simply that the soul is that principle in virtue of which the bodily organism realizes its potentiality to live. The inert, nonliving is in potency (or potentiality) to life. The living body is actualized; that is, it is able to do things to realize its specific nature. The soul is that actuality, the principle of the organism's life. The Aristotelian argument is simply that to know the matter constituting a thing is not enough. There is a principle by which this thing is alive and endowed with human powers. By the human soul, this matter—this flesh and bones, this organic matter—is made to be a human being, because organic matter is not in itself sufficient to constitute something as a living human being. (Were this so, then a corpse would be a human being.) For Aristotle and Aquinas, soul is to body as form is to matter. The soul is "joined" to the body in the same sense as the impression is "joined" to the wax seal.[46] So regarded, there is no question of the integration of soul and body. The soul is not a something else that is added on to the body or that somehow inhabits it. In this Aristotelianism moves away from Plato's conception of a soul that inhabits and guides the body, rather as a sailor does a ship. While Plato's *Phaedo* strongly suggests (at least) that the soul can exist and live independently of the body, Aristotle has the soul as most intimately united with it.

Since the soul is the living thing's life principle, Aquinas says that we know "by experience" that we have a soul, simply because we know that we are alive.[47] Therefore, whatever it is that is this life principle is the soul. If what makes the organism to be alive is its nervous system, or perhaps some state of the nervous system, then that is the soul. To put it crudely, once Dr. Frankenstein attached the brain to his creation and jump-started it with the lightning, the monster came to life. One could argue therefore that its activated brain was, in effect, its soul. Thus, the Aristotelian definition does not of itself constitute an argument that the human soul is immaterial, immortal, or in any other way different from animal souls.

45. Aquinas, *Aristotle's "De Anima" in the version of William of Moerbeke and the Commentary of St. Thomas Aquinas* (New Haven: Yale University Press, 1951), L. §233. Henceforth *In De Anima*.

46. Aquinas, *In De Anima*, §234.   47. Ibid., §6.

More problematic for modern conceptions of science and human nature is the Aristotelian conception of substance. It is worth our while and, indeed, important for this investigation for us to explore the comparison and contrast between the modern and Aristotelian conceptions at some length. For Aristotle, the living organism is a unity, one that has a particular kind of life. The form, which is the principle not simply of the human organism's life but of all its activities, makes it to be a specific kind of thing. Substance for Aristotle and Aquinas is intrinsically dynamic, for each substance has its specific perfection which it realizes by its proper operations. Negatively we may put it this way, that to know any substance it does not suffice to know what it is made of (its material cause) and how this matter is arranged, but also what the thing's operation is, what its perfection is. The perfection of a plant is to live, grow, and to bear seed. That of a wolf is to live, hunt with the pack, and bear young. So too the human being has a specific perfection, a suitable good proper to humans that they are called to realize. According to the Aristotelian conception, a substance has four causes: material, formal, efficient, and final (or with respect to the good),[48] and none of these can be reduced to or explained away by the other. For our purposes, what this means is that, as far as Aristotle is concerned, to know what we are made of, how our bodies are constructed, and how evolution may have brought us to be does not fully account for what we are. The human being has a specific perfection or good, and therefore its characteristically human operations.[49] The soul is the human being's principle of operation, by which he is ordered to characteristically human behavior and the specifically human good.

We may contrast this with the position adopted by, among others, Peter Singer, who argues that since an individual's properties of rationality, self-awareness, and autonomy come (in early childhood) and go (after brain trauma or as senility advances), then one's human personhood, regarded other than simply as membership in the species *homo sapiens*, is variable.[50]

---

48. Aristotle, *Metaphysics*, I, 2; Aristotle, *Physics*, II, 3 and 7.

49. Aristotle, *Nicomachean Ethics*, I, see especially chapter 7 on the "function" of a human being.

50. Peter Singer, *Rethinking Life and Death: The Collapse of Our Traditional Ethics*, (New York: St. Martin's Press, 1994), 205; see also his *Practical Ethics*, 2nd ed., (New York: Cambridge University Press, 1993), 85–86.

As he sees it, the human being is a particularly complex animal, endowed with a uniquely large and sophisticated brain, as well as erect posture, opposable thumbs, and so on—properties that are all programmed into it by human DNA. An effect of these physical traits is that most human beings, for the largest parts of their lives, become rational, conscious of themselves existing through time, and concerned for their continued existence. This rational state, however, does not belong to the human being as such. Indeed, nothing—strictly speaking—belongs to the human being as such. It is certainly conceivable that by the appropriate manipulation of the human DNA, one might develop a new animal with capabilities that surpass those we recognize as human, or that humans with limited intellects but other useful capabilities might be bred, as Aldous Huxley famously suggested in his *Brave New World*. The underlying conception is that physical nature is fundamentally uniform. While we find it useful, both in practical and in scientific matters, to distinguish the human from the nonhuman, the animal from the vegetable, the living from the nonliving, these differences can ultimately be explained in terms of material interactions. Life arose out of "dead" matter; chance variations brought complex organisms out of the simpler, and eventually human intelligence evolved from the lesser intelligence of our ancestral primates. In other words, all nature is a continuum in which different things are distinguished by their differing degrees of complexity.

This contrasts sharply with the Aristotelian notion of substance. Even if the human substance loses its capacity for reason, according to the Aristotelian conception, it remains a human being, a rational animal. To say that the human becomes a brute animal or that the brute becomes human is to posit a corruption of one substance and generation of a new. Aquinas writes that "no substantial form is susceptible of more or less; but addition of greater perfection constitutes another species." Either a thing is, or is not, an animal or a human being. One substance cannot continuously "morph" into another. To add intelligence to the brute animal is to make it a new kind of being, to put it within a new species and not simply to give it a new quality (as would, for instance, changing one's color by getting a dark tan).

As a consequence, the Aristotelian position is realist, and the scientific materialist is nominalist. Why "nominalist"? For Aristotle a word can name a substance in such a way that the definition of the word expresses the essence, which is what the thing is. For the scientist however, words, convenient though they may be, do not most accurately express what things are. What things are and the relationships among them are best expressed mathematically, in terms of quantifiable characteristics and spatial relationships. The most accurate account, best stating what is really going on, is in mathematical and diagrammatic terms. Let us consider a couple of examples. Carbon is a kind of stone, soft and slow-burning, which is good not only for fuel but also for drawing and writing instruments. Oxygen is a gas, invisible but vital for life. Any Aristotelian could tell the difference. The chemist does not so identify them (except in a basic chemistry class). To understand carbon and oxygen adequately it is necessary to know not so much that the one is a black solid and the other a colorless gas, but that the one has an atomic number of six and the other of eight. The differences between carbon and oxygen can be explained in terms of their respective nuclear weights and, especially, the number of electrons in their outermost orbital shells, for it is the configuration of this outer shell that determines the kinds of chemical relationships the atom can enter into with other atoms. While the ordinary lay person finds the differences between carbon and oxygen to be as great as can be, the scientist knows that the two are in many respects quite similar. What the scientist understands is that the tangible properties of color, odor, and solidity are not decisive of what each is. Rather, both carbon and oxygen are but two possible combinations of protons, neutrons, and electrons. It is in virtue of these that one is a solid and the other a gas at room temperature, that the two release energy when combined chemically, and that carbon, when compressed, crystallizes into diamonds. Let us take the discussion a step further and ask why there even are carbon and oxygen atoms. The answer (to put it *very* briefly) is that when the universe was young and most matter consisted of protons and electrons (which is to say, hydrogen atoms), clumps of matter, collapsing under the weight of gravity, generated great heat energy, which triggered the fusion of hydrogen atoms into helium. Then, ever so rarely, helium atoms would collide and fuse to form heavier elements. And so it went on. As chance atomic collisions occurred within stars, new elements came into being. In short, all the elements we know, all the different kinds of matter, result from random collisions of basically three kinds of particles under extreme conditions. The wonderful variety of elements—helium and lithium, gold and titanium, boron and uranium—all result from the possible combinations of three little particles. Matter is no longer to be classified according to the properties known only to sense experience. Indeed, it is the chemist with his knowledge of subatomic particles and electron orbit levels, who can put to rest the alchemist's projects of combining base metals to create gold—even as the chemist transforms crude oil into ingenious plastics.

If differences among physical things are mathematical, of degree, then one kind of thing can be transformed (in principle, at least) to another by degrees or accretion. This is important in biology, where, according to Darwinian Theory, the various species have arisen by accumulated minute changes. Darwin's theory of minute changes has been questioned of late; it seems inadequate to account for periods of rapid, explosive evolutionary development. Nevertheless, we know now that the "engine" governing much of biology is DNA, a kind of molecule that allows for great articulation and almost infinite variation. Minute changes in the genetic code can lead to readily observable differences in the organism. It is well known that human DNA differs from that of chimpanzees by less than 2 percent. To us from our ordinary point of view this difference is significant. Let us consider the scientific implications. If all the respective properties of carbon and oxygen result from the arrangements of their protons, neutrons, and electrons, then is it not likewise the case that the respective properties of human beings and chimpanzees result simply from their respective DNA sequences? Just as the outer electron shell determines how carbon and oxygen shall combine chemically, so does the DNA determine how the organism will grow and develop into a mature adult and how it will respond to environmental stimuli. Fascinating as we may find comparisons of human behavior with that of chimps, the true protagonist is the molecule of DNA. Just as the differences among the chemical elements and the compounds to be created from them is explained by understanding atomic structure, so too will animal behavior be accounted for by genetic understanding.[51] If this is the case, then it is true that the only difference between

---

51. I am aware that I am simplifying here, that biology is not so simple as chemistry and will not become so in the foreseeable future.

human beings and the simians is of degree, by which we mean that the one differs from the other only in the articulation of the genetic sequence.

Distinctions among *kinds* of things must therefore be ultimately conventional, created by human minds for human purposes. The Aristotelian, by contrast, holds that certain things differ from others by their very nature, that certain properties cannot be lost or changed without destroying the one kind of thing and generating another. A distinctive name for a species is justified because in reality that species is fundamentally different from others. If the Aristotelian position is right, then the soul—as the form of the living substance, its principle of life—is real and not reducible to the body's arrangement of matter. To a great extent therefore, the question of the soul is also the question of the reality of human nature. Can the gap between the human being and the simians be bridged by a series of physical modifications, or is the difference between them absolute, so that no chimpanzee, no matter how gifted, could attain to humanity? If the materialist position is right, then the soul is little more than a useful fiction.

This distinction between differences of degree and those of kind can be decisively grasped with reference to final causality. Different *kinds* of things have different *goods*, and this fact will be especially important—indeed, decisively so—for this present investigation. According to materialism, nothing has its own distinctive inherent good, natural purpose, or end. To be sure, animals act in such a way as to preserve their lives, and even plants respond to sunlight and water. Although these activities are end-directed, they do not reflect an end that is "written into" the very nature of living things as such. They are, rather, the development of the same patterns of interaction that gave rise to these beings in the first place. We might say that the instinct for self-preservation is the first characteristic selected by natural selection. Richard Dawkins writes: "The true process that has endowed wings, eyes, beaks, nesting instincts, and everything else about life with the strong illusion of purposeful design is now well understood. It is Darwinian natural selection."[52] On the other hand, Aristotelian realism holds that implicit in the form of the substance is an orientation toward the natural good for that substance.[53] What are we to

---

52. Richard Dawkins, "God's Utility Function," 81.

53. Aquinas, *Summa Theologiae*, Ia 5, 5; Aquinas, *The Disputed Questions on Truth*, Robert W. Mulligan, S.J., trans. (Chicago: Regnery Co., 1952), 22, 4. Henceforth *De Veritate*.

make of this? In an obvious sense, modern science exceeds the capability of Aristotelian science to explain natural elements and inanimate things. It is hard to see how an Aristotelian account of carbon could explain its chemical relationships, provide a basis for organic chemistry, or explain why a diamond and a block of coal are made of exactly the same stuff, much less show how adding another proton/electron combination or two would transform the carbon into a gas (either nitrogen or oxygen). Chemistry seems to get on well without the notions of *form* or *appropriate good.* It is when we turn to biology—and Aristotle was a biologist—that these notions get their conceptual "bite." He understood the plant or animal to be more than a complex protein machine that develops and behaves according to the laws governing its constituent parts. From the Aristotelian perspective, the behavior of the parts, the material components, is to be explained in terms of the form of the whole substance. Scientists today actively investigate whether and how life could have arisen from the chemical interactions among organic compounds. If this is so, then the line between living and nonliving becomes blurred (as indeed the very existence of borderline entities such as viruses suggests), so that living and nonliving reduce to being two different stages on a continuum of complexity. This continuity of structure, however, does not mean that differences of kind do not exist. Even having accepted materialist presuppositions as definitive, scientists can distinguish between kinds of things on the basis of behavior, and therefore on the basis of final causality. Carbon and oxygen are distinguished as solid is distinguished from gas. Lions are carnivorous and oxen herbivorous. A decisive factor in determining whether two similar animals belong to the same species is whether they can mate. We may then say that structural differences of degree can become differences of kind as they affect the thing's characteristic behavior and the apparent finality to which its acts are directed.

We cannot, in this present work, delve into this difficult question in its general form. What we will do is investigate it insofar as it pertains to the human being. Our contention in this book is that the physical mechanisms described by biology, chemistry, and physics cannot account for human nature, that the human being is not merely a physical variant on the chimpanzee, occupying what is now the highest spot on a continuous gradient of increasing complexity. Rather the human being is a different kind of be-

ing—radically different—because it is ordered toward goods that lie outside the natural order.

Aristotelianism offers an alternative to the sharp dualism between a
self-contained material body governed by laws of biology, chemistry, and
physics and an immaterial soul that somehow inhabits it. In particular,
Aquinas defends (as his interpretation of Aristotle) the notion that the
soul is joined to the body as its form and not merely as a mover—certainly
not something extrinsic—and that by this soul the organism is distinctively and irreducibly human. Aquinas further maintains that this soul is capable of continued existence separate from the body it informs, even though
this is not the soul's natural condition. It is this kind of response that this
work will develop. Before doing so, it is helpful to take note of some modern theorists, who have developed Aristotelian-Thomistic accounts of the
human person, beginning from perspectives outside the traditional Aristotelian stream.

Karol Wojtyła and Phenomenology

In his *Osoba i Czyn*, translated into English as *The Acting Person*,[54] Karol Wojtyła (Pope John Paul II) addresses the question of the integration of
the human person by a phenomenological analysis of the human act as at
once conscious and efficacious. For an act to be human, it flows from one's
interiority, from reason and the power consciously to decide. It does not
suffice, however, to qualify as a human act that something happen in consciousness, that one feel in a certain way. Rather the efficacy of the act is
also essential to its being a human act. More simply, when we act, we try to
effect change, to exercise efficient causality within the world. A human act
is, therefore, a mixed reality that cannot be reduced to either an event in
consciousness or to a sequence of occurrences in the world. The phenomenological essence of the experience *a human being acts* is that it is both
mental (conscious) and efficacious.[55] Thus, the human person experiences

54. Reimers, Adrian J., *An Analysis of the Concepts of Self-Fulfillment and Self-Realization in
the Thought of Karol Wojtyła/John Paul II* (Lewiston, NY: The Mellen Press, 2001). The analysis
summarized here is developed at much greater length in this work. This work also includes a
brief discussion of the difficulties with the English translation of Wojtyła's book.

55. Wojtyła, *The Acting Person* (Dordrecht, Boston, London: D. Riedel, 1979), Part One,

himself as irreducibly mental and physical, both body and spirit. This implies further that one's bodily presence in the world is decisive for human subjectivity. Because one acts on the basis of conscious decisions, he is responsible for the results of those actions. In acting, one chooses, even if only to a small extent, what kind of world there will be. He realizes (or attempts to realize) his values in the world.

It is bootless to object that this efficacy is an illusion, that one's organism will do what it will do, with consciousness following upon.[56] Wojtyła's point is that such an objection misses precisely the experience of *acting*, an experience that each of us has countless times every day. While one may object on theoretical grounds that mental intentions, conscious states of mind, have no causal relationship with one's activities, no one can deny that when the cook reminds himself, while preparing an omelet, not to add so much salt this time, he is aware of himself as responsible, as the one who will render the dish tasty or rubbery. Remembering a previous act, one might say, "I was not responsible. I couldn't help myself. I could not control what happened," but in the process of carrying out an act one ordinarily experiences himself not as the detached observer, but as the efficacious agent. The concept of acts and experiences that are irreducibly mental and physical is inextricably part of our understanding of ourselves and the world.

In his Encyclical *Veritatis Splendor*, John Paul II both affirms the Aristotelian-Thomistic conception of the unity of the human being as soul and body, and connects this with the moral life, that is, with one's acts as a responsible agent.[57] It is only as a unified being, both rational and effectively engaged in the world, that the human being can be regarded as a moral agent. Against those who would affirm human freedom over against a fixed nature, John Paul II argues that it is only as a responsible bodily being that one can exercise freedom, properly understood. The body is not so much "raw material" on which freedom acts, but it is the condition of one's being

---

Chapter Two. See also Wojtyła, "The will in the analysis of the ethical act," 3–22, and "The personal structure of self-determination," 187–195, in *Person and Community: Selected Essays* (New York, San Francisco: Peter Lang, 1993).

56. See Roger Wolcoll Sperry, "Consciousness and Causality."

57. John Paul II[Karol Wojtyła], *Veritatis splendor,* Encyclical Letter, 5 October 1993, (Boston: Pauline Books & Media, 1993), §48.

able to act at all.[58] In a series of public audiences from September 5, 1979, until November 28, 1984, John Paul II laid out his "theology of the body," an interpretation of human sexuality. Although the presentation was pastoral (the Pope teaching the Church) and the context theological, the philosophical underpinnings are significant to our project. John Paul II's purpose is to develop an "adequate anthropology,"[59] that is, a philosophical conception of human being implied by Scripture and yet doing justice to our experience of our human nature. In these audiences he contends that in its "original condition," the prelapsarian state, the human body, as male and female, is endowed with meaning, that it expresses the person. The "nakedness" referred to in Genesis 2:25 is a state of openness and full communication between the original man and woman, one in which it was possible for them to know and love each other freely. This state is distinguished from that of "historical man," that is, human beings after the Fall. Philosophically we may (following John Paul II) distinguish the original from the historical condition by the fact that for "historical" human beings, the relationship between persons has been altered by the fact that one person tends to use another as an object. In the context of the "theology of the body" audiences, the principal manifestation of this use is sexual lust,[60] although John Paul II makes it clear that the application is broader.[61] In other words, although the body in its original and proper condition (as God intended it) adequately communicates the person, it is only because of human misuse or abuse (theologically identified as sin) that the body conceals the person and his intentions. John Paul II comments that this concealment implies different levels of the "spiritualization" of the body before and after the fall, involving "another composition of the interior forces of man himself, almost another body-soul relationship."[62]

In what surely counts as a surprising development, the Roman pontiff

58. Ibid., §46–48.

59. John Paul II [Karol Wojtyła], *The Theology of the Body* (Boston: Pauline Books& Media, 1997), General Audience of January 9, 1980, 61.

60. John Paul II [Karol Wojtyła], *The Theology of the Body*, Audiences of April 30 and May 7, 1980, 108 ff.

61. Ibid.

62. John Paul II [Karol Wojtyła], *The Theology of the Body*, Audience of February 13, 1980, 73.

addresses the issues of human sexuality and sexual behavior not by accent-
ing the purity of the spiritual soul with respect to which the body is a cor-
rupting agent, but by arguing that the body itself is spiritual precisely in that
it can (in principle, that is, in its "original condition") adequately express
the person.[63] Indeed, throughout these audiences, as well as in related doc-
uments (such as, the Apostolic Letters *Salvifici Doloris* and *Mulierem Dig-
nitatis*, and the Encyclical *Evangelium Vitae*) he rarely uses the word "soul."
For the philosopher-turned-pope, there can be no question of a dualism
of substances, or of embracing Descartes's "thinking substance" as the true
core of human being. For Karol Wojtyła, the key metaphysical term is not
soul but *suppositum*,[64] by which he means the metaphysical subject that underlies experience and action. Wojtyła writes: "Metaphysical subjectivity,
or the *suppositum* as the transphenomenal and therefore fundamental expression of the experience of the human being, is also the guarantor of the
identity of this human being in existence and activity."[65] This *suppositum* is
therefore the human subject taken as a whole, as *some one thing*, which both
experiences and acts in the world. Further, by referring to it as "transphenomenal," Wojtyła indicates that the human *suppositum* can be fully known
only through metaphysical reflection. In his remarks on the "human *suppositum*," Karol Wojtyła comes close to a metaphysics of the soul.

Charles Sanders Peirce

One of the most innovative thinkers in modern philosophy, the American Charles Sanders Peirce insisted that all reality has a threefold charac-

63. George Weigel, *Witness to Hope: The Biography of Pope John Paul II* (New York: Harper Collins Books, 1999), 342. Calling the theology of the body a "theological time bomb,"
Weigel writes: "If it is taken with the seriousness it deserves, John Paul's *Theology of the Body*
may prove to be the decisive moment in exorcizing the Manichaean demon and its depreca-
tion of human sexuality from Catholic moral theology."

64. Wojtyła, "Person: Subject and Community," in *Person and Community: Selected Essays*, Theresa Sandock, O.S.M., trans. (New York, San Francisco: Peter Lang, 1993), and *Osoba
i Czyn*, Cracow, 1969, 93–95, 105, 120–126, 128–130, 132–135,passim. Unfortunately, the English
translators of this work chose to suppress this Latin term, indeed not even translating it with
a single English term, but with expressions such as "basic ontological structure," "ontological foundation of action," "ontological basic structure," etc. Thus, its technical significance is
lost. See *The Acting Person*, (Dordrecht, Boston, London: D. Riedel, 1979), 71–75.

65. Wojtyła, *Person and Community*, 222.

ter, which is manifest in ordinary experience, the structure of material beings in the world, and in the signs and symbols by which we express our
thoughts. He named the three basic categories "Firstness," "Secondness,"
and "Thirdness."[66] Although these admittedly curious categories have never caught on in contemporary philosophical writing, the understanding
they express amounts to a recapturing of an integrated pre-Cartesian vision of reality and human being. In this work we will make particular use
of Peirce's conceptions of sign and habit. Before doing so and in order better to grasp their import, let us first consider these three basic categories.

- *Firstness:* A "First" is what it is simply in virtue of itself. It is any thing
  considered as a monad. Firstness in phenomenology is pure feeling,
  without variation or contrast.[67] Among signs (things that represent),
  icons, which represent in virtue of some similar properties to their
  object, are "Firsts."[68] Qualities are Firsts. Aesthetics, the science of
  what is admirable in itself, is the normative science of Firstness.[69] In
  logic the term, which conveys or expresses meaning, is a First.[70]

- *Secondness:* A "Second" is what it is in virtue of its interaction with
  some other thing. It is one side of the dyad.[71] In phenomenology
  Secondness is manifest in effort and surprise. That a Second cannot
  reduce to a First is evidenced by the fact that the human being's interaction with things cannot reduce to a series of sense impressions. The
  door's resistance to the pushing shoulder is not simply a sensation,
  but is a Second that stands over against the shoulder. Among signs,
  the index, which represents in virtue of some causal connection with
  its object, is a "Second."[72] Ethics, the science of performing acts that
  are good or evil, is the normative science of Secondness.[73] In logic the
  proposition, which expresses a fact as true or false, is a Second.[74]

66. Peirce, "The Categories in Detail," in *Collected Papers,* 1 (Cambridge: Harvard University Press, 1965), Sections 300–353, 148–180. Henceforth citations from the *Collected Papers*
will be given by volume and section, for example 1.300–353 in the present case.

67. Peirce, *Collected Papers,* 1.303–305.

68. Ibid., 2.276.

69. Ibid., 1.573–574, and especially 5.129–136.

70. Ibid., 2.250.   71. Ibid., 1.322–326.

72. Ibid., 2.305–306.   73. See chapter 1, note 67, above.

74. Peirce, *Collected Papers,* 2.251.

- *Thirdness:* A "Third" is what it is in virtue of some second that stands in relation to something else.[75] Laws and signs are Thirds. A law is something general in virtue of which individual things behave regularly. The electron veers toward the positive charge because it is governed by the laws of electromagnetism. The electron and the positive pole are Seconds to each other. That they always relate in the same way means that they are subject to a law, a Third. Among signs a symbol is a Third.[76] It is a conventional sign that represents its object in virtue of a general rule or law. It represents something to someone in virtue of some interpretive key. Logic, which is the science of evaluating representations as capable of expressing truth, is the normative science of Thirdness.[77] In logic, an argument, which expresses a general relationship between two propositions (Seconds) is a Third.[78]

To be sure, there is no pure First, Second, or Third given to experience. The very fact of experiencing entails Firstness, because the experience manifests itself in *sensation* or *feeling*, and Secondness, because the experience involves an encounter with *something* other than the subject. What is important to Peirce, however, is that there is always a Third. A conception of reality in terms simply of Firsts (or reducible to Firsts), reduces to phenomenalism, and the notions of interaction and causality are either excluded or reduced to useful fiction. (Hume's philosophy comes very close to this.) A philosophy with only Seconds is pure materialism and unable to account for either subjective experience or laws and general kinds. A philosophy purely of Thirds reduces to idealism.

Without going further into Peirce's analysis of these (rather idiosyncratic but also remarkably useful) categories, let us examine their relevance to our current investigation. Peirce's insistence on three distinct aspects of reality constitutes a rejection of every form of reductionism. If the law of mind[79] is the law of general kinds and their regular behavior, then it is impossible coherently to separate matter absolutely from mind such that the two are incompatible. Rather, the fact that the elements of an individual

75. Ibid., 1.337–348.
76. Ibid., 2.307–308.
77. Ibid., 5.137 ff.
78. Ibid., 2.252–253.
79. Peirce, "The Law of Mind," in *Collected Papers*, 6.102–163.

fact (such as the rolling billiard balls on the table) admit of general descriptions and their behavior admits of general characterizations means for Peirce that they manifest the operation of mind. This mind may turn out to be an evolutionary mind governing the universe or it may be the mind of a god (be this god personal, impersonal, or superpersonal),[80] but it is a mind. In virtue of this manifestation of mind, things can be understood by our human minds. Indeed, Peirce remarks that the truly amazing evidence of the mind's adequacy to reality is that we can so frequently hit on fruitful hypotheses to explain nature.[81] Peirce argues that only a mind can understand mind, because mind functions with meaning and inference. Therefore the human thinker interacts with the meanings that lie present before him in the world he considers.

The objective of the present study, of course, is not to analyze in depth the thought of Charles Sanders Peirce. This introduction of him serves two purposes: First, we note that this scientifically minded thinker, whose philosophical and scientific studies took place in the heyday of positivism, was convinced—on the strongest possible bases, he argued—that body and mind, matter and spirit, were not antithetical, but that an adequate account of the world and thinking beings within it requires an integrated understanding of intelligence and material structures. Second, we will make use of two central themes of Peirce's study: his theory of signs and that of habits.

David Braine and the Anglo-American Tradition

If Karol Wojtyła attempts to recapture the integrated Aristotelian conception from a continental, phenomenological starting point, philosopher David Braine proposes recapturing the Aristotelian conception from the perspective of Anglo-American philosophy of mind: "In brief, it is the human animal, who is a 'spirit,' an intellectual being or substance."[82] Similar to Wojtyła, he argues, "The truth that we have to bring out is that the

---

80. See especially Peirce, "A Neglected Argument for the Reality of God," in *Collected Papers*, 6.452–493.

81. Peirce, *Collected Papers*, 2.753 and 5.172–174.

82. David Braine, *The Human Person: Animal and Spirit* (Notre Dame, IN: University of Notre Dame Press, 1992), 6.

events and goings on which we refer to as perceptions, sensations, emotions, and intentional actions are *irreducibly hybrid, the mental inextricable from the physical.*"[83] Braine's argument is that there are no raw data that intelligence then interprets, that at its most basic level, even perception is interpretive. Likewise, intentions are not mental events somehow added to motions, but are present in and expressed by acts themselves.[84] At root, Braine rejects *physicism*, the notion that physical reality ultimately reduces to brute matter without teleology, and admitting of adequate description by invariant mathematical laws. He argues that such a conception is inadequate, not only to account for human mental life, but even for scientific understanding.[85] The mechanistic explanations of seventeenth-century science were to replace explanations in terms of substantial forms; what they did in fact, according to Braine, was to replace multiple such forms with one, that of matter or—better—material particles, into which all other things could be analyzed.[86] Concerning the modern rejection of teleological explanation, Braine notes that this rejection is usually the result of confusing teleology with efficient causality, of treating the end as an efficient cause.[87] The only way satisfactorily to account for human being and behavior, in Braine's view, is to regard the human being as an integrated whole. In particular, that distinctively human behavior—linguistic understanding—demands a nonmaterialist account that integrates the physical human activities of expression with rational understanding.[88] Language is the bodily behavior that manifests intellectuality.

THE PRESENT PROJECT

The goal of this present study is to determine, as precisely as the subject matter allows, the nature of the human soul. I argue that the human powers to know the truth and to desire the good require the existence of an immaterial aspect or part of human nature, one that is not destroyed when the person dies. The argument parallels that found in the philosophical

83. Ibid., 29. [emphasis added]   84. Ibid., 140.
85. Ibid., chap. 8.   86. Ibid., 255 ff.
87. Ibid., 230 ff.   88. Ibid., chaps. 10–12.

psychology of Thomas Aquinas. Indeed, one could call this work a kind of translation of Aquinas's understanding into contemporary modes of thought. The attentive reader will note that I rely heavily on the thought of C. S. Peirce, especially his analysis of habit and sign. The fundamental empirical fact supporting the argument is that some physical thing—the human being—is rational. Even if one might argue that it is not the human being as a whole, but only some part, such as the brain or the entire nervous system, that is rational (although by implication I argue that this is unlikely), it remains that something physical is governed by laws of reason. This means that the human person can be understood not only as a thing in the world but as a sign and indeed author of significance. He is, in a way that we show, governed by logical as well as physical laws.

Since our starting point and foundation is human experience, Part Two, consisting of chapters 2 and 3, determines the experiential bases of the material and the spiritual, respectively. What do we mean when we say of a thing that it is "material" or "spiritual"? Therefore Part Two constitutes a metaphysical groundwork for the remaining analysis. Part Three, consisting of chapters 4 and 5, develops the results of Part One by integrating the material and the spiritual and showing how the powers to know and to love (or desire) constitute the human person as both spiritual and bodily. Although this is not primarily a study of the "mind-body problem" or the problem of mind and brain, these chapters show how many of the puzzles that arise in contemporary discussions arise in the first place, and how they may be resolved. My contention, which should become evident from that analysis, is that the contemporary problem is generally miscast, because mind is seen to be a function of consciousness. Approaching the same terrain from a different direction—a more Aristotelian one—the problem melts away. Part Four, consisting of chapter 6 and the Epilogue, characterizes the nature of the soul and then offers some speculative reflections on the possibility of an experiential afterlife.

PART TWO THE MATERIAL AND THE

SPIRITUAL

CHAPTER 2

The Existence and Essence of Material Things

MATERIALITY AND MATTER

Ordinarily we do not regard *matter* as a particularly problematic concept. Matter is the "stuff" of what lies all about us. Material things are, in a way, paradigmatic of reality. When we want to affirm that something is real, we most commonly appeal to material things and experiences: "as sure as you're standing there," "as real as this chair I'm sitting on." Matter is a "no nonsense" kind of reality. Material things are what they are and do not slip away as thoughts and feelings seem to so often. Nevertheless, the nature of matter, or rather the material, important as it is, proves difficult to define.

We note first that *material* is not coextensive with or equivalent to *sensible*. One can see a mirage or a rainbow, neither of which is a physical thing. On the other hand, certain very important material things—ultraviolet rays, black holes, and beta particles—are imperceptible to human senses. It is tempting to define the material as that which physics studies. Since science uncovers the nature of things, it is the task of physics to determine what matter is, whether this be earth, air, and water, or fermions and mesons. However, if we define physics as the science of matter and motion, then we cannot simply define matter as that which physics studies.

Nevertheless, although such a formulation is clearly circular, it does point us in a helpful direction.

The experience of matter

The notion of materiality arises from common human experience. One has the experience of being *here* and *not there*. To arrive at *there* he must exert some effort in the limbs. Indeed, one may fail to arrive *there*, for a door or mountain or some person may interfere with his movement. Other things impinge upon the human being, causing him to react, inflicting pain or giving pleasure. In short, we experience ourselves as in a world resistant to our efforts, one which directly impacts upon us and upon which we may impact. A yearning for freedom may wash across society, sweeping the oppressed up in a revolutionary fervor. A desire for true love may inflame a young man's heart. But neither political freedom nor the encounter with love can stop me here and now with the same force and immediacy of a blow to the solar plexus or impel my muscles as quickly as touching a hot iron. One finds himself to be a material thing surrounded by material things. Their materiality is manifest by their directly impinging on the person in a way that is independent of his thoughts, ideals, beliefs and desires. An ear-shattering shriek causes the same shock whether the screamed words express terror or joy. The first referent, therefore, to materiality is one's own self as a bodily being, located now in this place and affected by these other things.

No matter what definition we may develop for matter, the genesis of the notion of materiality is thoroughly concrete. The notion of materiality originates in and rests on the experience of the body's reactivity to factors in the environment. This is why no argument alone can suffice to prove that matter exists. The "proof" that material things exist is in the direct encounter with them in one's environment. Because there is that which is outside my control, which impedes the exercise of my will, I know there is matter. This is what materiality is. Peirce writes, "Now mere qualities do not resist. It is the matter that resists."[1] The discovery of the material is the discovery that one material thing impacts upon and affects another, first

---

1. Peirce, *Collected Papers*, 1.419.

one's own body and then that which lies about one. The characteristic of materiality is obtrusive resistance. To be material is to be "in the way," first of all to me and secondly to things around me. The ghost in the haunted house is immaterial because the thrown brick passes through it. The radiation that Roentgen did not perceive and that did not impede his activity is known to be material, for it fogged the photographic film. Overexposure to such radiation could have made him fatally ill.

To characterize materiality in terms of reactivity is not to say what *matter* is. Although it is tempting to define matter as a kind of primordial stuff from which all formed things are made, any such *Urstoff* turns out to be an abstraction. Aristotle held that matter must be formed to be known, for it is only through its form that anything can be known at all.[2] Furthermore, the notion of an ultimate *Urstoff* has been irredeemably discredited by contemporary physics. Yesterday's fundamental building blocks—once atoms and later their protons, neutrons, and electrons—are found to be constituted of strange, almost ephemeral sub-particles, some of which vanish in fantastically short periods of time, and none of which can properly even be called a "particle," if by that we mean something analogous to a grain of sand. The photon seems to be a packet of waves (but what, then, is waving?), and an orbiting electron has no definite location but only a location probability. Matter, which we take to be the most real aspect of reality, seems to slip from every effort to grasp what it ultimately is. The Pre-Socratic philosophers sought to answer the question in terms of earth, air, fire, water, or some combination of these. This notion of a common underlying *stuff* reappears in Newton, who effectively identifies it with mass, that is, "quantity of matter." Contemporary science has turned away from the notion of matter as a kind of continuous stuff and instead toward the particulate ideas of Leucippus and Democritus. Although no one claims to have identified the truly ultimate constituents of matter, scientists today expect to find an account in terms of tiny, ephemeral particles whose behavior is unlike anything on the macroscopic level. It may yet turn out, of course, that the best account of these particles will be in terms of the behavior of continuous fields. However, whatever matter is (if indeed one definition of matter is even possible) must be ultimately discovered by

2. Aristotle, *On the Soul*, II, i, 412a7 ff.; Aristotle, *Metaphysics* IV, v, 1010a24.

scientific investigation, the result of inquiry into material things. It is not something that philosophical tools alone can determine.

Space and time

Even if, properly speaking, there is no such "stuff" as pure matter and we must leave it to the physicists to determine the nature of matter, the philosopher can discover certain general characteristics of material things. Evidently material things are spatial and temporal. Wherever there is material being, there is space and time. If to be material is to be reactive, obtrusive, this reaction presupposes a change, an encounter between the reagents. The materiality of the rock is not abidingly evident, but becomes so at the moment the foot kicks against it. The foot, at one moment swinging freely, is abruptly stopped and deflected. To grasp my sandwich I must move across the room. The batter has only a brief moment to swing so as to hit the ball. In short, the reaction-event presupposes the contrasts between here and there, then and now. Reaction is an event with a place and a time. Plato's Idea of the One is outside space and time, unaffected by any other being. The One and Duality may give rise to the Many, but this is not by the One's having reacted upon Duality. The one rock, however, is shattered in a moment by its interaction with the swinging hammer. Material things are extended in space and endure through time. The fact that an interaction has taken place or can take place requires that material objects encounter each other. The ball makes contact with the bat. The wind moves the weathervane. The magnet deforms the space around it; its magnetic field is an aspect of its extension in space. The material thing is conceived as extended, for it must admit of a here and there, which are more than mathematical points. Similarly the material thing endures through time, for it must admit of a then and a now. Were we to try to conceive of a material interaction as somehow an instantaneous "flash," then the interaction as such would be destroyed. There would be no encounter between two things—only the flash. The conception of materiality depends on the experience of interaction, and this interaction presupposes the interacting things' endurance—however brief—through time.

Two cautionary notes are in order here. First, the correlation of materiality with space and time does not of itself determine the structure and extent of space and time. Whether space is curved, whether time had no beginning or an asymptotic beginning "after" the Big Bang, and whether there are additional spatiotemporal dimensions are questions whose answers depend on appropriate scientific investigation. Second, from the *then* and *now* of material interaction we cannot immediately infer the *yet to come*. The principle of materiality directs us only to the present, the now in which material things are encountered. The future is not given in that encounter, that interaction. Lacking predictive power, materiality alone does not reveal the nature of a thing.

MATERIALISM

It follows, then, that materialism is more than a science based on materiality. Materialism needs not only a theory of matter, a scientific account of matter, but also an account of why matter is all that there is. The history of science amply demonstrates that we do not know from direct experience exactly what matter is, what are its fundamental properties and the laws governing its behavior. Indeed, just as the Pre-Socratic philosophers allowed that there might well be three or four mutually irreducible forms of matter, so today there is reason to believe that *matter* is not some one thing. Today more than ever in history, we are accustomed to the notion that scientists may well discover strange new forms of matter. But the existence of an account of matter is not all that materialism needs. Materialism claims to be self-sufficient, capable of accounting adequately for every real thing, including human beings. Now this is not a scientific claim and cannot be. The claims of materialism are not based on a complete understanding of matter, but on a preconception of what might count as an explanation of reality. However, if materiality is reactivity, then materiality itself does not answer the question of how material things will behave. Materiality (as reactivity) does not entail uniformity of behavior, and in particular it does not entail precise obedience to mathematical laws. To know how material things behave—whether electrons and neutrinos, hurricanes and volcanoes, or orangutans and rhinos—it is necessary to investigate them. It may well be the case that the behaviors of some things can be adequately accounted for in terms of their constituents, as chemical bonding is explained by the valences of the electron levels, but we have no *a priori* reason to believe that such an explanation is always possible. The scientific explanation must address the nature of the thing under investigation.

BEING AND EXISTENCE

Existence

C. S. Peirce writes: "The existence of things consists in their regular behavior."[3] This somewhat puzzling statement sheds important light on the concept of existence. Clearly existence so conceived cannot be equivalent to *being;* since for something to behave regularly it must in some sense *be* and that in a sense prior to its behaving. This act or state of being, however, cannot be separated from its existence. If we seek to speak of a thing's *existence* without knowing or being able to specify its behavior,[4] then we find ourselves at a loss. As soon as we begin to attempt to think of its mode of being we find ourselves forced to discuss behavior (broadly understood). Except in natural theology, when we attempt to specify *pure being* we come up empty. Let us examine this more closely.

For a star or a lion or a stone to exist is for it to carve out its space in the world by its properties and characteristic ways of interacting. The thing's "regular behavior" includes not only its motions—the lion's going out to hunt or the star's emitting light—but also its ability to occupy a particular space in a particular time period and its qualities, such as hardness, impenetrability, rigidity, shape and so on. Whatever exercises some regular behavior (including the susceptibility to any kind of observation or measurement) can, to that extent, be said to exist. Bigfoot, if he exists, must move about the Northwest, eating, sleeping, and procreating, leaving his droppings here and there, and possibly knocking branches off trees or kill-

---

3. Peirce, *Collected Papers,* 1.411.

4. It is important to note that the notion of *pure being* has found effective application only in natural theology. If God is a being beyond all others such that no predicate is ever adequate to him and such that he is literally incomparable with any other thing, then he cannot be said to exist in the sense of having some regular behavior, some qualities or patterns of interaction that can be detected and considered scientifically. His is a being that must be beyond all existence (in our present sense of that term). We may say of God that he is Pure Being (*ipsum esse subsistens*), but this expression gives us very little information about him.

ing smaller animals. If there is no behavior, then Bigfoot does not exist. The requirement that the behavior be regular is simply the requirement that the thing be one. If Max of 4th Street and Edna of 10th Street both get sick on Friday, we call that coincidence, until we learn that both had eaten Thursday at Typhoid Mary's Diner. The disease is one; an epidemic resulting from the infection of one person or source exists. If two events are connected, then there is an existent that connects them. When the northern lights appear, radio reception is poor, because both are caused by one thing, the sun's electromagnetic radiation. But a shooting star over Indiana is unrelated to the drowning of a man in Germany. If the existence of things consists in their regular behavior, then our knowledge of them is through that regular behavior. We determine what things exist by encountering them (either ourselves or through instrumental proxies) and observing their behavior. By investigating this behavior we come to learn what they are, what kind of things they are. In determining that the behavior is regular, we give ourselves ground for future expectations. In virtue simply of a thing's being material, all we can say is that it has, at some place and time, interacted with something else. To say of it that it is an existing thing, however, is to attribute to it—albeit implicitly—an essence, a nature according to which it behaves in regular ways. The study of this nature constitutes the science of that kind of thing. The sciences investigate the manners of things' existence by investigating their behavior.

Being

Existence is not the only kind of being, and we do well to note briefly here the wider senses in which certain kinds of things are said to *be*. Every day we speak routinely of things that cannot properly be said to exist. Political candidates promise "law and order," and the voter may well respond more favorably to these abstractions he cannot see than to the promise of "a chicken in every pot." Crabgrass exists, but love does not; we try to kill the former and will die for the latter. Law and order, love, good grades next semester, the vision of oneself as a successful attorney, and a quiet determination to set things right are all realities that do not exist. So too are blindness, knowledge and ignorance, nothing, and logic. Some of these—for instance, "nothing"—are beings of reason, which have no positive being in anything but which can be referred to meaningfully. In any case, the realm of being is evidently larger than that of existence.

Furthermore, among beings we may distinguish between those that are real and those that are not. Peirce characterizes reality thus: "The reality of things consists in their persistent forcing themselves upon our recognition. If a thing has no such persistence, it is a mere dream. Reality, then, is persistence, is regularity."[5] Since existing things persist in time and interact with other things, existence is a way of being real. Cows are real; they moo and give milk. Unicorns are not real, although the idea of unicorn is real in myths and legends. Some nonexistent beings, however, also manifest this "persistent forcing (of) themselves upon our recognition." One could speak eloquently here about fundamental human needs and the deepest longings of the human heart. We do need love. We may also speak, however, about beings of reason: ideas and theories. Consider, for instance, the atomic theory. The notion that matter may somehow be broken into ultimate parts has ancient roots. In the fifth century BC Leucippus of Miletus proposed an atomic theory. Democritus picked up on it and tried to develop it. Kant worried about its implications in the "Second Antinomy of Pure Reason."[6] In the late nineteenth and twentieth centuries the atomic theory came to fruition and is now accepted as true. This idea of ultimate atomic parts of matter has persisted for 2,500 years; even without proof and in the face of substantial objections, the idea persists. The idea of atoms is real, because it has exercised an unremitting pull on the human mind. To be sure, it is necessary to understand how this pull is exercised, in what this persistence consists. This understanding might be in terms of the structure of our minds or, more likely, that of material reality itself. At this point it suffices to note that the idea of *atom* is real. It has structured the minds of scientists, provided them hypotheses, and helped to guide their inquiries. One might argue, on the other hand, that the proletarian consciousness is not a real being, for every effort to tap into it, develop, and foster it eventually failed.

To a great extent, the project of this book will be to discuss the real being of the human soul.

5. Peirce, *Collected Papers*, 1.175.
6. Immanuel Kant, *Critique of Pure Reason* (New York: St. Martin's Press, 1965), A434–5, B462–3.

ESSENCE: WHAT A THING IS

The question, "What is it?" seeks to categorize the thing, to classify it among things that are known, asking its properties, what its characteristic behavior might be. The questions, "What are its properties?" and "What are its regular or characteristic behaviors?" are equivalent insofar as they both express the question of the thing's essence.[7] The existence of a thing is directly related to its essence, taking this term in its Aristotelian sense as "what the thing is." Furthermore, we can classify things (that is, say what they are) according to their patterns of behavior. This is the procedure of the physical sciences, in which things are defined by precise formulae according to which their behavior can be accurately predicted. To the extent that things share the same kinds of behavior, they are the same kind of thing. Conversely, to the extent that they behave differently, to that extent they are different kinds of things. We classify things according to their regular behavior, or in Peirce's term, their habits.[8] Peirce defines "habit" as follows:

Let us use the word "habit". . . to denote such a specialization, original or acquired, of the nature of a man, or an animal, or a vine, or a crystallizable chemical substance, or anything else, that he or it will behave, or always tend to behave, in a way describable in general terms upon every occasion . . . that may present itself of a general describable character.[9]

The term *habit* therefore applies not only to animate things, to which we normally reserve the term, but indeed to any existing thing. Any regular behavior of a thing is a habit. Using this definition, Peirce characterizes the laws of science as habits, albeit degenerate ones.[10] Peirce's point is not that inanimate things are somehow really animate, but that what we call habit

7. Here we are essentially restating and working with Aquinas's conception of *res* as one of the transcendental predicates of being. "We can, however, find nothing that can be predicated of every being absolutely, with the exception of its essence by which the being is said to be. To express this, the term *thing* (*res*) is used; for according to Avicenna, *thing* differs from *being* (*ens*) because *being* gets its name from *to-be* (*esse*), but *thing* expresses the quiddity or essence of the being." Aquinas, *De Veritate* q. 1, a. 1.

8. Peirce, "A Detailed Classification of the Sciences," *Collected Papers,* 1.203ff.

9. Peirce, "Belief and Judgment," *Collected Papers,* 5.538.

10. Peirce, "Variety and Uniformity," *Collected Papers,* 6.97 and 101.

in animals is conceptually continuous with the law-governed behavior of stones and crystallizable substances. The difference we notice between animal habits and the laws governing inanimate things is that animal habits develop and change, whereas, as Aristotle famously noted, you can't train a rock.[11] Although he did not want to exclude the possibility that nature's laws may have evolved,[12] Peirce called such laws "degenerate" habits. Let us summarize his definition as:

"When Z obtains, a occurs."[13]

By Z we mean any state of affairs falling under a general description. Z need not be the thing's entire environment, the totality of factors that may affect that thing. Z is a state of affairs that falls under a general description. This can be as simple as "It is raining," without specifying whether the rain is warm or cold, in the city or the country, accompanied by high winds or calm. Similarly, the behavior a is specified in general terms. It may be "vibrate at 440 cycles per second" or "secrete salty fluids."

Although scientific laws are not usually presented in this format ("When Z obtains, a occurs"), this formula captures what these laws express. Newton's first law of motion ($F = ma$) specifies what any physical body of determinate mass will tend to do when force is applied. When this law is combined with the law of gravitation, $F = Gm_1m_2/r^2$, it is possible to state how a falling or orbiting body will behave. The mathematical factors F, m_1, m_2, and r, constitute the state of affairs, Z.[14] The acceleration a is the behavior a. In general scientists of every stripe formulate their discoveries in terms of how a specific kind of thing will behave under well-defined circumstances. The "well-defined circumstances" may themselves be relatively complex; they may consist in interrelated force fields, each of which is defined by a complicated differential equation. The behavior a is determined only when all the variables in those equations have been specified. We ought further to recall the proviso that Z is not an exhaustive description of the entire physical environment. In determining the orbits of artificial satellites, scientists

11. Aristotle, *Nicomachean Ethics*, II, 1.   12. Peirce, *Collected Papers*, 1.409ff.

13. Strictly speaking, this should read simply, "When Z obtains, *a*," where *a* is not a substantive but a verb. My intention here is to use a shorthand and not to develop an algebra.

14. "F" is the gravitational force; "m_1" and "m_2" are the masses of the two bodies, "r" the distance between them, and "G" an empirical, invariant constant.

ignore the small but real gravitational effects of the outer planets and neighboring stars. No scientific law or principle provides us with an exhaustive picture of anything. To put it more broadly, knowing what a thing is and its regular behavior does not constitute a thoroughgoing knowledge of the thing's history, its future, and its relationships with every other thing in the universe. What a scientific law tells us is that given the relevant circumstances in which a thing is found, its behavior is determined in a particular way, to the extent that no other unspecified factors intervene.

If the existence of each thing consists in its regular behavior, and if that regular behavior can be stated in the form of scientific laws, then there exists *ipso facto* an order among things in the universe. The electron exists in relation to electromagnetic fields and protons. The lion exists in relation to grasslands, zebras, and cheetahs. The existence and nature of each thing necessarily stands in relation to other things. Each physical object is, in this respect, a part of the whole. It is the task of the physicist to discover and formulate as precisely as possible the laws governing the simplest and most basic physical parts and aspects of the universe.

The issue immediately at hand is the nature of the physical thing. We note that every physical object manifests a range of typical behaviors. Even the simple electron has not only a specific charge, but also mass and spin. Therefore, we can refine the formula as follows: "Q: When Z_i obtains, a_i occurs," where Q designates the object and i ranges over the known properties of that kind of thing. In virtue of this modification to the formula of habit, it is possible to classify things according to their shared properties. That is, we identify a class of objects Q_a such that "When Z_1 obtains, a_1 occurs." Within that class we may find Q_b and Q_c such that

Q_b: When Z_2 obtains, a_2 occurs, and
Q_c: When Z_2 obtains, a_3 occurs.

For instance, Z_1 in this case might be experimental conditions relating to mass and spin and a_1 the appropriate electron behaviors. If Z_2 is the presence of an electrical field, and a_2 and a_3 are "veer to the positive" and "veer to the negative," respectively, the formulae distinguish between the electron (Q_b) and the positron (Q_c). This kind of hierarchy of formulae underlies ordinary qualitative analysis in chemistry. By differences in behavior we can distinguish sub-classes of larger classes.

Thus, each physical object falls within a class of objects that share common behaviors and therefore properties. If a particular object fails to behave according to its characteristic habits, then an explanation is required. Either something has intervened to hinder its behavior (the water was impure; the friction was not negligible after all) or the object belongs to a new class of objects. Scientific discovery frequently occurs when things do not behave as expected under the determined conditions. What this says, in other words, is that every object conforms to law, to general rules by which it relates to other objects and in virtue of which it can be known. Science recognizes no surds. Confronted with a deviation from predicted behavior, the scientist reexamines his experimental apparatus and conditions. Failing to find any reason for the deviation and unable to repeat it, he chalks up the deviation to unknown error. This means that each physical object has its own teleology, its law, which is to behave according to the laws governing the behavior of its kind.

A historical note may clarify the point of the foregoing argument. Philosophers early in the development of modern science—thinkers such as Descartes and Newton—tended to think of matter as inert and formless "stuff." The Cartesian view was that matter's properties come from its extension, that is, from the size and shape it is found in. The material universe for Descartes was mathematical, indeed, geometric. To Descartes' extension, Newton added the notion of mass or "quantity of matter" subject to the laws of motion and gravitation. From these conceptions it was not hard to extrapolate the hypothesis that the properties of all material things could be accounted for in terms of the simple properties of inert Cartesian-Newtonian matter. Thus Laplace could formulate his celebrated hypothesis that, given the position and velocity of matter in the universe, he could (in principle) know its entire history. Along the same lines, D. M. Armstrong writes: "It seems increasingly likely that biology is completely reducible to chemistry which is, in its turn, completely reducible to physics. That is to say, it seems increasingly likely that all chemical and biological happenings are explicable in principle as particular applications of the laws of physics that govern nonchemical and nonbiological phenomena."[15] The truth is that such a conception of matter and the universe is not justified by the evidence. Neither science nor philosophical reflection warrants

15. D. M. Armstrong, *A Materialist Theory of the Mind*, 49.

the belief in an inert matter or material substratum from which everything is made and in terms of whose mathematical interrelationships everything can ultimately be understood. Rather, experience indicates that different kinds of things exist and behave according to their kinds. It is the task of human experience and the various sciences to determine how many such kinds there may be and what they are.

With this point we have reached what is, in an important sense, the heart of the issue: *How is the development or evolution of habit possible?* Whether or not one accepts Peirce's conception of physical laws as degenerate habits which admit (in principle, at least) of development, we see that certain things—animals and human beings, for example—adapt, developing new habits and changing old ones. What factors, principles, or causes underlie such development? The materialist explanation reduces essentially to this: What we call "habit" in living things is a nexus of interactions governed by invariant laws.[16] At the macro-level the human being or animal exhibits a degree of freedom, choice, and adaptability as it makes its way through the world. However, the behavior of neurons as they fire, or of post-synaptic receptors as determinate quantities of glutamate stimulate them[17] is (or is expected to be) invariant, law governed. Materialist reductionism hopes adequately and entirely to account for the apparent flexibility and adaptability of complex entities by appealing to the determinate behavior of their ultimate constitutive parts. Our ultimate goal in this present work is to show that the development of human habits requires a nonmaterial explanatory factor, the soul.

First, however, we must consider the meaningfulness of things in the world.

SIGNIFICANCE AND MEANING

Because things can be classified, they are bearers of significance. That is to say, in virtue of a thing's essence, it can represent or signify other things.

---

16. In speaking of "invariant laws," I do not at all intend to deny that some laws may well be statistical. A statistical law is also precise and enables accurate prediction.

17. Joseph LeDoux, "Small Change," in *The Synaptic Self,* chapter 6. LeDoux here describes this interaction within the brain.

It is precisely this meaning, this significance that makes the sciences possible. The scientist actually examines very few specimens of his object and then under very controlled conditions, but on that basis he characterizes an entire class. Even though most of what goes on in the universe happens outside of scientific laboratories and under conditions that preclude exact measurement or observation, scientists confidently claim to understand the principles and mechanisms making those things behave as they do. Physicists maintain that matter and energy are neither created nor destroyed, but how do they know that on Wednesday, April 17, 2002, the Colorado River did not lose a milligram of matter or an electron volt of energy? How does the earthbound scientist know so confidently how things stand in a galaxy whose light traveled for 2.5 million years to get to him? The answer is simply that one member of a real class—that is, a class of things sharing the same essence—is like another. What holds good for the lab specimen holds good for the same kind of thing in the Grand Canyon or in the Great Nebula of Andromeda.

To say that one entity represents another is to say that it is significant, meaningful. Indeed, scientists speak in precisely these terms. The subtle variations of light coming from the star 51 Pegasi, along with a slight "wobble," *indicate* that it has a planet orbiting it. The patterns in the spectroscopic analyses *mean* that the planet is gaseous.[18] Cores of ice drilled from glaciers in Greenland *tell* scientists about environmental conditions in earlier geologic ages. This significance is genuine; otherwise, scientific results would simply be fictions. One member of a class—whether this be an electron path, a star, a milliliter of sulfuric acid, or a zebra—is taken to represent the entire class. From the careful observation of one nascent solar system, scientists hope to learn much about the formation of all such systems, including our own. Successfully to observe the hunting habits of one leopard yields knowledge about all leopards. The individual is a *sign* of other members of its class.

This significance can arise in two different ways. One thing can be an *icon*[19] of the other in virtue of some resemblance between the two, on the

18. Bill Arnett, "Other Planetary Systems?" University of Arizona, Students for the Exploration and Development of Space, http://seds.lpl.arizona.edu/nineplanets/nineplanets/other.html.

19. Peirce, "The Division of Signs," and "The Icon, Index, and Symbol," in *Collected Papers*, 2.227–273, and 2.274–307, respectively, for a detailed discussion of icons and indices.

basis of a common structure. In the early stages of modern atomic theory, the structure of the solar system was taken as a model for the structure of the atom. The house cat is an icon of the lion. As both these examples suggest, the iconic significance of a thing as representative of another is limited. It turns out that an atom is more unlike the solar system than like it, and a house cat is such precisely because it can be domesticated, as a lion cannot. Nevertheless, images are suggestive and typically lead investigators to deeper understanding of things they investigate. The *iconic* significance of things is especially important for the forming of hypotheses, for developing possible connections among things. This iconic significance of one thing with respect to another is real; that is, it is in the things themselves. One thing is an icon of the other in virtue of some common shared feature. It images the other, at least in some respect.

More important for the scientist is the *indexical* significance of a thing, that one thing can, in virtue of its causal relationships, indicate another and reveal its own properties. Black holes, which are by their very nature imperceptible, can be detected by their bending light rays that pass by them. Behavior is an *index* of one thing in relation to other things. On the basis of a thing's behavior, we attribute properties to it. If a surface resists scratching and denting, we call it hard. An animal that kills other animals for food is carnivorous. Because the electrons move toward the positive pole, they have a negative charge. The thing's properties are posited to account for its behavior. Through experimentation, science investigates the behavior of things to determine their inherent properties and therefore what kinds of things they are. Because materiality is based on the thing's interactions with other things in its environment, indexical significance derives directly from the materiality of a thing.

The inherent significance of things, including inanimate physical things, is real, but limited. It is real, because what meaning these things have is there to be discovered by the intelligent observer and is not imposed. One might object, of course, that such significance is simply imposed or created by the observer, by the scientist. Fuffy T. Cat, who eats from a dish and chases yarn, is one individual and a lion of the Serengeti is another. That one might draw inferences about the lion from observing the house cat does not justify saying that the latter somehow *means* the former, that he is a *sign* conveying information about his leonine cousin. But that he does convey such information is precisely what makes him a sign. Peirce insists: "A sign, or *representamen*, is something which stands to somebody for something in some respect or capacity."[20] To be a sign is simply to stand in relation to some other thing that, according to some interpretive principle, the first conveys some understanding of the second. But, it may be objected, this interpretive principle lies in the thinking mind of the observer who compares the lion with the house cat. Between the two felines there is no intent on the part of one to represent the other. This is indeed true, but it does not negate the character by which the one is a sign of the other. The interpretive principle—in this case a common physical structure—is based on what the individuals share. In our cat-lion example, one could also note that the house cat resembles certain other things, including a puppy, a sack of potatoes, and a rabbit; all these things are about the same size and weight. Are we then to say that the cat is a sign of the puppy, potatoes, and bunny? In fact, it is. However in this case, because the interpretive principle is size, we find that the cat is of very limited usefulness for understanding the other things. On the other hand, a close study of the house cat can yield promising hypotheses about the lion.[21] If things could not represent other things— be *signs* of them—then we could not know any more than what we have actually experienced. This does not mean, of course, that things themselves *intend* meanings, but only that their shared structures and patterns of causal interaction constitute interpretive principles in virtue of which one thing can signify another to the intelligent observer.

THE NATURE OF PHYSICAL THINGS

The physical entity has a physical nature that gives rise to its habits and is the basis for its law-like behavior. Because it has a nature, the simplest way to know if a particular kind of physical thing is present is to test for it, to set up the required conditions and see whether the typical behavior is observed. If the solution darkens upon exposure to light, then it may contain silver iodide. However, if an inappropriate response is observed,

20. Peirce, "Division of Signs," in *Collected Papers*, 2, 228.
21. For example, it turns out that males of both feline species kill the infant offspring of other males, if they can.

then we suspect that a different kind of physical entity is present. In its materiality the physical thing is known to be present by the sheer fact of its interacting. Its form and future behavior are not determined by materiality alone. This makes dreams and horror stories possible. The knife on the floor may moan and secrete blood by the gallon. The pill may transform the girl into a giant, or—as more typically happens in dreams—a tool shed may have long corridors and bathrooms inside. That such things are fictions of the mind is not required by their materiality but by the natures of real things. The brute fact of interaction verifies only that the thing is there. Nevertheless, we expect—indeed, we *know*—that it has a nature. If its behavior is unusual or unexpected, then its nature can be found and understood. (We might note that every good writer of horror and science fiction knows this. The monsters and unexpected phenomena they create do obey "laws"; their behavior can be understood. The efforts of the story's protagonists to understand what they are and how they behave are ordinarily central to the plot.) There is no purely brute and inexplicable existence. In Aristotelian terms, matter, to exist, must be informed.

These considerations lead directly to a central question of metaphysics: Why do things behave as they do? A physicist shoots a stream of particles through the accelerator. Upon entering the target chamber, the proton veers toward the negatively charged pole. We ask "why?" The answer is that protons have a positive charge. To be positively charged is to be attracted to the negative pole; this is what *positive charge* means. The explanation for the particle's behavior is that it is a proton. But we may ask further, "Who says so? Why does *this* proton have to veer to the negative?" On the face of it, such annoying questions seem to betray an ignorance of physics. The question remains, however, why it is absolutely certain that *this* proton must behave the way every other proton behaves. Of course, it can happen that the physicist may find a particle that does go the wrong way. Precisely this phenomenon led to the discovery of positrons, electrons with a positive charge—a kind of anti-electron. It turned out, however, that the existence of positrons is theoretically demanded by the same theory that accounts for electrons. It is possible to determine when to expect electrons and when positrons. The question we are asking is why *this particle* has to obey all the proton laws. Aristotle notes that one cannot train a rock to ascend on its own.[22] Why is this so? Aristotle would say that such is the nature of inanimate bodies. Newton would say that the stone is subject of the law of gravity. Whether from Aristotle or Newton or Einstein, the answer is that this is how this *kind* of thing behaves.

Lurking in the background of this question is the analogy of nature's laws with human positive law. Why does the motorist slow down? He has glimpsed the police car lurking in the trees ahead. He knows that disobeying the laws regarding speed will cost him. Who says he should travel under 55 mph? The legislator does—and the police officer enforces the law. Who legislates for inanimate things, and why do they obey? In his "Fifth Way" to prove the existence of God, Aquinas refers to a direction given to inanimate things by another: "Now whatever lacks intelligence cannot move towards an end, unless it be directed by some being endowed with knowledge and intelligence; as the arrow is shot to its mark by the archer."[23] And we call this being "God." This end is not, in the first instance at least, some cosmic purpose. This end is the natural behavior of the thing; it is, in Aquinas's words, "evident from their acting always, or nearly always, in the same way." Aquinas's point here is that the directedness of inanimate things is written into them. The falling rock or orbiting moon, the deflected electron and the devouring black hole behave as they are supposed to. The law of a thing's behavior and existence is written into it. Even if one is not inclined to accept Aquinas's conclusion that the author of this end-directedness is what we call "God," he cannot deny that this is written into the nature and existence of things without also affirming that their behaviors are fortuitous. Things have their natural ends, for which they behave as they ought. Why do the stars shine in the night and the nightingales sing in the morn? Because it is their respective natures to do so.

Nevertheless, the great successes of classical physics resulted from the deliberate decision to ignore final causes. In his *Novum Organum*, Francis Bacon wrote, "Thus, however, . . . (the mind) falls back to what is actually less advanced, namely final causes: for they are clearly more allied to man's own nature than the system of the universe, and from this they have wonderfully corrupted philosophy."[24] And indeed, one might wonder at the medieval ascription of appetite to inanimate things, where the falling stone is said to have an *appetitus* for the earth, its natural place. I suggest, however, that this is too facile a reading of the ancient and medieval authors. *Appetitus* and its Greek counterpart *entelechy* do not mean *desire* or *appetite* in their usual English senses, but instead refer to the natural tendencies of things to behave always or for the most part in the same ways. The early physicists and their contemporary successors have erected an impressive science by describing in precise mathematical terms what those ways of behaving are. These ancient and medieval concepts were not so much discredited as shown extraneous for the work of building modern physics.[25]

That the notions of end-directedness, *appetitus,* and final causality are not necessary for the everyday work of physics does not mean that they are unnecessary *tout court*. When in his Fifth Way Aquinas adds the phrase "so as to obtain the best result," after citing regular behavior as evidence of action for an end, he relates regular behavior to the good. He is not one to argue that this is the best of all possible worlds, nor is he prepared to deny the reality of evils, as if to say that the death of one who has fallen (according to the strict law of gravity) from a third story window is "the best result (*quod est optimum*)." The crux of the argument is that inanimate things are ordered and that this in itself is for the best. For his purposes it suffices to note that mosquitoes behave regularly, without having to defend the existence of disease-carrying insects.[26] The good of any thing is to attain its proper end, which is founded on its form.[27] Nevertheless, this phrase "so as to obtain the best result" clearly points to an order external to the thing that is so ordered. What Aquinas has in mind is that each thing fits into an ordered universe, as part of a whole in which everything has its own proper behavior. Teleology, properly understood, is an expression and result of a thing's obeying general laws, of its realizing its nature through its characteristic habits. A thing's teleology is its ordination to a future result describable in general terms. For the simplest entities, this ordination is

---

24. Francis Bacon, *Novum Organum* In *Great Books of the Western World*, (Chicago, London, Toronto: Encyclopedia Britannica, 1952), First Book, No. 48.

25. E. A. Burtt, *The Metaphysical Foundations of Modern Science* (Garden City: Doubleday, 1954), 15 ff.

26. See Thomas Gilby, O.P., "The Five Ways" in Aquinas, *Summa Theologiae,* vol. I *The Existence of God,* Thomas Gilby, General Editor (Garden City, NY: Image Books, 1969), 262–273.

27. Aquinas, *Summa Theologiae* Ia q. 5, a. 5; *De veritate,* q. 21, a. 6.

simple in the extreme. The massive body moving through space *will* continue in a straight line at constant velocity until it should fall under the influence of other body's gravitation. For more complex entities, this ordination is correspondingly more complex. In the evening, the hungry panther *will* set out to hunt, following scents and sounds and using the experience of previous hunts. Her behavior is to be explained in terms of her need for food and the consequent objective of finding and capturing prey. To be an asteroid is to move through space under the influence of gravity; to be a panther is to be a nocturnal predator. The fact that different things have different but constant natures makes possible an order among them. If the natures of some things are changed, or if new natures are introduced into a system, then the "natural order" changes. We know only too well by now how the introduction or the elimination of species from an ecosystem can disrupt the system as a whole. If you kill the coyotes, the jackrabbits will ruin the crops. And hospital administrators now have to grapple with the fact that powerful antibiotics allow only the most virulent bacteria to survive and thrive, thus unwittingly turning healthcare facilities into breeding grounds for super-germs. The order of nature is an order established by the respective teleologies of the different kinds of things that are found in nature. It is in this sense that the law-like behavior of the electron or planet is "for the best."

CONCLUSION

The question before us is the human person. What is a human person? How, in what manner, does a human being, a person, exist? According to the principle stated earlier in this chapter, the existence of the human person must consist in his or her regular behavior. This brings us to the question of habits, their formation and development. If the question is about the characteristic behaviors of the human person, one might well object that there are no such behaviors—or perhaps that there are too many. Some argue that to be human is nothing distinctive, that *human* is a relatively minor variation of *animal*, since much human behavior can be interpreted as a sophisticated variant of animal behavior. Let us note here that it is precisely the task of biology to determine what are the structures and laws underlying all living things, the principles governing bacteria and brains. Alternatively, some, such as Sartre, argue that to be human is to be radically free, that *no* behavior is characteristically human, because freedom precludes the very notion of the "characteristically human." Our strategy, therefore, will be to examine the bases of habits in general and then of human habits and their development.

The point of this chapter has been to characterize the material, for if—as indeed I intend—we are to argue that materialism is unable to account adequately for the nature and behavior of the human being, then a characterization of the material is demanded. The fundamental achievement of this chapter is to characterize the material itself in terms of reactivity. This characterization is based on an analysis of the fundamental human experience of bodily existence in the world. Matter is given to us in every moment of our lives, and our bodies bump up against reality as we exert ourselves against and are impacted upon by the environment. This does not mean that matter reduces to subjectively experienced resistance, but only that such experience reveals the material. I have further argued that the philosopher as such cannot determine what matter is; this is a task for the physical scientist.

If the existence of things consists in their regular behavior, then the existence of human beings consists in their regular behavior, in their habits. The fundamental question is: Do human beings exist? And we can regard this question in two very different but complementary ways. As indicated before, on the basis of scientific evidence, one might deny that the human animals differ in any significant way from their less-sophisticated cousins among higher primates. Thus, human beings may be said to exist as a kind of variant on primate animals. This hominid sub-species might even evolve into a new, higher species than that with which we identify ourselves. Indeed, precisely such a perspective follows upon the strategy of the sciences, which do not examine the human being as a whole, but rather the fundamental biological structures by which he is constituted—proteins, DNA, different kinds of cell, and so on. Any study of human nature as a whole is regarded as a kind of stopgap, as we await the completion of a complete account of the human being's biological constituents. Complementing this is the approach based on consciousness, according to which the radical freedom of the conscious human being renders superficial and, indeed, dangerous any definition of a human nature. The freedom of the conscious human person is so fundamental that it is not legitimate to characterize any set of habits as constitutive of human nature. I am what today I autonomously choose. The question then remains how to reconcile the two—the determined biological nature of us higher mammals as discoverable by the biological sciences, and the freedom to choose and define oneself according to the imaginings of consciousness.

In this study I maintain that neither of these reductionist alternatives is correct, that the dichotomy is false. My thesis is that the human being can neither be reduced to a system of predetermined habits nor to a center of pure consciousness, but rather that the formation of a human being's habits and his consciousness arise from the same source. Searle writes, "We think of ourselves as *conscious, free, mindful, rational* agents in a world that science tells us consists entirely of mindless, meaningless physical particles. . . . How, for example, can it be the case that the world contains nothing but unconscious physical particles, and yet that it also contains consciousness?"[28] The answer, in a nutshell, is that the world does not really consist only of "mindless, meaningless (and) unconscious physical particles." Among the things the world contains are rational animals, by which I mean not simply beings that have a reasoning power inside (analogous to the computer inside a spacecraft). Rather, the human being is a rational being, a kind of being, an animal, whose fundamental governing principle is rational, whose body and life are a sign representing something further. The question is whether there are human behaviors fundamentally and intrinsically different from purely material processes and irreducible to physical laws. To be a rational animal, I shall contend, is to be able rationally to form one's habits and therefore the laws one is subject to. In other words, the human being is spiritual as well as material. However, the terms, *spirit* and *spiritual* admit of a variety of interpretations and (mis)understandings. It behooves us, therefore, to examine them closely, and we do so in the following chapter.

28. Searle, *Minds, Brains, and Science*, p. 13.

CHAPTER 3

Spirit and the Spiritual

THE CHARACTERISTICS OF THE SPIRITUAL

Just as we find the conception of the material to be rooted in human experience—in the resistance of things in the environment to our efforts—so do we also find the spiritual in experience. Even more than as material, we commonly regard ourselves as spiritual beings. Indeed, most people consider the spiritual to be the most characteristically human, to be that which makes us most authentically what we are. What, then, is a spirit or a spiritual being?

We may start by considering our use of these terms *spirit* and *spiritual*, not in philosophical, but in everyday contexts. Any athletic coach will aver that physical ability and strength are insufficient to win regularly. Winning athletes have to have spirit, and indeed the testimony of countless "underdogs" who have won when hopelessly outclassed testifies to the importance of *spirit*. When we ask such athletes about their spirit, they speak in terms of never giving up, of believing that with focus, commitment, faith in themselves, and their best effort they could win. Napoleon said that in war, "the moral is to the physical as three to one." In war as in sport, there is no victory without spirit. In other areas of endeavor we speak of *spirit* as a motivating ideal. For example, even after his assassination, Martin Luther King Jr.'s spirit was said to live on in the struggle for civil rights. Although this spirit is vague in many respects (which is why members of a movement may argue vociferously about what or who most truly respects the spirit in question), we can normally identify certain essential features of it. Martin Luther King's spirit, for instance, requires uncompromising commitment to the ideals of equality and nonviolence, and it would certainly exclude armed revolt or violent efforts to establish an African American aristocracy. We may even speak of a national or ethnic spirit. Characteristically, Americans value personal freedom, and the Chinese value social order. In ordinary usage, the notion of spirit invariably refers to the values, the goals governing the behavior of those who embrace or have that spirit. To be spiritual, therefore, is to be governed by ideal, rather than material (or physical) factors. What does this mean, to be governed by *ideal* factors? (We remain, for the moment, in the realm of ordinary usage.) To act for an ideal is to form one's actions according to a kind of mental vision, an idea of how things can be. This ideal can be the realization of a particular state of affairs: victory over the stronger team or removal of the corrupt political machine from City Hall. Or it can be a transformation of oneself or a group, as is the case with every student undertaking a course of study. Whenever people speak of acting for an ideal, implicit is a contrast with the physical. By dint of discipline, intelligence, loyalty, commitment, or superior desire they will overcome the physical obstacles to the realization of the vision.

Although *ideal* is etymologically related to *idea*, the two (as we understand them here) are different. An *ideal* is some sort of desirable future state, condition, or value that guides the actions of those who adopt it. Whether the ideal is a personal pledge to care only for oneself—"As God is my witness, I'll never be hungry again," [1]—a commitment of a leader to foster democracy—"We do highly resolve . . . that this government of the people, by the people, and for the people shall not perish from the earth,"[2]—or a pledge to resist a powerful enemy to the utmost—"We shall fight on the beaches, we shall fight on the landing grounds, we shall fight in the fields and in the streets, we shall fight in the hills; we shall never surrender," [3]—or whatever else one might propose, the ideal is some describ-

1. Scarlett O'Hara in the film *Gone with the Wind*, Directed by Victor Fleming, 1939.
2. Abraham Lincoln, "Gettysburg Address," Roy P. Basler, ed., *The Collected Works of Abraham Lincoln*, (1853–1855), vol. 7.
3. Winston Churchill, Address to the House of Commons, June 4, 1940. Accessed from

able condition, value, or state of affairs in terms of which human beings form their actions. The ideal is known, therefore, through a representa-/ tion, most often verbal, of that state. And here is the philosophical issue. The pledge of oneself (or of the community; for simplicity we shall speak in terms of the individual's ideal here) to the ideal is accomplished by formulating a vision, a representation of the desirable state, condition, or value. This representation is itself a material, physical thing—marks on a page or sounds in the air—which is physiologically "recorded" in a human mind in the form of memories. In what sense is it spiritual? That is, we maintained earlier that to be spiritual is to be governed by an ideal. How does the representation one makes to himself or community govern spiritually? How is Scarlett O'Hara's defiant hilltop proclamation or Lincoln's inspired pledge related to the physical, historical situation that each faced?

Before moving into this analysis, two ancillary points are worth noting. The first, which is evident from the O'Hara quote, is that although we normally think of ideals as high-minded and noble, they need not be. Very selfish people can have clear ideals. (One is reminded of reports that Iraqi dictator Saddam Hussein modeled himself on Soviet dictator Joseph Stalin.) Second, is that an ideal, while general, also entails possible plans of action. Lincoln believed that the attainment of the ideal stated at Gettysburg required the successful prosecution of the war to preserve the Union. Churchill's address was accompanied by meetings with generals to draw up battle plans. The coach of the underdog team spells out the steps to victory in his game plan. The ideal, the ultimate vision has practical consequences, intermediate steps toward its attainment.

To say that the ideal governs one's life is to say that without it life would proceed differently. And indeed this seems factually to be the case. This governance, however, is not material. We do not allege that the actual representation of the ideal so interacts with its hearers that it causes them to realize the state represented by the ideal. (It is true, of course, that the rhetorical impact of a statement of ideals can stir up the ardor of its hearers to attain the lofty goals it sets out.) The ideal works, instead, by guiding and thereby forming the future activities of the one who accepts it in such

The Winston Churchill Centre Website, http://www.winstonchurchill.org/i4a/pages/index. cfm?pageid=388#in.

a way that that attainment of the ideal state or condition is fostered. One conforms himself to the ideal, in a sense, in order to realize it. For this to occur, two things are necessary. The first is that the representation have to do with reality. By this I do not mean that the ideal has to be realistic, in the sense of attainable for this person with his resources. Rather I mean simply that the ideal is capable of representing things as they really could be, that it be capable of being *true*. The second is that the representation be desirable or of value. To pursue an ideal is to act to attain something whose existence is "only mental" rather than something actually existing. Scarlett resolves to put aside every sentimental or romantic impulse that might interfere with her resolution to be rich and secure. Churchill proposes that the English put aside their normal fear in the face of a powerful enemy.

The ideal has meaning, and this concept of meaning depends on two further, fundamental concepts: goodness (or the good) and truth (or the true). This is to say that we seek meaning because we are fundamentally ordered to good as good and to true as true. These notions will lead us to that of being as such. Indeed, more frequently from this point on it will be necessary to consider the transcendental predicates of being, as discussed in Aquinas's *Quaestiones Disputata de Veritate*.[4] It is in virtue of this orientation to truth and the good that we are spiritual beings. Karol Wojtyła writes: "The faculties that express and actualize the soul's spirituality, and thus the human being's spirituality, are reason and free will."[5] The connection, as we shall see, between the physical behavior (and hence existence) of the person and the ideals lies in the ideas that found the meaning common to the ideal (a representation) and the existing situation within which one acts.

To examine this notion of the spiritual, therefore, we turn our attention to the good and the true and the relationship of these concepts to ideas.

4. See my discussion in Adrian J. Reimers, "St. Thomas's Intentions at *De veritate* 1, 1," in *Doctor Communis*, vol. 42, no. 2, (Maggio-Agosto 1989).

5. Wojtyła, "Thomistic Personalism," in *Person and Community*, p. 168.

THE GOOD AS GOOD

By *good* we understand something to be desired.[6] This is to be construed as broadly as possible. Whatever can be desired for whatever reason is in that respect a good. Food is a good for maintaining life. Exercise and fresh air are good for maintaining mental and physical health. Knowledge is good because it enriches and empowers the mind. But we may also say that a "zip gun" is good for holding up liquor stores, and the rack was good for torturing prisoners. Although we can (must!) distinguish among genuine, illusory, and false goods, it is important to recognize how the logic of good is to be related to desire. When a thug describes a holdup as a good job, we say that he is wrong about what is good, but we understand what he means. This means that anything whatever can be described and experienced as a good (or an evil). A scientific researcher may value dung or dust as good. The archeologist finds a strange artifact and asks what it was good for. The engineer reads of a chemist's discovery and thinks how it may be of use—that is, good for something. The mold spoiling melons in a Peoria, Illinois, fruit market was exactly the kind needed for producing penicillin. Such goods are *goods for* something else, that is, goods in relation to some further good. Further, the *good as such* refers to that—whatever it may be—which is desirable in and of itself and in terms of which any other good can be judged and desired.

We come into existence wanting and loving. To value is innate. The doomed infant in the ultrasonically filmed abortion, *Silent Scream,* squirms to evade the abortionist's tools. The newborn protests at the light in the delivery room and soon seeks the breast. The baby wants comfort and attention, and later develops curiosity about the world and a predilection for play. From very early in life, the human being desires good things; his behavior is directed by values. The living human body strives in every respect for life. Cells take in nourishment, grow and reproduce. The heart beats to nourish the body, and the lungs take in air. The immune system fights off infections, and the digestive tract breaks down sugars and proteins to build the body up. All this is beyond the reach of human willing, but it is part of

6. Aquinas, *De Veritate,* 1, 1; see also Aquinas, *Commentary on the "Nicomachean Ethics"* (Chicago: Henry Regnery Co., 1964), Book I, Lec. 1, 9–11; Aquinas, *Summa Theologiae,* Ia, q. 5, a. 1, and Aquinas, *On Evil* q. 1, a. 2.

being human. The human being is naturally ordered toward life. The body, in virtue of its biological structure and functioning, has an innate desire for life and the things that support life. Beyond life itself, other values, such as comfort, knowledge, and acceptance by others, become quickly evident. Although we come into the world oriented to certain goods, it is not true that life—or any other good of human experience—is the one thing that all humans by nature desire and cannot help desiring. The desire for life is innate insofar as the human organism is born valuing it, but it is not foundational. By suicide, one can repudiate life itself as a good. Indeed, as we look more closely at the way human beings live, we find that the task of determining what is truly good is an important aspect of every human life. While the question of suicide puts the issue most dramatically, the question is faced in a myriad of different decisions that every one of us makes. We need only to consider the decisions people make every day about diet and exercise, choice of career, hobbies, smoking, choice of friends, and so on. Some people choose a particular line of work, such as firefighting or race car driving, in part precisely because it is dangerous to life and health. Many knowingly disregard the dangers of overeating and an idle lifestyle, because they want a life of ease and physical satisfaction. The Christian martyrs and national war heroes sacrifice their own lives for the sake of something they value more than life itself. The question of the nature of goodness becomes central as one's life proceeds. One can seek not just the good as known or experienced, but the good absolutely considered. One can, as it were, choose to pursue the *highest or perfect good*, whatever that may be.

Two faulty claims

Let us note briefly here that we must reject the claims that (1) the notions of good and evil are founded entirely or solely on the experiences of pleasure and pain, and (2) the human person is incapable of acting except on the basis of self-interest. Both of these claims effectively reduce the notion of good to a material relationship and therefore evacuate the notion of good.

(1) Pleasure and pain.   That good and evil are founded on the experiences of pleasure and pain flies in the face of common human experience,

and defenders of this thesis have to resort to complex rationalizations to make the theory fit the facts. Why does one man sit at ease in his home, enjoying friends, family, and the comforts of the middle class, while another risks life and safety to work for the rights of an oppressed minority? One can respond that the second is trying to earn a place in heaven, or is so constructed psychologically, that helping the oppressed gives him pleasure. Such explanations have the dubious strength that they are irrefutable. One can always say that any person you choose acts on the basis of desires the attainment of which he finds pleasurable. This is true, as it stands, but if the criterion for desire is pleasure, then the explanation has become circular. One can legitimately ask why more people have not picked up on the pleasure of caring for the dying on the streets of Calcutta. Mother Teresa's own testimony was that the work itself is unpleasant. Quite different, but equally problematic for the pleasure-pain thesis, is the phenomenon of masochism. There are people who desire intense pain, who take pleasure in pain. Even if one calls this perverse, it is still real. If pain is a pleasure—at least for some people—then how do pleasure and pain stand as the basis for all human action? If the argument that ultimately only pleasures and pains motivate human persons is to be subject to evaluation, then the first step is to define what constitutes a pleasure and what a pain. Then we can look at different cases and determine whether the theory holds.

The most serious objection to this position, however, is that one can legitimately and reasonably ask whether the attainment of *any* pleasurable state you may name is good. In other words, the concept of goodness is simply not reducible to that of pleasure. Although it is certainly true that pleasure and pain powerfully influence the way human beings behave, the very concept of the good entails a relationship with human action. This is precisely why Aristotle found virtue so important for the good life.[7] The good is what is worth realizing. The overweight glutton mutters as he downs the cheesecake, "I really don't need this," and in doing so acknowledges the good that is different from his pleasure. There is an alternative course of action to indulging the desire for pleasure. The good is to be pursued; its relation to pleasure is a separate matter.

7. Aristotle, *Nicomachean Ethics* II, 3 and especially 9.

(2) Self-Interest. That, ultimately, a human being can act only in his own self-interest suffers similar flaws. For this argument to work *self-interest*, like *pleasure*, has to be so defined as to include any interest that a self may have.[8] This claim ultimately flows from dualism, an abstract conception of human nature, that human subjectivity is constituted in a consciousness fundamentally separate and distinct from the body, the world, and other human beings. Descartes conceived of himself as a thinking substance, absolutely different from his body and other extended substances. Empiricism conceived of a human subjectivity consisting of sense impressions and the recollection of them, such that there was no getting past the phenomena to the true natures of things. In general, as David Braine has cogently argued,[9] modern dualist and materialist philosophies come to the same results. One of these is that the person as a center of consciousness becomes detached from the physical world in such a way as not to be part of it. According to such a conception, it is difficult to understand how genuine human communion, sympathy, or concern is even possible. If the human person exists as an isolated consciousness, then he cannot genuinely enter into another's experience, suffering, and desire. Therefore, the only interest one can have is his own; if someone claims an interest in another, then that must reduce to self-interest. However, we often feel joy, outrage, relief, sorrow, and excitement about things that do not touch us directly. Whether Agassi wins at Wimbledon will affect my life not a bit, but I care. Collectively we breathe a sigh of relief if a child lost in a distant state is found safe. The advocate of the self-interest theory must construct accounts by which such shared interests are actually self-interest. As with the first claim, concerning pleasure and pain, it is certainly true that by taking an interest in something, one makes the interest his own. However, what is needed for the self-interest theory to work is to specify in advance, as it were, what constitutes self-interest. Otherwise, the theory reduces to saying that everything a person is interested in is what he is interested in.

Fundamentally, this argument to individualism fails by narrowing the concept of good. The good is that which is worth realizing, worth striving for and attaining. Although that which benefits oneself may well turn out

8. On this and the preceding paragraphs, see Peirce, *Collected Papers*, 5.354–355 and 382.
9. David Braine, *The Human Person: Animal and Spirit*, 2 ff.

to be good, the notion of good is not restricted only to self-interest. There is no reason why one cannot desire and strive for goals that do not relate to or even conflict with one's own self-interest. Although one may well feel a sense of satisfaction in having contributed to the greater good or in having done something altruistic, there is no reason to believe that the act reduces to the act of self-satisfaction.

At the root of these two faulty claims is an implicit reduction of good. The first claim is that good reduces to a material or physical relationship, that the dynamism underlying every human striving and action is physical, the response of the physical organism to the conditions of its environment. This is tantamount to holding that pleasure is a kind of optimal state, which the animal organism naturally seeks to attain. Perhaps as a result of evolutionary pressures, the organism experiences as pleasant that which maintains its own and its species' existence. Humans would then differ from the other animals only in that our pleasures are more varied and sophisticated. The second claim reduces goodness to a purely subjective ascription. Only that is good which the agent determines for himself to be good. The good is not truly shared or independent of the desiring agent. Contrary to both these positions, however, the notion of good transcends the material and the purely subjective. The good as such is worth pursuing and attaining, whether or not this be pleasant or to one's personal advantage. Whether one actually pursues it or not, he is capable of recognizing its reality and of orienting his life to it. *Good* is, in other words, a transcendental predicate.

The reality and relativity of good

This discussion of the notion of good would be incomplete were we to ignore the related issues of the reality of good and its relativity. If the good is not something real in things or if good is entirely relative to subjective desires, then the notion of the spiritual is undercut, shown to be in one crucial respect itself unreal and relative.

Good as real.   The principal reason for holding that the good is unreal is that science has no need of the good, that an adequate and true account of the world can be given without reference to good or purpose. John Searle notes that because Darwin effectively removed teleology and purpose from evolution, we cannot speak of the *good* of natural structures. Searle considers the following sentences.

1. "The heart causes the pumping of the blood."
2. "The function of the heart is to pump blood."

Although both assert exactly the same facts, the second "assigns a normative status to the sheer brute causal facts about the heart, and it does this because of our interest in the relation of this fact to a whole lot of other facts, such as our interest in survival. . . . All of the teleological features are entirely in the mind of the observer."[10] That is to say, the beating of the heart is not in itself objectively a good. We regard the heart as having a "function" (and therefore serving some good) because we subjectively value our lives. In the order of nature, however, this beating is valueless and purposeless. Because hearts beat, mammals with beating hearts survive and thrive; a heart that can beat is a successful adaptation in that species that have such hearts survive and reproduce. Failure of a heart to beat is not an evil; it simply ends the ability of a particular organism to function. Searle's graphic and colorful example illustrates a principle dating back to Bacon,[11] that to understand the natural world we have no need of final causes, that a complete and adequate explanatory account of the world can be given without recourse to purpose, end, or good.

What this argument shows, however, is not that the concept *good* is inapplicable or of merely subjective interest, but only that it has no application in contemporary physical sciences, as these understand their task. Aquinas actually addresses the issue in his treatment of *good* in *De Veritate*. To the proposition that being and good are interchangeable, it is objected: "In mathematics being is found, but not good."[12] Aquinas's response is instructive:

The things which a mathematician studies are good according to the existence which they have in reality. The very existence of a line or of a number, for instance, is good. But the mathematician does not study them according to their

10. Searle, *The Rediscovery of the Mind*, 52.
11. See note 16, chap. 2.
12. Aquinas, *De Veritate*, q. 21, a. 2, Obj. 4.

existence but only according to their specific formal character. For he studies them abstractly, though they are not abstract in their existence but only in their notion. . . . And so the note of goodness does not belong to a line or a number as they fall within the purview of the mathematician, even though a line and a number are good.[13]

What is interesting here is that, unlike the parallel passage in his *Summa Theologiae* (Ia 5, 3 obj. 4 and ad 4), Aquinas does not argue on the basis of the abstract character of mathematical objects. In *De Veritate* he grants them whatever existence they might have and maintains that, in virtue of that existence, they are good. The reason, therefore, that *good* does not appear in mathematics has not to do with the nature of its objects but is because of its method of studying things, which is "[not]according to their existence but only according to their specific formal character." Lines, angles, and numbers might be good, but mathematicians simply do not consider this goodness. Mathematical reasoning simply does not make use of the notion of finality.

The pertinence of this to our current discussion is that contemporary physical sciences proceed precisely by reducing physical systems to mathematical structures. Every mechanism admits of mathematical description, and the task of the scientist is to determine how the various components of a system may be quantified and related mathematically to other factors. The scientist then studies the system and its associated objects "[not] according to their existence but only according to their specific formal character." Therefore, the scientist finds no goodness within his scientifically understood world. This proves that the good is unreal (or merely subjective) only if scientific knowing is coextensive with knowledge *tout court.* The world we experience, however, is full of goods to which one must respond appropriately. This ordinarily means intelligently, that is, with knowledge. One needs to know not only if 10W30 motor oil is good in this climate but also if accounting is a wise career choice. In other words, there is no prima facie warrant to accept the scientific exclusion of finality from our knowledge of good about how things are.

13. Ibid., ad 4.

Good as relative.   Equally serious is the objection that every evaluation is relative only to the individual center of desire, to the subjective preferences of the individual person. If this position is to be maintained, then it requires proof. Our experience, both personal and corporate, has been that human beings can and do universally recognize certain things—a mother's care, adequate food, knowledge, love between a man and a woman, laughter, shelter from inclement weather—as goods. Failure to recognize the reality and relevance of certain basic goods is ordinarily taken to indicate that a person is somehow deficient, perhaps mentally ill or immature. Radical relativism, which holds that all goods are so only because of subjective evaluation, is not supported by ordinary human experience. This is not to say that we enjoy universal agreement about what is ultimately good or what the highest or most important goods are. In fact we do not. Indeed, some of the most significant conflicts that human beings enter into, both individually and corporately, concern fundamental disagreements about what is good. However, the significance of such conflicts and disagreements is not necessarily that *good* is relative but that goods can be compared and evaluated. As we have already indicated, a fundamental task for every human person is to determine what goods are to be striven for more than others. The hierarchy of goods and the highest good are not given immediately and indubitably to human experience. There is no a priori reason why such a hierarchy and highest good may not be real.

THE TRUE AS TRUE

Concerning the true we can argue in much the same way as we do concerning the good. Any representation that corresponds with reality, representing it as it really is, is true. Professor Joseph Pieper once posed the issue[14] by asking his hearers, "What would it take for this to be true: that there are men on Mars?" Students responded with a variety of proposed responses—that radio transmissions had been received, that astronomers had observed artificial structures on the planet's surface, and so on un-

14. Joseph Pieper, In a series of lectures delivered at the Internationale Akademie für Philosophie, Liechtenstein, Winter 1988.

til finally one responded that there actually be men on Mars, which was the response Pieper was looking for. His point was simply that truth is, in the final analysis, constituted by the representation's agreement with how things stand in reality. The representation may be a sentence, a theory, a picture or a map, a perception, a hand gesture—anything that purports to represent how things stand. To be sure, any discussion of truth will entail difficult issues concerning how truth is known, the criteria for establishing that something is true, verifiability, and so on. If it is true that there are men on Mars, then to know this truth we must see their artifacts, receive their transmissions, or observe the Martians themselves. But the truth itself of the statement consists not in its verification or validation, but in its correspondence to the way things really stand. This is what "truth" means. In his *Language, Truth, and Logic,* A. J. Ayer proposes that the very concept of truth is redundant, that "in all sentences of the form 'p is true,' the phrase 'is true' is superfluous."[15] The obvious objection to Ayer highlights the point. Mothers of mischievous children, attorneys on cross-examination, and incredulous customers in the auto-repair shop ask, "Is that true?" That is, "Does what you propose for my belief really correspond with how things stand?" For truth is a property of representations; of any representation—be it verbal testimony in a court, the written records of an ancient event, the readings on a mechanical gauge, or one's own perceptions—one can ask if it is true.

Like goodness, this relationship of truth is nonmaterial. It is not constituted by any dyadic physical interaction (by which we mean an interaction fully accounted for by the natures of the two entities and the physical laws governing such interactions) or combination of such interactions. However fruitful it may be to account for human knowledge and reasoning in terms of adaptation to evolutionary pressures, this adaptation does not account for the truth of what human beings come to believe. The reason for this is simply that of any perceptual or physical interpretation we can ask the further question, "Is it true?" The representation is never self-validating, but must be understood or interpreted, and the goal of the interpretation is to establish the truth. What the representation shares with its object, in virtue

---

15. Alfred Jules Ayer, *Language, Truth, and Logic* (London: Victor Gollancz Ltd., 1938), 122.

of which it may be true, is not something physical or perceptual, but something ideal. Indeed, as we remarked earlier, a representation can serve as an ideal. At this point, therefore, we turn to the question of ideas, for an ideal is so in virtue of an idea or ideas.

Ideas

An idea is the principle of an intellectual representation. A representation is a sign of some other thing. It is a thing—marks on paper, sounds in the air, sticks arranged on the ground, hand gestures, or virtually any other kind of gesture or artifact—which stands for some other thing to the mind of an observer who knows how to interpret it.[16] By idea I do not mean a kind of picture, although every idea will call up in the mind some image, whether visual or aural or tactile. This mental image, however, is not the idea, but only a representation of some thing corresponding to the idea. The idea is that which constitutes a rule for any representation of that being. This is to say that although the word "car" may evoke in one's mind the image of a green sedan, the idea of car encompasses automobiles of any color and model. *The structure of the idea is not sensible but logical.* Ideas are not physical or perceptible beings. Ideas are conceptually and therefore logically governed, which is to say that they have meaning. The idea of *car* is conceptually related to other ideas, such as *vehicle, street, passenger,* and *self-propelled.* It is appropriate to speak of cars as traveling on streets, but not on the information superhighway. Furthermore, as the principle of intellectual representation, the idea is a principle of unity by which diverse predicates can be applied to one subject.

Words, signs, and images—all of which are perceptible—express ideas. Ideas structure thought by relating representations logically to each other as the things they represent can relate in reality. The great advantage of signs and symbols, especially mental signs, is that they are almost infinitely malleable, governed only by the rules of meaning that we find for them. It is precisely in virtue of this that creative imagination is possible. To build a shed, one needs tools, materials, and a few hours. To represent a palace nestled in a hidden Asian valley, nothing is needed but a few sounds or

16. See Peirce, "Division of Signs," in *Collected Papers*, 2, especially 2.228.

marks on paper. Thus, representations can represent any thing, any relationship, or any property that may be conceived. Ideas themselves, however, do not admit of direct inspection or perception to determine their
contents. An idea is known, as it were, by the company it keeps—and the
manner in which it keeps that company. To know an idea extensively is to
know how the concepts it governs are used, what other ideas it relates to
and how it relates to them. Of course, what we know are not, in the first instance, ideas but things—electrons, walruses, ancient civilizations, and the
like. And our knowledge of these is expressed in signs of various sorts. The
ideas govern the use of the signs. If there is a principle of unity in the world
by which certain phenomena of experience are drawn into a whole, if there
are existing things to experience, then the knowledge of these is governed
by ideas which order the signs logically as the nature of the real things orders them in relation to each other. Thus things are known through the
ideas.[17] The reality of the idea consists not in its physical instantiation but
rather in the representational or logical relationships among signs it governs. An idea is therefore a kind of rule regulating how signs relate to each
other. The capacity of a representation to be true of the object represented
derives ultimately from its ideal and not its physical characteristics. Truth
is an ideal relationship, not a material or physical one.

It is said that teaching is the task of communicating ideas, of inducing
others to adopt ideas that they have previously not had. What the student
gains in reality, however, is an understanding of things in the world. Rather
than to speak of communicating and learning ideas, it is more accurate to
describe education as forming student minds according to or by ideas. The
student cannot know by direct inspection whether he has grasped the idea,
nor can the teacher observe it directly. Rather the knowledge of the idea is
manifest in the student's behavior, in how he speaks of the reality at issue
and how he behaves in the laboratory or discussion. Because we can represent ideas by—and can therefore unwittingly reduce them to—mental images, we can and often do fail to develop their full implications. Common
stereotypes illustrate this. Until fairly recently the mental image one had of

17. See John P. O'Callaghan, "The Problem of Language and Mental Representation in Aristotle and St. Thomas," *Review of Metaphysics* 50, no. 3 (March 1997): 526, and O'Callaghan,
"Abandoning or Modifying a Tradition: Interpreting Aristotle's *De interpretatione*" (unpublished).

'quarterback' in football was of a white man, an echo of a persistent cultural stereotype. In the realm of science, the image of electrons as tiny balls (most likely red!) so shaped the understanding of atomic physics that Born's hypothesis of quantum states—with its implication that electrons can move from one level to another without passing through the intervening space—seemed to be so much nonsense. Thus the infinite malleability of mental images can be limited by unexamined habit. When this occurs, the grasp one has of the idea, or better, the use one can make of it is accordingly limited.

BEING AS BEING

Here we may reflect further on Peirce's principle: "The existence of things consists in their regular behavior."[18] To the extent that this is true, existence reduces to capacity to interact with other things. The issue with the human being is whether and how his behavior can be nonregular. That is to say, if we accept Peirce's principle, which has been helpful to our investigation, as definitive of *being,* then it seems to follow that the human being can exist only insofar as his habits (regular behavior) can be given. If the human person is not ultimately the resultant of regular patterns of behavior, but of some ordered orientation to truth and the good (and the meaning of this ordering is yet to be specified) then he is more than "an existing thing." Indeed, it may be that in an important sense he does not fully *exist* as a person. To put it less obscurely, if the existence of the human being consists in his regular behavior and nothing else, then he exists as an entity within a causal system which he in no way transcends. There is no "real me" beyond the factors that determine "me." As we shall see later on, this issue goes to the question of the unity and identity of the self.

Our considerations of *spirit* open to us the notion of metaphysics, the science of being as being. By the very fact that we can characterize materiality as such, we open the question of being as such. That is to say, we can conceive of modes of being that are not material, raising the question of the status of being *qua* being, and not simply *qua* material (or physical). If

18. Peirce, *Collected Papers,* 1.411.

indeed it is possible meaningfully to raise the question of truth or to strive for good absolutely considered, then there is admitted, in principle at least, the conception of being that is in some sense immaterial. If truth *qua* truth can be found, then ideas, on which truth is founded, are real; that is to say, there is an ideal order underlying or governing the material. Similarly, if a good that transcends every limited or material good can be sought, then good is real. To affirm the reality of good as good, therefore, is to transcend the material order. The order of good presupposes some factor that is outside the realm of the physical. Because truth and goodness are the bases on which human beings relate to each other, the human being is a being that cannot escape metaphysics. Before developing this account further, however, we do well to consider the related topic of beauty.

BEAUTY

Manifestations of the human spirit come to a distinctive kind of unity in the creation of art. Human beings create images through visual representation, tone and rhythm, storytelling, and poetry. Humans furnish their worlds with art. The early human cave dwellers in southwestern France are distinguished from their subhuman hominid neighbors in part by their cave paintings. Animal parents care for and nourish their young, but human parents hang Richard Scarry pictures in the nursery and dangle a plastic Pooh Bear over the crib. The cat eats the same kibble every day, but its master expects variety and that his meals conform to minimal artistic standards. Foods have significance; Szechwan pork or *arroz con pollo* is almost unthinkable for an American Thanksgiving feast. Similarly, in their sexual activity—so frequently thought to be the most characteristically *animal* form of human behavior—human beings follow rituals and carry out their love making in a way involving far more than genital response and copulation.[19] Setting and accentuated physical beauty—in short, aesthetic considerations—are important elements in human lovemaking. The artis-

19. It is worth noting that it is characteristically women who bring the artistic element to activities such as eating and sexual intercourse. It is men who hasten intercourse simply for the sake of sexual satisfaction; the woman *requires* a prepared setting. Someone who eats meals straight out of the can at an unset table is either severely depressed or a male living alone.

tic impulse flows, in fact, from the metaphysical thrust that characterizes the human spirit. The Greek word, κοσμος, which means *order,* and by extension both *ornament* and the *universe as an ordered whole,* is the common root for the words *cosmos* and *cosmetic.* In ornamentation one reflects, as it were, the order of the universe. Art serves no useful function as art. Steel-frame warehouses protect from the elements as well as buildings by Pei. A story is not ordinarily as useful as a road map or a recipe. Nevertheless, we humans *need* art. This need is not just a superfluous emotional preference (if indeed there can be such) but is rooted in our rationality, in our power to understand. John Paul II, himself a poet and actor, writes: "Every genuine artistic intuition goes beyond what the senses perceive and, reaching beneath reality's surface, strives to interpret its hidden mystery. The intuition itself springs from the depths of the human soul, where the desire to give meaning to one's own life is joined by the fleeting vision of beauty and of the mysterious unity of things."[20] To understand beauty will shed important light on the spiritual.

We start by saying what beauty is *not.* Although the perception of something beautiful is pleasurable, beauty is not identical with being pleasant or agreeable. A very unpleasant thing—such as a frigid arctic landscape or a volcano spewing rivers of molten lava—may well be very beautiful. We may notice something similar concerning human artifacts. The loveliness of Johann Strauss's *Blue Danube Waltzes* contrasts strongly with Stravinsky's frequently harsh and sharply percussive *Rite of Spring,* marked as it is by dissonant chords, irregular rhythms, and disturbing phrases. To appreciate Stravinsky's masterwork, one must learn it and strive to enter into it. And of the two, it is undoubtedly the greater work of art. Similarly, although El Greco's *Toledo in a Storm* is not as lovely as any landscape photograph in *Country* magazine, its artistic value—its beauty—is far greater. Neither can beauty be identified straightforwardly with goodness. The tragedy of the man taken in by the beautiful but treacherous woman has become a dramatic cliché. Don José is betrayed by Carmen and (in the Scottish folk song) MacPherson laments: "'Twas by a woman's treacherous hand / I was condemned to die."

What I propose here is that a being is beautiful in relation to the in-

20. John Paul II [Karol Wojtyła], "Letter to Artists," 4 April 1999, (Chicago: Liturgy Training Publications, 1999).

tellect's intuitive power, its power of understanding. *Beauty is the being grasped as a whole according to a single idea.* The beauty of a thing consists in its order. In the first question of his *Quaestiones disputatae de veritate,* Thomas Aquinas offers a deduction of the predicates of being.[21] After discussing the predicates of a being considered in itself (*one* and *res*), Aquinas considers them in relation to the rational soul. In virtue of its relation to the intellect, the power to know, a being is called *true.* Truth is the correspondence or agreement between intellect and thing. In Aquinas's analysis, however, the intellectual faculty has a twofold operation: intuition, by which the intellect grasps a being's essence, and "combining and dividing," by which intelligence attributes a predicate to a subject. Strictly speaking, therefore, there is no truth in the first act of the understanding. Truth is in question only when one thing is predicated of another. One such predication, of course, might be that of an essence to a particular: "Fido is a dog," and "Socrates is a human being." To remain faithful to Aquinas's analysis, from which this conception is drawn, beauty must, in the first instance, pertain to the proper essence of a thing, to its intelligible structure or form. The true beauty of anything is based in its form. Therefore, beauty is an ideal character pertaining to the operation of the rational power. As such, beauty is a correlate of truth. Where truth is there must be beauty, and truth is found in the context of beauty.

The intellectual experience of beauty is certainly well known. Mathematicians speak of "elegant" proofs of theorems. Chess players admire the simplicity and beauty underlying complex combinations. The philosopher is struck with admiration by the subtle unities in Plato's dialogues. Indeed, most scholars are drawn into their respective fields by the beauty they find in ideas. Notwithstanding the experiences of scholars and chess players however, beauty is most commonly associated with sense experience, with the perception of sensible things. It is the sight or the sound that is most commonly described as beautiful. In one obvious respect, a human being who realizes the full perfection of human nature should be most beautiful. Such perfection would be constituted (in part, at least) by physical health and strength and moral virtue. However, this is not the way we usually speak. Violetta Valéry, the consumptive prostitute heroine of Verdi's *La Traviata,* was reputedly the most beautiful woman in Parisian soci-

---

21. See Adrian J. Reimers, "St. Thomas's Intentions at *De Veritate* 1, 1."

ety.[22] Her beauty lay in the proportions of her body and the structure and coloring of her face, physical attributes doubtless enhanced by her graceful carriage and smile, as well as flattering clothing and makeup. In short, her beauty consisted in the order of her physical appearance. We may say in general that the beauty of any visible thing lies in the apparent balance and harmony of its visible parts. The beauty is seen when one recognizes or perceives the sensible thing as a whole. Such beauty, however, is of the thing as visible. An internist might well have found the state of Violetta's lungs horrifying, and Monsieur Germont, *père*, was shocked by her moral character. Thus, physical beauty is to sense perception as formal beauty is to the rational power. In a way, our analysis confirms that beauty is in the eye of the beholder. Beauty is the form of the thing as apprehended by the cognitive power, whether this be perception or the understanding. In discerning a thing's form, the cognitive power perceives its beauty. If the form is not grasped, then the thing does not appear as a beauty. This is why what may strike a novice as unremarkable appears to a connoisseur as beautiful. The detective may admire the schemes of a master criminal, even while joining in others' moral outrage at the crimes. More to the point, this is why one has to learn to appreciate classical music or jazz.

Although beauty has the aspect of truth (at least in the first instance), the response to beauty is one of admiration. This is different from the desire of the thing itself as a useful good, but it points to the goodness of the thing in its own right. John Paul II connects beauty with the transcendental predicate *good*: "In a certain sense, beauty is the visible form of the good, just as good is the metaphysical condition of beauty."[23] Let us again consider the beauty of a human being. It is not beauty itself that stirs sexual desire. Of course, the physical attributes that relate to fertility can be powerfully attractive to one of the opposite sex. However, the young man's attraction to a woman's rounded hips or ample breasts is other than the impression of beauty. Such attributes appear as a good to be possessed, promising pleasure and indicating fertility.[24] This experience of desire, with its

22. It is bootless to object that Violetta is fictitious, since Verdi drew her from the life of a beautiful historical courtesan, who did indeed die of consumption.

23. John Paul II [Karol Wojtyła], "Letter to Artists," §3.

24. What was evident to our ancestors is being discovered anew by contemporary science, namely that sexuality and sexual desire are directly related to fertility.

concomitant impulse to possess, is distinct from the experience of admiration, of the encounter with another as beautiful. This distinction underlies a frequent and characteristic conflict in the minds and hearts especially of the young. The admiration evoked by the encounter with one as beautiful expresses itself in the desire to remain in the presence of that beauty, to "drink it in" and to wonder at it. This is not the same as sexual desire; indeed, one may well experience such beauty as too pure to be touched—in Romeo's words, "beauty too rich for use, for earth too dear."[25] Thus, the desires awakened by specifically sexual attractiveness can conflict with the contemplation of beauty. In her manifest fertility, a beautiful woman is desirable as a good to be possessed sexually, but in her grace and appearance she appears as a beauty to be contemplated untouched. She is desirable for the offspring she can bear and for the pleasure of union, but also admirable in herself for her beauty, her perfection of form. These two aspects can be harmonized if the two concerned come to a genuine personal knowledge of and love for one another. Neither the admiration of beauty (which can lead to placing the one admired on a pedestal) nor the craving of sexual pleasure (which can quickly degenerate into lust) can of itself constitute a healthy human relationship. Simply to admire a woman's physical beauty is neither to know her nor to love her.

The apprehension of a thing as beautiful has important consequences. Beauty pertains to the intellect's grasp of the thing's essence. However, the intellect does not immediately grasp the essence of the thing it encounters, for to know what a thing is often requires extended study and research. (It is only comparatively recently that we have learned, for example, what the sun really is.) It is more appropriate to say that in considering a thing the mind regards it as a unity according to an idea. We have noted earlier in this work that an idea brings unity to a multiplicity. It ties disparate things together. Grasping the idea, the mind admires its beauty and is fascinated by it. The scholar's response to a new theory often resembles that of the admiring lover.[26] When one has discovered an idea, then one's experiences make new sense; they have a fuller meaning, because they are

25. William Shakespeare, *Romeo and Juliet*, in *The Oxford Shakespeare*, W. J. Craig, ed., (New York: Oxford University Press), Act I, Scene V.

26. It is not unknown for mathematicians to express a mild resentment when physicists or engineers find—as they often do—some practical application of their pure mathematics.

related to each other in a coherent whole. In the new idea, the intelligence can rest from the work it has been engaged in, for the idea is the achievement of the unity of explanation being sought. This is the satisfaction of the *wonder* that Aristotle characterized as the beginning of science.[27] Thus, the experience of beauty lies not only at the root of art, but of science as well. Whitman's complaint about the "learn'd astronomer" with his charts and figures is profoundly wrong.[28] Like the poet, the astronomer proposes to enter into the starry skies by the power of his mind. Science, like art, is founded on the human being's fundamental desire to see things as a whole, to find the structure and simplicity—the elegance—within the chaos of human experience. Further, this impulse to grasp things as integrated wholes extends to all reality. We speak of the cosmos, the world, the universe, as a unity. To conceive the world as an integrated whole is characteristically human, rooted in the very nature of human intelligence. Wittgenstein stated that the world is the "totality of facts, not of things,"[29] and although he held these facts to be mutually independent, he characterized the world as a whole. Even when Bertrand Russell writes of the world as "purposeless" and "void of meaning,"[30] he does so to give it an integral significance, a unity. In Russell's world, one finds no aberrant pockets of genuine purpose and authentic meaning. In his essay, Russell describes a world governed by an idea, the principles of science, and which therefore responds to scientific inquiry. I cite Wittgenstein and, especially, Russell, because they in particular are reluctant to confer upon the world as a whole any metaphysical status. But can one not see and appreciate the cold beauty of Russell's purposeless cosmos, a realm of hard facts, accessible to human reason but uncompromising before human yearnings? The human mind, even when it resists the impulse, is impelled to search out the characters that pertain to the whole. To be a rational animal is to be a metaphysical animal.

27. Aristotle, *Metaphysics,* I, ii, 982^b 12.

28. Walt Whitman, "When I Heard the Learn'd Astronomer," *Leaves of Grass: The First (1855) Edition,* Malcolm Cowley, ed., (New York: Penguin Books, 1959).

29. Ludwig Wittgenstein, *Tractatus Logico-Philosophicus* (New York: Routledge & Kegan Paul, 1961), 1.1.

30. Bertrand Russell, "A Free Man's Worship: Mysticism and Logic," cited in E. A. Burtt, *The Metaphysical Foundations of Modern Science,* (Garden City: Doubleday, 1954), 23.

In this lies a promise and a danger. One can be seduced by an idea so perfect it has to be true, the key to explaining everything. One wants to abide in the idea and trace out its implications. The experience of beauty constitutes an essential aspect of reality in truth, but it is not necessarily the truth of the thing. Just as the physical beauty of a person or a thing can mislead the observer concerning its inner integrity and goodness, so can the elegance of an idea be mistaken for the true essence of the thing it is taken to represent. The idea brings the various aspects of reality into an unexpected but harmonious unity. This unity may turn out, however, to be false or superficial, because the apprehension of the idea is but one moment in the acquisition of truth. It is a vital moment, however, often the decisive one, and precisely in this does beauty open the door to the spiritual. The experience of beauty, of admiration for the perfection of form, is the primordial or foundational manifestation of spirit, urging the person to seek true knowledge of the good revealed as beautiful. The beautiful opens the door to metaphysics precisely in that the beautiful is objective; it stands over against the admiring subject as a good inviting him to the knowledge of being as such.

STATUS AND CHARACTERISTICS OF THE SPIRITUAL IN HUMAN NATURE

The foregoing presents the central concepts on which our understanding of the spiritual is based. If *true, good, beautiful,* and *being* can be legitimately applied as transcendental or universal terms in the way suggested above, then the spiritual is real. The issues before us now are twofold:

1. How and to what extent is this spiritual element or factor related to the material?
2. How and in what way is this spiritual factor separable from the material components of human nature?

We identify the soul as this spiritual factor. If the human being is a *rational animal,* the soul is that in virtue of which this kind of animal is rational. If, as Peirce writes, "The mind is a sign, developing according to the laws of inference,"[31] the soul is the idea-using (and therefore logically competent) principle of this development.

When he writes that "the mind is a sign," Peirce's argument makes it clear that it is the man himself who is a sign. Let us parse this sentence, which will become the linchpin of the analysis in succeeding chapters. The human being is a sign-maker, of course, but not only when he is deliberately creating signs and symbols. In fact, every human act is significant, for it interprets the reality with which the human being is engaged. In the essay from which our sentence is drawn, "Some Consequences of Four Incapacities," Peirce offers a detailed analysis of the deductive, inductive, and hypothetical aspects of human action, the point of which is to show how the various modes of the syllogism form the logical structure of human behavior. We shall discuss this in detail in chapter 4 of the present work. Here let it suffice to say that by his actions the human person interprets the world about him. His acts and habits are thus signs, and just as a nexus of propositions constitutes[32] an argument, so do one's acts and habits constitute him as a sign. Furthermore, this sign, which is the person, develops (or, to continue the analogy, the argument unfolds), and the fact and nature of this development is a central issue in our present investigation. Peirce states that this development is "according to the laws of inference," that is, logical. This is to say that the human person is an ideal reality, one somehow formed and governed by ideas, a physical living organism that behaves according to the laws of reason. This is another way to say "rational animal."

We call this the principle by which the mind (that is, the human being as a self-conscious whole) so develops the soul. As such the soul is not a material principle, but an ideal one. Were it material, then the laws of logic would be reducible to physical laws and the relationship of the mind and its representations with truth would be physical. The human person is related immaterially to the world about him, as is evidenced by the objects of his rational power and will.

31. Peirce, *Collected Papers*, 5.313. For a more detailed account of my interpretation of this, see Reimers, "The Human Act and Its Context," in Reimers, *An Analysis of the Concepts of Self-Fulfillment and Self-Realization in the Thought of Karol Wojtyła–Pope John Paul II*, chap. 3.

32. In principle, *any* set of propositions constitutes an argument. Whether the argument is interesting or useful, much less valid or cogent, is another issue.

Having characterized the material and the spiritual, we need now to integrate these into an account of the human person. Although one can argue—as the foregoing has done—that the notions of the true and the good, which constitute the spiritual, have real significance, it remains to be shown how these ideas actually work, how a being that is evidently material is also spiritual. The next two chapters, respectively on the powers to know and to strive for the good, address this question. In particular we will consider the notion of habit and the practical syllogism, showing how reason unfolds in the life and behavior of the human person.

PART THREE SPIRITUAL ACTION OF

THE MATERIAL BEING

CHAPTER 4

The Power to Know

Human beings want to know, to understand things. Scientific materialism, beginning with Darwin,[1] argues that the human capacity to know is simply a more developed and more sophisticated variant of animal cognition. Analysis of its structure, however, shows that human reason is more than a survival adaptation. The difference between human knowledge and animal cognition is founded on the human ability to understand, which is the power to grasp what things are (their essences) and form cognitions and behavior according to this understanding. This power to understand, we shall argue, cannot be only a material state or capacity. Although everything a human being does is indeed physical, this behavior is determined not only by physical conditions, but also by the understanding formed by ideas.

Knowledge—human cognition—has to do with truth. To be human is not simply to have and use cognitions, but to know them as true, to evaluate them according to rational criteria. Unlike all other animals, human beings create symbolic means of expression, most notably language, to represent to themselves and each other what they believe to be true. The power to know requires, first of all, the ability to believe things can be true. As a consequence of this capacity for truth, the human person stands at a

---

1. Charles Darwin, *The Descent of Man,* ch. 21.

certain distance from his cognitions. Because truth has a contrary, simple cognition cannot stand on its own; the human subject can call every cognition into question. Nothing that is known or believed or proposed for belief is given infallibly. The rational power, furthermore, goes beyond simply believing vital facts about the environment. Humans are theorists, given to speculation about what lies behind the facts. Knowing how things stand, we construct mythical, scientific, and artistic visions to explain the facts we know. The primitive tribe, after a successful day's hunt, gathers in the village to celebrate by dancing and retelling stories. Scientists in the twentieth century developed the microchip and genetically engineered grain . . . as well as the cinema and television. Beyond survival, human reason seeks to envision the world as a whole and its underlying principles. We need, therefore, first to investigate human belief and then understanding.

BELIEF

What belief is

Belief is the commitment of mind to something as true. To believe is to stake one's conscious activity on something's being the case and as such is expressed to oneself or others symbolically, whether in language or through a drawing, diagram or gestures. Expression alone, however, is not sufficient to constitute a belief. Most people will not approach too close to a cliff's edge if there is no guardrail. This natural fear expresses a kind of implicit belief in the danger of accidentally falling. In avoiding such dangers one need not—and most often does not—think to oneself, "I recognize a danger here and therefore will keep my distance," although when asked, he could so explain himself. We accept many things as true without expressing them, except when questioned or when the issue is otherwise brought to consciousness (as when teaching a toddler). There is a sense in which a belief is accepted prior to conscious thought or awareness of it. We may speak of "implicit beliefs" or better "proto-beliefs." Therefore, the proposition is not itself the belief, but it expresses the belief, for one may not have brought a particular belief to consciousness. Furthermore, as the phenomenon of lying shows, it can happen that what one professes to believe differs from what he believes in fact. Indeed, a person's habitual behavior may well belie beliefs that he professes in good faith. If the marketing manager who lectures about the advantages and safety of air travel breaks into a cold sweat when required to fly, his friends question whether he truly believes what he says to his audiences.

At issue is the relationship between habits and beliefs. As a disposition of mind to act, a belief constitutes a habit. Since, as Peirce holds, "the true meaning of any product of the intellect lies in whatever unitary determination it would impart to practical conduct under any and every conceivable circumstance, supposing such conduct to be guided by reflexion carried to an ultimate limit,"[2] every belief can conceivably affect one's behavior. A stated belief that would not under any conceivable circumstances change or affect one's behavior either is not truly believed or is meaningless. To believe that something is true is to prepare oneself to act. In the formula for habit, "When Z obtains, a occurs," the conditional clause is founded on a belief. Human behavior is mediated through the mind according to what the mind believes to be true. Therefore, in order to trigger the habit, it does not suffice that Z obtain; the agent must believe that Z obtains. In this respect a belief affects habits. On the other hand, habitual behavior manifests a kind of acceptance of something as true. It manifests a particular understanding of the world.

There results a kind of dialectical interaction between a person's beliefs and habits. The expressed belief may constitute a proto-habit, by which we mean simply the germ of a habit. As the person responds existentially to the belief, it will develop into a habit. Any kind of practical training begins with factual instruction, which forms the proto-habits. By using imagination and studying instructional diagrams, the trainee can begin to see how his new habits will unfold. Even after the first day of instruction, the habit is there, albeit neither strong nor proficient. Indeed, the distinction between habits and proto-habits is not sharp, for one can embrace different habits to varying degrees. The driver makes a mental note that construction has started on the expressway, which will delay his trip home from work and decides to take a different route. But leaving the office, he for-

2. Peirce, *Collected Papers*, 6.490. This is, in effect, one of the ways in which Peirce expresses his pragmatism (which, it should be noted, is significantly different from that of William James).

gets and takes the expressway. The mental note led to the proto-habit of taking another route, but on the first day of construction, the old habit proved stronger. Tomorrow he will probably not forget. Because habits can be stronger or weaker, so too can beliefs vary in strength. There are those beliefs one holds firm to and others that one can easily change. At any state of its development, belief is a disposition of the mind with identifiable existential consequences. In other words, the belief is a property of the person, a more or less important aspect of his existence in the world, a constituent of his regular behavior patterns.

Because any habit can be brought to symbolic expression, by which it constitutes a belief, the totality of one's habits implicitly express an interpretation of his life and of the world. By reflecting on one's interaction with the world, these habits are brought to consciousness and one gains knowledge. Furthermore, as habits are brought to expression, they can be judged and modified.

Truth of beliefs

As a disposition to act, a belief must be oriented toward things as they are, if the act is to succeed. Therefore one wants beliefs to be of things as they are. To believe what is false is to set oneself up for failure. One can, of course, lie and not only to others but to oneself as well. However, the end of belief is truth, and therefore truth is the criterion we apply to beliefs. Aristotle characterizes truth thus: "to say that what is, is, or that what is not, is not, is true,"[3] defining truth as a relationship between what is said (the sign or symbol) and what is (the object). This relationship between sign and object is dyadic, admitting of only two values: *true* and *false*. For a sign to be a belief, it is essential that it admit of such correspondence and evaluation, that it be applied to a concrete existential situation and be evaluated in relationship to it. This is not to say that the correspondence between sign and object needs to consist in a kind of isomorphic mapping, as though for each element in the state of affairs represented there must be a corresponding element in the symbol representing it. The sign may be iconic like a road map, which expresses the belief that the streets lie in rela-

3. Aristotle, *Metaphysics* Book IV, ch. vii 1011^b 27.

tion to each other as the lines on the map, indexical, like the usher's gesture to the empty seats, or symbolic, representing not in virtue of some direct correlation or likeness, but rather in virtue of its meaning.

Because the proposition represents or purports to represent some state of affairs in the world, it has an indexical character, which is distinct and even somewhat independent of its meaning. Because reference to existing things in the world is essential to the notion of belief, every expression of belief has at least one component that refers to an existent. If "the ball is on the table" expresses a belief, it must refer to a specific ball, the one we were playing with or the one Babe Ruth autographed for Grandpa. It refers also to a specific table, one that we could point to. This reference is essential if the statement is to express a belief. And the reference must be clear. "Andrew landed in Florida," could express a false belief concerning a member of the British royal family or a true belief about a devastating hurricane. The belief may, of course, be indefinite or general, as when one says that hurricanes are common in the summer or that lithium occupies the leftmost position of the second row of the periodic table. The periodic table is a cultural artifact, developed by Mendeleef, exemplars of which can be found in any chemistry text. Lithium is a chemical element with atomic number 3, which anyone can isolate by following known laboratory procedures and recognize by its specific characteristics. Anyone who has taken a beginning chemistry course can connect the belief stated above with his own experience, even if only in a rudimentary way, by following certain instructions. Beliefs refer to the existing order and implicitly express the existence of things. A man tells his wife that he sat in the shade of a tree. She responds that it was not a tree but a cactus. He replies, "Whatever. I was comfortable." She knows what he meant. Indeed, it is a matter of common experience that without knowing the proper terms for things, one can nevertheless know all sorts of truths about them and communicate successfully. If one knows how the terms indicate their referents, then one can know what is meant. The misstated proposition can be understood and acted upon—the misuse of terms notwithstanding.

This dyadic relationship between belief and object is decisive when the belief is expressed in action. If belief constitutes a predisposition to a kind of action, then truth is manifest in success. Often the quickest and easiest way to determine whether a statement is true is to act on it. As a commitment of mind to something as true, every belief entails the disposition to act in a particular way when presented with a situation of a particular generally describable character. Because a belief is that things in the real world are in such and such a way and not in some other, the belief is intrinsically tied to the person's existence in the world as a physical entity. Even theoretical beliefs may have proximate behavioral implications. That the subtraction of a larger number from a smaller results in a negative number has a direct implication for budgeting and spending. To believe that the Earl of Oxford wrote the Shakespearean plays and sonnets is not only to be prepared to engage in heated arguments at literary conferences; it is also to expect that should the Earl's secret diary ever come to light or should an Avon householder happen upon some lost correspondence by William Shakespeare, the discovery might well refer to Oxford's authorship under Shakespeare's name.

Because a belief is a disposition of mind toward action, to adopt a belief is to adopt or modify a habit. One holds a belief to the degree that one is prepared to act in a certain way, according to the belief. The status of a belief as a mental state or conscious event is secondary. To believe that winter will be cold is not simply to have mental images of snow and ice, but to expect (among other things) that light clothing will be insufficient to keep warm and that one's car will need extra attention to run smoothly. Since the existence of things consists in their regular behavior, there is a sense in which the existence of a human person consists in his or her beliefs. By their very nature, one's beliefs determine how he will behave, and conversely his regular behavior—habits—are at the least proto-beliefs. To adopt a belief is to change oneself, even if slightly. This point will prove critical in our discussion of the question of a specific human nature, and we shall return to it toward the end of this chapter.

The purely dyadic characterization of truth as correspondence is not too far from materialism, because the truth of a belief appears to be tied closely to the success or failure of certain actions. The preceding two paragraphs are not far from William James' conception of truth as something that happens to an idea that makes it true.[4] James' point is precisely that

4. William James, "Lecture Six: Pragmatism's Conception of Truth," in James, *Pragmatism* (Buffalo: Prometheus Books, 1991), especially 90. The difference between Peirce and James

what matters about an idea is not some kind of metaphysical relationship, but rather that it help us get through the situations we face directly. An idea that meets our needs is true; when it ceases to work, we reject it as false and find a better idea. As such, beliefs are simply tools, and therefore their significance is material. The capacity to think, to form and hold beliefs would arguably amount to nothing else than a particularly clever biological adaptation to the environment.

Truth and understanding

Thomas Aquinas characterizes truth as the *adequatio intellectus et rei*, the correspondence of the understanding and thing.[5] This definition goes significantly beyond saying of what is, that it is, and of what is not, that it is not, for Aquinas attributes truth in the first instance not to the symbolic expression but rather to the understanding. It is the intellect—the understanding—that is judged to be true or false in relation to the thing. The proposition, as an expression of the understanding, is said to be true if the understanding it expresses is true. Thus Aquinas characterizes Aristotle's definition as a formal determination of his own.[6]

To understand is to grasp the essence of a being, and this is the first act of the intellect. The second act is "composition and division," that is, in predicating something of a subject. Therefore, following Aristotle, Aquinas holds that in the first act of the intellect there is neither truth nor falsity.[7] Aquinas compares the act of understanding to vision, which cannot of itself determine truth or falsity. If to understand is to grasp the essence of a being, then it is most appropriately and best expressed in the being's definition. Although a perfect knowledge of the essence is expressed in a scientific definition, understanding is generally evidenced by one's knowledge of the meaning of a term, by the ability to use it appropriately. To un-

---

thus becomes sharp. For Peirce, pragmatism offers an ultimate test for meaning, while James makes it a direct test for truth.

5. Aquinas, *De Veritate*, q. 1, a. 1.

6. We may remark that this is precisely Aquinas's intention, as he makes clear in the body of the *De Veritate* article.

7. Aquinas, *De Veritate*, 1, 3; *In De Anima III*, Lec. 11, §§746–751; cf. Aristotle, *De Anima*, III, ch. vi, 430a 26, and *Metaphysics*, VI, ch. iv, 1027b 26.

derstand is to grasp the essence of a *being,* that is, of whatever can be said in any respect to be. Aquinas will go on to argue that *being* applies primarily to substance and to everything else in relation to substance. But every being, whether substantial, accidental, or relative, whether real being or a "being of reason" has an essence.[8] Whatever *is,* in whatever sense, has an essence that intellectual power can grasp.

This grasp of the essence does not consist merely in the knowledge of a term, the ability to recite a definition of it, a mental image, or some more-or less appropriate behavioral response, even though all of these may well constitute aspects of such grasp. This is evident from the experience of teaching. The language arts teacher is not content with the students' ability to recite the definition (*agricola* means "farmer"), but requires them further to be able to use the word in an original sentence. Beginning calculus students learn the definition of *limit* in one hour; then for the next week the teacher assigns problems and exercises on limits. This concept, which some students never adequately grasp, becomes for others the key to powerful, new (to them) ways to reason mathematically. To educate, to bring others to understanding, is more than to impart facts or to train for tasks. It is to empower learners by leading them to understanding, by which they can come to the truths of things on their own. To grasp a being's essence means, therefore, to bring into unity one's experiences and expressions with respect to that being. In other words, it is to have an idea, a principle of thought. The idea is neither a conscious event nor an experience, but a power of mind. One can understand an idea poorly while thinking he does so well, and his understanding of an idea can develop. A child can understand *justice,* but Aristotle distinguishes "commutative" from "distributive" justice, while John Rawls relates justice to an abstract conception of fairness. If, as Aristotle said, the soul is, in a way, all things, it is so precisely in that the mind is formed by ideas of things.[9]

This conception of truth, however, as agreement of the understanding (as opposed to a single proposition) with the essence of a thing (as opposed to a singular existing fact) allows for degrees of truth and falsity in this sense, that one's understanding and expression of ideas can agree

8. Aquinas, *De Veritate,* 1, 1.

9. See Fulvio Di Blasi's discussion of the *adequatio intellectus et rei* in his *God and the Natural Law* (South Bend, IN: St. Augustine's Press, 2003), 95–96.

more or less adequately with how things are. If truth relates essentially to the understanding, then the possession of truth cannot be a simple dyadic relationship, as the history of science makes clear. Believing the earth to be the center of the universe, ancient and medieval astronomers accurately plotted the stars and predicted the motions of the planets. Thinking whales to be fish, nineteenth-century whalers successfully hunted them, bringing their flesh, fat, and bones to market. Certainly the astronomers and whalers of old knew much of the truth; their beliefs worked well for them. Nevertheless, their knowledge was, in an important sense, false. The universe is not a series of concentric spheres with earth at the center. Whales are mammals, not fish. The history of science illustrates what logicians and philosophers of science recognize,[10] that our understanding is always provisional, that today's established theory may be overthrown by tomorrow's discovery and next year's new conception. The correspondence (*adequatio*) of intellect and thing leaves us with a dilemma. It seems now that truth must be only provisional, an approximation, subject to future correction or even rejection. Since the Ptolemaic astronomy worked for navigation, but not for sending a man to the moon, must we say it once was true but now is false? If so, then "truth" seems to be variable.

We can begin to address this by asking what may be the point of understanding. One could answer simply that understanding gives us the power to move on to new truths, to infer what might be so from what is already known. Today's theory (which is perforce provisional) is a ladder by which we generate further useful results. Newton showed how white light is composed of all the colors, and Doppler discovered his famous shift; with these results and some help from chemical spectroanalysis, astronomers were able to discover that the universe is expanding. The goal of understanding, so conceived, is the discovery of new facts. However, human inquisitiveness never stops with the simple fact. To understand is to grasp the essences of things, to know what sun, wolves, earth, and electrons are. The *wonder* that Aristotle spoke of is precisely this curiosity about the "why" of things, to understand what they really are, how they came to be and from

---

10. Cf. Karl Popper, *The Logic of Scientific Discovery* (New York, Evanston: Harper & Row, 1968), 108, 278, and especially 281: "It is not his possession of knowledge, of irrefutable truth, that makes the man of science, but his persistent and relentlessly critical quest for truth"—a quest that Popper makes clear will never attain its goal.

what and for what purpose. Even if a legitimate purpose of understanding is to generate useful facts, there remains nevertheless the human experience of wonder, the desire to know for the sake of knowing. The "ladder" by which we arrive at new facts, the true understanding of things is more important to us than are the facts themselves. But where does understanding come from? How do ideas originate? To answer these questions we examine the human being's perceptual, practical, and intellectual interaction with the world.

IDEAS AND HABITS

As existing beings, human beings find themselves in the world, interacting with other existents. Because the existence of a thing consists in its regular behavior, which is bodily action and interaction governed by habit, the human being's existence consists in his relationships with the world about him—in his habits. We can distinguish three main classes of human habit: (1) perception, (2) work or practical activity, and (3) reasoning (or the manipulation of symbols to express meanings).[11] As the discussion proceeds, how these classes of habits are distinguished will become clear. At the start, however, it is important to note how they are not distinguished from each other, that is, what they share in common. All three kinds of habit are bodily, involving the actions and reactions of the body as it encounters things in the world. The stargazer and the scholar are engaged bodily with the world around them, just as is the carpenter. Although perception and ratiocination characteristically call on certain organs and muscles, these habits are not mutually distinguished—nor is either distinguished from work—by the bodily motions and responses themselves. It is, rather, by their respective finalities that perception, work, and reasoning are characterized.

---

11. An explanation of method might be useful here. Picking up on Peirce's phenomenology of Firsts, Seconds, and Thirds, I identify three classes of habit: (1) habits that image a possible object, (2) habits relating causally with an existing object, and (3) habits that interpret objects as representative. The inspiration, if not the classification, is from Peirce.

Perception

We commonly think of perception in terms of a kind of passive mental recording of sensible characteristics in the environment. Just as the camera records the image on film and the tape recorder copies the sounds onto the cassette, to be accessed later, so, it seems, are the processes of seeing and hearing. The visual image is projected onto the retina (albeit upside-down) and there the brain reads it. As a result of this metaphor, we tend to see the memory and imagination as a kind of storehouse of images, similar to a large photo and sound recording library, from which pictures, smells, sounds, and feelings from the past can be accessed and recalled or recombined into fantasies. This seems to be the model Hume uses in the opening chapter of his *Inquiry Concerning Human Understanding*. Based not only on such phenomena as the fallibility of memory (even very recent memory) and learning to perceive, but also on what we now know about the brain's functioning in perception, a different kind of account is needed. Here I propose that perception is a class of habits.

Human perception is the habit of ordering environmental stimuli into coherent images of things. Perception is a response to the influences in the world by which we image it to ourselves. The human organism responds to certain subtle influences from the environment; the physical properties of things affect our perceptual organs, stimulating nerves, whose momentary physical and chemical alterations trigger the transmission of weak electrical signals to the brain. In the brain, these signals are further processed and interpreted. These responses, both of sense organs to stimuli from without and of brain to nerve impulses within, follow regular patterns. They are kinds of regular behavior and therefore, according to the definition we have been using, habits. The point is more than merely terminological, however (as if to say that they are habits simply because I have arranged in advance to call them such). We know that the sense organs can be trained (vintners and perfumeries hire those who are accomplished smellers), and there is good evidence that internal structures in the nervous system also develop habitual ways of responding on the basis of experience.

The nature of perception, however, does not derive from the simple responses of the organs, but from the purpose they attain. Perception is not the passive reception of images, whole and entire, from without the body.

Although our perceptions seem to be whole, continuous, and derived directly from their objects, the process of perception is significantly more complex than the transmission of a moving picture. The act of seeing a car passing by is not simply the mind's recording of an image moving across the retina. Light reflected from the object and focused by the lens stimulates the nerve cells of the retina, which in turn send weak electrical signals to the brain. Research has shown that different parts of the brain process different aspects of the same image. Different areas of the brain process shape, color, and motion. Furthermore, there appears to be no one area that integrates the data provided by the shape, color, and movement sections.[12] What seems to us (as perceiving people) to be simply the internalization of the physical images of things turns out to be a complex neurological process of integration and interpretation. What the perceiving person thinks he is doing and what his brain is actually performing are two very different things. The result of this nervous activity—neurons stimulating each other both independently and in coordination—is that the person sees a car passing by. Philosophers ask how the physiological events are related to the perception event, how the physical processes of the nervous system cause the mental process of perception, and what the status is of the mental image, the conscious product of the body's perceptual activities. What I propose here is that the perceptual image is constituted by a unified response to the sense stimuli. We see, feel, hear and smell *things*. The image is, if you will, in the person's rationally or ideally formed response as the sense organs interact with the environment. As these organs react to light, sound, or other stimuli, they do so interpretively. The kind of interpretation the person develops is an image, an iconic representation of the source of the stimuli. To perceive is to interact with things iconically, to form images of things on the basis of how they have affected one physically.

From this it follows that physical stimuli do not constitute the sufficient cause of the mental process of perception. Since perception is interpretive, our bodies do not simply react mechanically to visual and auditory stimuli. Even at the neuronal level, the body's response is geared toward imaging, towards interpretation. Antonio Damasio comments: "Brain cells, at every level of the nervous system, represent entities or events occur-

---

12. See Floyd E. Bloom, Arlyne Lazerson, and Laura Hofstadter, *Mind, Brain, and Behavior*, 62–77.

ring elsewhere in the organism. Brain cells are assigned by designed to be *about* other things and other doings."[13] Every act of perception involves the stimulation of a part of the nervous system, evoking a response which, in human beings, is geared toward the mind's need to perceive things according to their kinds. This response is not isolated, as though one could consider a single neuron or retinal cell and determine how it (and others like it) will always react. The part responds according to the context of the whole, specifically according to the need to fit it into an overall image. This is why, even though the distance between rods and cones is greater than the minimum visible distance and there is a "blind spot" in each eye, we see a continuous visual field. Despite the fact that each color of light has its own wavelength, the color of an object under different lighting seems to be invariant (the Land effect).[14] Seeing is neither something that the eyes do nor something that the brain does. Seeing is a complex activity of the eye-brain system, in which each rod, cone, and neuron responds as it does within the purposeful context of imaging the environment.

The responses to stimuli are ordered according to some idea. I do not say that perception is a matter of the mind's imposing order on raw sense data. The point, rather, is that sensation is interpreted according to ideas. Merleau-Ponty notes, "Now the sensations and images which should be the beginning and end of all knowledge never make their appearance anywhere other than within a horizon of meaning."[15] Earlier we characterized an idea as an intellectual principle by which a thing may be represented. Since an idea is that by which a representation can be made of that thing or kind of thing, the act of perceiving is governed by ideas. By means of ideas, the acts of the body in responding to sense stimuli are unified into meaningful wholes. Thus humans can learn to perceive. Soldiers and spies are trained to discern camouflaged enemies and forged photographs. Wine tasters learn how to recognize subtle differences in bouquets. In the early

13. Antonio Damasio, "How the Brain Creates the Mind."

14. See Christof Koch, "Towards the Neuronal Substrate of Visual Consciousness," adapted from Koch, "Towards the Neuronal Substrate of Visual Consciousness," in *Towards a Science of Consciousness: The First Tucson Discussions and Debates,* Proceedings of the 1994 Tucson Conference, S. R. Hameroff, A. W. Kaszniak, and A. C. Scott, eds. (Cambridge MA: MIT Press, 1996).

15. Maurice Merleau-Ponty, *Phenomenology of Perception* (New York: Humanities Press, 1962), 15.

1990s Americans amused themselves with cleverly drawn patterns which, if stared at with eyes unfocused, would eventually yield three-dimensional images. What is of central importance is that perception is not a matter of imposing order on unformed stimuli; perception is itself ordered. Even at its most rudimentary level, human perception is shot through with rationality. When the human subject perceives, he perceives a "something," a being that has an essence, which can be described. As perceived, this being is material, for perception is also a material interaction (sound waves striking the ear, molecules entering the nose), and as material, the perceived object exists in space and time. One expects it to have future existence. (Imagine stepping on a Lego block in the night. You expect to see it lying on the floor after you turn on the light.) What is perceived immediately fits into some general category of things. The perception is an image, an iconic representation that one makes for himself. We experience perception as image, so that when we perceive something we say, "It looks like . . ." or "What I see (or hear) is a . . ." The fact that we can call up previous perceptions in memory and imagine things we have never experienced suggests that we somehow have these images in our minds, rather like a theater in the head. However, the image cannot be in one's own head or mind, for if it were, how could one person point something out to another? If one says, "Did you see the feather in the boy's hat?" he refers his hearer to something common to both their experiences. On the other hand, one can see what another misses. This is common in training situations, where the student is learning to recognize subtle symptoms or characteristics and in those apparently random patterns that seem to be an image of Jesus or Ho Chi Minh. ("See that white space? Imagine that is the left eye, and then you can see the whole face.") Perception is not mechanical but ideal; that is, it is a process formed and guided by ideas.

If perception is a habit of imaging, it is an action of one's body that results in an image. The action of the body is the unified collective response of the sensory system; the image is the perceptible object as understood, that is, as represented to oneself. One appropriates the image perceptually by adapting one's sensory apparatus to the thing perceived. Thus, we do often see what we expect to see.[16] It is in this respect that the image is,

16. This is why proofreading is such a difficult task. The reader has to see the marks that are actually there and not the words he expects.

as it were, reflected in one's subjectivity. This also makes it clear how memory and imagination function. To recall the image of—say—one's mother is not a matter of pulling a picture out of mental storage, but of rehearsing the sensory responses one performed when actually seeing her. This is why to recall something we often have to "get a running start" by recalling the process leading up to the image one is looking for and why one sensation, such as a smell or a song, can bring back specific memories.

If the purpose of perception were simply to detect environmental dangers and opportunities, then its operation could perhaps be mechanical or univocal, like that of the sensors on a robot. As a habit of imaging, however, perception is not directly linked to action. Perception mediates between stimulus and response. This is true in animals as well as in human beings. The gazelle recognizes the lion from afar, but does not bolt until she judges the lion to be dangerously close. She can, of course, be wrong. As habit of imaging, perception has its own internal criteria, which are independent of causal interactions with the world. The responses by which the image is formed need to coordinate in such a way that the image is of some one thing, that it have a unity that accounts for all the stimuli relating to it. To an extent, of course, stimuli may be disregarded, if they belong to another image or do not immediately serve to constitute the perceptual image at hand. So it is that the fans at the sporting event may not even notice the plane flying overhead. (This may relate to a difficulty that persons with autism have. Unable to "filter" sounds, they become very agitated with stray noises, such as the hum of a fluorescent bulb or the sounds from road construction nearby. Their frustration—and, indeed, the inability to filter—may result from a need to incorporate *all* their stimuli into one coherent whole.) The criteria by which we judge perception are not functional, but aesthetic. That is, hearing *as hearing* is not in the first instance about warning one of danger, but rather about forming an image of the aural environment. Good perception ties the image together according to some general conception. Therefore the perception has its own proper aesthetic impact on the person, independent of the existential significance of the thing perceived; one can gaze in awe at the beauty of an exploding volcano. A perception can be more or less beautiful, insofar as it is more or less well formed, and in virtue of that has an impact on the feelings of the one perceiving. This is a result of the ideal character of the perception, of the act by which one perceives.

This view, that perception is about imaging the world according to general characters, stands in contrast to scientific naturalism, which is well expressed by Daniel Dennett: "It is *not the point* of our sensory systems that they should detect basic or natural properties of the environment, but that they should serve our 'narcissistic' purposes of staying alive."[17] Yet, this seems to be precisely contrary to our common experience. What is distinctive about human sensation is its disinterestedness. The human being perceives things whether they impinge on his own life and needs or not. Although many animals enjoy remarkable sensitivity of perception, they do not have the capacity to learn new ways of perceiving; the deer never learns that a stationary human figure in hunting garb represents danger. Most important, animals do not perceive what is not relevant to their instinctive needs and desires. Charming as the children's story may be, Ferdinand the Bull will not give up his aggressive ways and take time to smell the flowers. Flowers are vegetation, useless to a bull if he cannot eat them. In general, brute animals are able to perceive a limited range of things in their world according to their instinctual needs. A dog responds instinctively to other dogs' barking, and, in virtue of training, to the master's voice, and the sound of the can opener, but not to the music on the stereo or conversations on TV. Animals perceive in virtue of innate abilities to relate form and motion and as a result of conditioning. What associations are not innate they learn by repetitive training. Pavlov's dog did not care about the bell, but only the food that the ringing announced. Animal perception differs from the machine's response to its input, to be sure, for the beast's perception is geared to the needs of the organism. We can say that the machine responds to inputs, but the animal to the things it needs.

Although animal perception is similar to the human—which is, after all, a kind of perception by an animal—it differs in its finality. For the animal, perception is ordered only to patterns and combinations related to survival and the continuation of the species. Human perception is more objective. During mating season, the lion seeing a lioness really does "just want one thing," whereas a man may regard a woman from a variety of perspectives: her dress suggests she is foreign, perhaps Asian, or her manner suggests she is a journalist. The man is able to see the woman in relation to something other than his own immediate biological or survival concerns. The human

17. Daniel Dennett, *Consciousness Explained,* p. 382.

power to perceive differs from the animal in that human perception is the act of imaging the world or the environment. The animal ignores an irrelevant stimulus; the human tries to "fit it into the picture." A sign of this difference is that human beings are subject to distractions, even while engaged in survival and reproductive activities. The logic of imaging is different than that of defending, seeking, responding to threats, and so on. The criteria for imaging simply do not reduce to the criteria of human needs. The image is to be an ordered whole, not necessarily the revelation of threats and opportunities. Human perception is directed finally toward imaging the world as world, and not simply towards identifying objects of interest or concern to the organism, such as enemies, potential mates, food, and shelter.

Perceptual images do not necessarily represent the world correctly and certainly not completely. We cannot see ultraviolet or infrared light and need special apparatus (a radio or TV) to detect and interpret electromagnetic waves of much greater length than light. A temperature inversion can create a mirage. One can hear ringing in his ears or feel a sharp pain in amputated limbs. Our ancestors found pictures of animals in the sky, and to this day astrologers attribute properties and influences to what are really random arrangements of stars. Nevertheless, more often than not our perception of the world is fairly accurate. By acting on the basis of our perceptions, we can get around successfully, which indicates that our perceptual image of the world is fairly accurate. It is not, however, the direct finality of perceptual habits as such to image the world accurately. Perception is the habit of forming images of the environment and what is in it. To know what is in the world, the knowledge gained through perception must ultimately be integrated and interpreted by that gained through habits of work and reasoning.

Formed by ideas, perception is also a source of ideas. The unity of the perceptual image is ideal and from it the rational subject can draw further notions. It is precisely here that the empiricists, having started well, fail to bring the analysis to completion. Hume argues that from the repeated sequence of two kinds of events the human mind infers a cause. From the simple ideas of "a body yellow, of a certain weight, malleable, fusible, and fixed," we form the notion of gold substance, according to Locke.[18] Yet

18. John Locke, *An Essay concerning Human Understanding* (Indianapolis: Hackett, 1996), Book III, chap. vi, 2, see also Book II, chap. X, xiii, 2ff.

whence come these *ideas* of cause and substance? By eventually locating them in the pure reason, Kant addresses what the empiricists missed, albeit at the cost of radically severing these ideas from the things in themselves. The empiricists passed over these ideas as subjective and, in a sense, unreal contributions of the mind. This, however, is to give ideas the short shrift. That these ideas are real is manifest already in their unifying the perceptual experience. The unity of the perceptual image is already ideal. In perception itself we find the ideas of subject and properties; the redness moves with the bullfighter's cape, and is perceived as invariant, despite changes in angle, lighting, and so on. (It is instructive to notice how children learning to color or paint see colors as flat. It takes a trained eye to pick up on the subtle variations in hue caused by shadows, surface texture, and such factors.) Similarly, although Hume is right to note that repeated patterns of experience can foster expectations in the mind, he does not account for the idea of *cause*. That the ball's motion follows upon that of the cue does not in itself suggest the idea of cause, namely that the ball moves only if the cue (or something similar) strikes it, communicating its motion to the ball. What we *see* is the cue striking the ball, an interaction of two things that affect each other. The motion, as well as the causality, is an aspect of the perceptual image.[19] The witness testifies that he *saw* the defendant strike and kill the victim. Even if the defense attorney disputes the accuracy of the witness's interpretation, he will not say that the testimony is nonsensical, which it would be if seeing the murder were not conceptually possible. ("Move to strike, your honor. All the witness could see was the defendant's fist traveling in an arc ending at the victim's head.") Sense perception is not preliminary to reason; it is imbued with reason.

Work or practical activity

Even if habits of perceiving provide us with images, they do not assure us of truth. By our work, however, we gain a distinctive and more objective access to the nature of the world and the things in it. By work or practical habits, I mean those whose purpose is to change something in the environment. To plant, build, and destroy are such habits, but so too are to

19. Maurice Merleau-Ponty, "Sense Experience," Part Two, chapter 1 in Merleau-Ponty, *Phenomenology of Perception*, especially 229–230.

play tennis and the piano, to walk in the park and to run a 10K. Practical habits engage the world bodily to make things different in the world and the body. The retina, sophisticated and sensitive as it is, is virtually powerless to change what lies in the visual field, but the calloused hands of the quarry worker can move heavy stones and powerful machines. Working does not image; it gets things done. The end of work is success or failure. Further, work is by its very nature engaged materially. Indeed, the material is "discovered" precisely in work, as things in the environment resist the agent's efforts to change them. Arguing against those who would reduce the human person to a center of consciousness, Karol Wojtyła notes that the *efficacy* is essential to the human act,[20] by which he means simply that a human act intends to effect change in the world; it is efficient causality at work. We cannot speak meaningfully of a human act, if what we speak of has no reference to an intended change in the physical world. As a result, it is precisely in working (or practical activity) that we discover the physical capacities and limitations of human beings in general and of specific individuals. Thus through practical interaction with the world, the human person learns the properties of things in the world and of his own body. We may even speak of work as a kind of knowing; the rancher knows cows, and the surgeon knows hearts and lungs.

Work is rational activity, formed by ideas. We cannot adequately explain human work simply in terms of the response to the environment, unless one includes in that response the ability to recognize general characteristics in the environment, characteristics that the worker can abstract and incorporate into his own life and activity. It is this power to abstract that has enabled human beings to surpass our animal neighbors. They seek water, as do we, but we create our own rivers for irrigation and eventually indoor plumbing; the canal and the pipe share properties of the river. Animals seek food, as do we, but we cultivate it in plots and prepare it in pots. The farmer and the gardener learn that what grows in the wild grows better if weeds are kept away and water and fertilizer provided. The properties that make plant growth possible in the wild are identified and used by the intelligent human farmer. The human worker makes nature's principles

20. Wojtyła, *The Acting Person*, chapter 2, "An Analysis of Efficacy in the Light of Human Dynamism." See also his essay, "The Problem of the Will in the Analysis of the Ethical Act," in Wojtyła, *Person and Community*.

his own and adapts them to his purposes. Therefore, although the finality of work is success, getting things done, work by its very nature involves an understanding of the world, an integration and interiorization of the principles by which things in the world around us exist. Ultimately it does not suffice that the worker know his task; he must act on the basis of how things are. This knowledge is not just experimental (that is, inductive) but ideal.

Practical action makes scientific knowledge possible. One of the key insights of the scientific revolution was that by intelligently and carefully manipulating things we can determine their properties. Modern science does not contemplate the world; it works with it, putting the questions to nature by acting upon her. The work of science is experimentation, activity guided by intelligence with the aim of bringing about expected changes. Thinking that lightning might be electrical, Benjamin Franklin sent aloft a kite with a metal rod connected to a Leyden jar. Lightning striking the rod should, if it is electricity, spread the gold leaves in the jar. Were lightning something else—perhaps a coagulation of light particles or some kind of fire—then the Leyden jar would be unaffected. Franklin's experiment was premised on the notion that electricity in any form will behave the same way. Whether in the field or in the laboratory, the experimenter expects that his targeted manipulation will reveal the true properties of things. The principle underlying experimental science is that interaction with a thing reveals what the object of investigation is, what kind of thing it is. Therefore, the experimenter tailors his actions and equipment according to the object under investigation. By experimenting, the scientist interacts with the object according to an idea, a conception by which the object is understood. He forms his own behavior and apparatus according to that idea in the expectation that, if the object instantiates that idea, the experiment will yield a positive result. This is precisely why the design of an experiment is crucial not to its success but to its validity.

Our knowledge, then, is not simply of concrete and discrete facts, a cognition of how things stand, but it is also a knowledge, structured by ideas, of the essences of things. To know the truth, then, is to know what things are, to know the essences of things, to grasp what things are. This understanding may well be imperfect and our knowledge therefore incomplete. Nevertheless, knowledge of the essences of things is an essential component of knowledge. Our analyses of perception and work reveal that this understanding is not in the first instance the possession of mental images or symbols. It is not simply the capacity to formulate propositions. To understand is, in a sense, to be conformed to the thing understood, so that one can perceive and work with it appropriately. Human art, whether exercised in farming, manufacture, domestic arts, or cultural creation, does not reduce to mere technique. The artisan works on the basis of a sense for the reality he deals with. This is why the good worker can adapt to the unexpected. Since Texas longhorns could not cope with harsh winter snows, northern ranchers sought out different breeds of cattle. Farmers learn which crops will replenish the soil and determine what planting patterns will best prevent erosion. The manufacturer and artisan find new materials to work with. The everyday creativity of the worker is rooted in the intellectual power to understand the essences of the things he works with, his appropriation of the ideas by which he forms his work.

Reasoning

Reasoning is the set of habits by which human beings represent things to themselves as possibly true or false. The reader may well find it strange to refer to reasoning as a kind of habit. Nevertheless it is. Reasoning, like perception and work, is a bodily activity. Indeed, we could give it the name "controlled sign-making." When one reasons, he uses his brain to create mental images and quite often his hands (for writing) or tongue (for speaking). Reasoning is done in language, but to speak a language is a kind of habit. The native language seems natural, while (for most of us) the foreign tongue is always somewhat opaque and not quite "'at hand.'" Furthermore we fall into habits of expression, patterns of speech, and customary conversational structures. We all know people who always seem to say the same things, and indeed, in certain situations, most of us fall into habits of expression. ("Since the event is a reception with my wife's colleagues, I will talk about my strawberry patch or our daughter's travels.") Even by ourselves we mull things over in our minds, imagining conversations, comparing one thought to another. One might object that this is not reasoning, that reasoning is more formal, more disciplined, more structured. To this I answer that the only difference between the free-floating mental activity when one is alone, the idle conversations at a cocktail party, and the careful analysis involved in writing out an argument is in the degree of focus and discipline. The scholar putting together an argument for publication reviews his paragraphs and sections for coherence and logical consequence. The process leading up to this, however, was considerably sloppier, involving recollections of phrases, happy discoveries, and—quite often—typing one trite word after another in the hopes that upon revision the whole thing will come together. In all this, we use habits—habits of language, of expression, of argumentation. The question is ultimately (and this is the question of this entire work) whether established habit is decisive.

The finality of reasoning is truth, just as the image is that of perception and success that of work. Reasoning is that process by which we determine whether the image or representation is true, whether it adequately expresses reality. Whatever we perceive, experience, or do can be expressed by symbols, by language. At the least, we can label what we encounter, if no better than by referring to "that," this "thingamabob," "that tingling in my elbow," or (while gesturing) a "motion like this" and in doing so, make ourselves understood to others. Furthermore, because our actions are derived from habits, we can use general terms to refer to the characteristic actions that make up our habits and the general circumstances under which we perform the acts. To be sure, verbal expression can be more or less precise; this is why we teach vocabulary in the schools. On the other hand, it is almost infinitely malleable, capable of expressing every nuance of human experience.[21] The goal of reasoning, however, is not simply self-expression or expression of one's mind, but to express things as they are, to represent things as true. Perception images the world, but does not of itself know that image to be true. Work knows only what succeeded or failed this time, not what can be expected to succeed in the future. We reason to determine how things really stand with the objects of our perception and work. Earlier we drew a connection between habits and beliefs. When brought to rational expression, habits become beliefs. The skills refined by the master craftsman can be observed and recorded symbolically in textbooks, not only so that others can imitate, analyze, and even improve the

21. This is not to imply that every human person can express every meaning exactly. This is why poetry writing is an art.

master's habits, but also so that the nature of his skills or of his materials can be better understood.

Like perception and work, reasoning is a bodily human activity, a kind of habit. The same parts of the body that image the world in perception and transform it by work participate in reasoning. We speak with our mouths (which also taste and eat) and write with our hands (which also feel and grasp). The body can gesture. Severely injured people can communicate by blinking their eyes. Even pure thinking "inside the head" is a physical activity that can be observed and measured with appropriate equipment.[22] Like perception and work, reasoning is a bodily activity, subject to the laws governing other bodily activities. (This is why it is possible to recite one's prayers absentmindedly, without attention or expression, mumbling at Morning Praise, "Come, let us sing to the Lord, and shout with joy to the Rock who saves us!") It is not simply by being verbal or mental that an activity counts as reasoning, even if most of us ordinarily do our reasoning mentally, that is, in the privacy of our imaginations. What makes an activity to be reasoning is that it intends to represent what can or might be or is truth. Words—whether "heard" in the mind, expressed aloud, or written down—are not ideas. Mental events are not ideas, and they can come and go, calling up other thoughts and images, which depend on the mental habits, experiences and idiosyncrasies of the thinker's psychic makeup. But these signs, even as they come, are judged by logic and rendered meaningful. Words and mental events express ideas, and ideas govern thought by structuring the way the thinker behaves in his conscious action. To be rational is not simply to have mental events that mysteriously correspond to or correlate with physical happenings. To be rational is to be logical, to govern one's behavior by the laws of meaning. It is to act on the basis of understanding.

Logic and understanding. We judge beliefs according to the canons of reasoning, that is, by logical laws or principles, whose foundations we need to examine. If to be human is to be rational animal, then to be human is to use logic. When we speak of understanding we are dealing not only with the relationship of an expressed belief with its referent, but also of its rela-

---

22. Michael I. Posner, "Seeing the Mind," *Science* 262 (29 October 1993).

tionship with other beliefs and states of affairs. Because a belief can be stated in the form of a proposition, it stands in logical relationship with other propositions, with other beliefs. One belief can be inferred from or contradict another, standing as evidence for or against the truth of another belief. This is most clearly and dramatically evident in the cases of those scientific discoveries which followed upon the postulation of an entity's existence, as in the cases of the discovery of Neptune and subatomic particles, such as the neutrino. Of course, it is not only in the practice of science that the logical relationships among beliefs come into play. The suspect's claim that he was shooting pool with his brother-in-law contradicts the police officer's belief that he was robbing the bank. The political officeholder infers from the facts about rising unemployment and falling stock prices, that he may lose the election. Beliefs stand in logical relationship with one another.

The logical character of beliefs means that their symbolic expressions consist of terms having general meanings. The belief is related not only to the existential situation it describes but also to the general characters of things that may or may not also exist. The suspect's reference to a brother-in-law in his alibi implies that either he or his pool partner is married and thus that there is a woman who may be able to offer testimony. The existence of such a relationship and the fact that the mutual activity is one normally pursued for fun suggests that the relationship between the suspect and his brother-in-law is close and congenial. A social scientist may subsequently study the case in order to establish some kind of theory concerning loyalties and cooperation within extended families or kinship relationships. Even a proper name or demonstrative pronoun will, in context of a belief, adopt or acquire a general character. Once we know that Andrew caused widespread devastation and loss of life in Florida, we know that the referent of *Andrew* is not a British prince but a storm. The *that* in "That is mine" must be an object that the speaker has fairly clearly pointed out. If the indication is unclear, one can always designate his referent in terms of the kind of thing it is.

Without realizing it, a person can hold beliefs that are incompatible or even contradictory. For instance, one may hold that innocent human life may not rightly be taken, but also believe that elective abortion is morally acceptable. One may profess to reject superstition but nevertheless faithfully check his horoscope in the daily paper. As long as the two beliefs are not set "side by side," as it were, one can affirm them both. It is not the case, however, that both are fully believed, when all their implications are faced. It can occur that the two beliefs come into an existential conflict, when in the same situation the two beliefs require mutually exclusive behaviors. Precisely this has occurred with nurses assisting with elective abortions, as they see that the procedure is the killing of a human baby. If upon reflection, one discovers that the two are logically incompatible, then he will reject or modify one of the beliefs. This is Aristotle's point when he insists that no one can believe two contradictories, "for it is impossible for anyone to think that the same thing both is and is not."[23] One can assert contradictories and even represent them to himself as true; were it not so, Aristotle would not have had to write so much in *Metaphysics* Book IV. The point is that since an actual belief informs thought and behavior, no one can hold to both a belief and its opposite. The belief forms behavior one way or the other.

In real life, of course, people do not hold themselves to a high standard of logical consistency. A politician professes himself an environmentalist and consistently votes against regulation of the polluting industries that support his electoral campaign. Another proclaims himself a proponent of free trade and yet regularly urges tariffs and import quotas. The characteristic failing of politicians, however, afflicts us all. The father lectures his son on thrift and responsibility while overextending his credit for expensive electronic equipment. The American poet Walt Whitman boasted, "Do I contradict myself? Very well then I contradict myself, (I am large, I contain multitudes)."[24] Although a person can certainly *express* contrary beliefs, expression is not the same as belief. If every belief entails a disposition to act in the world in a certain way under certain general conditions, then that beliefs contradict each other means that they entail a disposition to do a thing and its contrary. One who asserts contradictory beliefs can ultimately hold only to one of them, because should the proper conditions obtain, he would have to choose one course of action. Ultimately the resolution of a real conflict between beliefs can be forced only by an encounter with the real world. The nurse must either assist with the abortion or with-

23. Aristotle, *Metaphysics,* IV, Ch. iii 1005b.
24. Whitman, "Song of Myself," in *Leaves of Grass* (1855).

draw. The politician must cast his votes and answer to the press and his constituency. (He may, of course, have no real beliefs about protecting the environment but only about the best ways to continue being elected.) The existential dilemma may be revealed by the logical analysis. Because one's beliefs refer both to the real world and to each other, they cannot conflict. Two conflicting beliefs cannot, in their entirety, both be genuine.

We turn at this point to consider the elements of logical inference. By doing so we can more sharply determine the role of ideas in rational activity.

(A) Universals.   The terms of any belief are or can be subsumed under universals. We have already noted how an indexical term, such as *Andrew,* must (implicitly, at least) be subsumed under a general category—*man* or *hurricane*—in order to be understood and used in a proposition. Even a strictly demonstrative term, such as *that* or *it,* must be so subsumed. Does *that* refer to an object, a color, a relationship, or event? "That is ugly!" "Do you mean the shirt?" "No, I mean the pattern in your tie." To understand logical inference we need first to grasp how universals are used and what they really are. Are universals real or merely conventional?

An African saying has it, "When elephants fight the ants get trampled." For most people this proposition calls up in the mind an image of large gray beasts with tusks and trunks in violent conflict as tiny insects scurry about beneath their large flat feet. This image can vary, of course, from thinker to thinker. The specific variations of mental images of different thinkers need not affect their ability to communicate with each other or to recognize instances of the proposition in real life. These mental images are themselves singulars with particular, albeit transitory, features. The mental image is itself not a universal. Indeed, the mental image can play its role in thought only if there is something about it that is universal. The universal, whatever it is, does not exist in the mind as a mental image. Indeed, we may take this a step further and note that the universal seems to determine the mental image in specific ways. Consider inverting the proposition to say, "When the ants fight the elephants get trampled." Although one can, with some cinematic imagination, picture to oneself monstrous ants trampling across the savanna, he realizes that this cannot be of real ants, of ants as we commonly understand them. One's first reaction to such a proposition is puzzlement, for *ant* carries with it the notion of very small size and *elephant* of great size. Although very few (if any) of us have ever observed ants being trampled by fighting elephants, we have no difficulty imagining a variety of scenarios in which this is taking place. On the other hand, an effort and some ingenuity are required to envision fighting ants trampling elephants. The universal meanings of the terms *elephant* and *ant* preclude us from forming an image of the proposition according to its manifest sense. The meanings prevent us from doing logically what their objects cannot do in real life. Violate the canons of meaning and the sentence is confusing, if not outright nonsense.

Let us next consider the words that express universals. In the last page or so, *elephant* appears ten times. Although each repetition of this string of letters has its own existence, taking its own space on the page, we say that *elephant* is one word. Normally one would say that the word *elephant* appears ten times prior to this paragraph: one word repeated ten times. It is not enough to say that the word represents a universal; the word *is* a universal, even if the sequences of ink marks are singular things. Although one may create and use the word-token or letter sequence however he wants, the word *elephant* as a word is governed by certain rules and principles. To suggest that "ants" can trample elephants is to misunderstand what *elephant* (or *ant*) means. Should one attempt to use *elephant* as a verb or possessive pronoun, the resulting sequence of words would be nonsense. The word *elephant* is, in fact, a universal, which governs the string of marks E-L-E-P-H-A-N-T, as well as the spoken, Morse code, and ASL representations of it.

The word is real. It determines the structure of thoughts and beliefs. In virtue of this word, its various printed and spoken tokens have effects in the world, including the effect of calling mental images to the minds of their hearers and affecting their behavior. Consider: As Walter lifts a piece of chocolate to his mouth, his friend says, "Gift!" If Walter is an English-speaking person, he will doubtless say, "Thank you." Should he speak German (in which language *Gift* means *poison*), he will hesitate or even drop the candy. The word has effects and evokes responses in oneself and others. The English *gift* is related logically to such words as *generosity, love, friendship, birthday,* and so on. Since it is usually used in contexts of happiness, friendliness, and peace, it tends to evoke good feelings. One may use these associations to evoke good feelings, as advertisers do when they describe a sales promotional item as a gift. The *meaning,* however, is the essence, in virtue of which the word behaves logically as it does. To be more precise, we should say that the word is the essence of the token and that the meaning is the explication of this essence. At issue is whether universals have real being in their real instances, for instance, whether there is a universal essence of "elephant-ness" in every elephant. The present argument is that the sequence of letters *elephant* is as real an object as any pachyderm in the zoo. The difference between the word and the animal is that any thinker can reproduce the sound or letters of the words almost effortlessly and in great numbers, while breeding elephants is hard and time-consuming and the managing of them difficult. The words—which are physical existents—have meaning. One can object that in the case of the word-token the meaning is placed there by a human mind, imposing an intention, that the word-token itself does not "contain" the meaning. Certainly, the word's meaning does result from human intention, but it does not consist only in the speaker's or thinker's intention. The meaning consists in its possible relationships with other words and with those things that it can represent. *Elephant* does not mean simply because I (or any other person) want or intend it to mean, but because it stands in logical relationships with other words, such as *animal, herbivorous, pachyderm, mammal, offspring,* and *large,* and represents or stands for certain entities to be found in India, zoos, circuses, and African plains. Its meaning is independent of any individual human mind or even of the community that uses it. This is evident from the fact that archeologists can successfully decipher texts in newly discovered dead languages. By examining the relationships among symbols in a document and determining from other evidence how the document was used, they can determine what the symbol means. Therefore, it is clear that the meaning of the word is real, that it attaches to the physical tokens that express the word. The essences of words are real. They are universals, which have real being.

The meaning of the word is ideal; it is an idea. But what manner of being does this idea, this meaning have? Clearly, it is not physical. Two very different ideas can attach to the word-token "Gift." Neither is it some kind of mental event, such as a feeling or mental image—even if it calls such images to mind. The idea is a principle in virtue of which mind operates as it does, a kind of law governing the thinking mind. The idea of elephant enables one better to come to grips with experiences involving certain large pachyderms. The oppressed peasants live with the simple fact that life is hard; then the revolutionary arrives with a new idea, a principle in terms of which they can understand their plight anew. What they formerly saw as hard luck now becomes *exploitation.* What they formerly saw as disconnected facts are joined into unity by this new idea. Because of her secretive habits of overeating and purging, a young woman is constantly ashamed and feels she is uniquely wicked or going crazy. Then she reads a magazine article describing *anorexia nervosa,* and a feeling of relief comes over her. Her secret compulsion is shared by others, and furthermore it is connected to and partly explained by her uncomfortable relationship with her parents. The mystery in her life has a name, and this means she can understand and control it. Ideas shape the mind of the thinker. To learn an idea is to expand the power of one's mind. The primary locus, therefore, of ideas is the intellect of the reasoning human being. In what sense can they said to be present in the physical tokens, in the words we see and hear? That words are conventional does not mean that they are unreal. Once a word has found its logical location in the language, no one thinker can readily dislodge it. Lewis Carroll notwithstanding, words cannot mean whatever one speaker decides according to his private mental intention. Thus, one is held responsible for his use of language. The sign betrays the thoughts, the ideas of its creators. Words have meanings, which are ideas.

Similarly, there is no reason to deny that the general natures—essences—of existing beings (that is, other than words) are real. In any one particular case, of course, we may wrongly identify an essence. For example, the ether, a rigid, permeable substance that is to have filled all physical space, does not exist. This concept of *ether* applies to nothing real. Existing entities can be erroneously grouped into a common class—as when children classify ants with spiders or nineteenth-century whalers classed whales as fish. Furthermore, that essences are real does not guarantee that human intelligence can grasp them quickly or accurately or with little effort of mind. Finally, we do not assert that essences themselves exist. Thus, the essence is not "in" the thing as in a physical location. The essence is of the thing, as that in virtue of which the thing exists as this kind of thing. We can express these essences in meaningful terms, with words. A correspondence obtains between the word and the object (or the class of objects) that it represents, not in virtue of any physical connection, but because of an ideal relationship. The word relates logically (or meaningfully) as the object relates in existence. What is real in the word—the idea—corresponds to the reality of the general (or universal) character of the object. The object can be taken to instantiate the idea expressed by the word. In this way we can speak of ideas as being in things. Therefore, we have no reason to deny that the belief is capable of representing real things as they are—that is, in truth.

(B) Inference   Because beliefs stand in logical relationships to each other, we evaluate our thoughts, in part, by their logical consistency. St. Paul argues that if the dead are not raised then Christ is not raised (I Corinthians 15:14). That is, the belief that no one is raised from the dead contradicts the belief that Jesus was raised from the dead. One must choose to believe the one or the other, because both cannot stand together. The human mind operates by inference, by moving from one thought to another. Because it is founded on the assignment of individuals and classes to classes designated by predicates, the syllogism is the paradigm for logical inference: "*A* is *B*. *B* is *C*. Therefore, *A* is *C*." The Aristotelian syllogism is founded on meaning; if *A* is *B* and *B* is *C*, then to deny *C* of *A* is to deny the meaning of at least one term. For if *A* is not-*C*, then neither can *A* be *B*, for to be *B* is to be *C*. The predicate *B* can be affirmed or denied of *A*. If it is affirmed, then whatever belongs to *B* is concurrently affirmed of *A*. The statement "*A* is *B*," states that whatever belongs to *B* belongs to *A*.[25] If all men are mortal and Socrates is a man, we can assert his immortality only by changing the meaning of *mortal*. If he were literally immortal, then he would continue to live and will not die, which constitutes a counterexample to the general statement that all men are mortal. Socrates' immortality, if we wish to ascribe it to him, must lie in the enduring influence of his thought and personality or something similar. Indeed, we may remark that the complaints about the rigidity and inadequacy of syllogistic reasoning are usually founded on an improper use of terms, on the inappropriate or

25. Peirce, "Some Consequences of Four Incapacities," in *Collected Papers*, 5.264 ff. See especially 5.279.

insufficiently accurate application of a predicate, or on the inaccurate characterization of the subject. If the validity of the syllogism be denied, then with it are denied truth and meaning. Conversely, if meaning or truth be denied—and we have seen that these stand and fall together—then the syllogism is but an arbitrary pattern. But the syllogism is not an arbitrary structure that we assume in order to construct arguments. The validity of the syllogistic form is not a kind of primordial assumption underlying all our arguments. Rather it is founded on and is a consequence of the possibility of meaning.

Inference is the process by which what is contained in a representation is brought to expression, by which one belief or representation gives rise to another. Copernicus admires the majesty of the sun as a perfect symbol of the majesty of God, and he proposes that the sun is more appropriately the center of the universe than the earth.[26] An English traveler observes that the peoples of the Caucasus are the most handsome he has seen and infers that they best exemplify the white race, which he calls "Caucasian." A man buys two automobiles of the same manufacture, and both prove unsatisfactory. He concludes that the automaker is incapable of manufacturing good cars. By analogy, repetition, similarity, or incidental association one thought can suggest another. This underlies the practice of "learning by heart." The pianist learning a piece not only learns its developmental structure, its logic, but he also drills himself to get it "into his fingers," so that they move to the right place at the right time. By mistake we say, "music hath charms to soothe the savage beast": by mistake—because William Congreve[27] wrote, "to soothe the savage breast." This process, by which one thought follows from another, need not be logical, following strict canons of correct reasoning. The sound of a word or even a mistake may suggest a connection between thoughts, which is—by definition—inference. The inference may or may not be valid, but it is an inference nonetheless. It is not sufficient, however, for us to draw inferences. One's inferences structure beliefs and form a conception of the world as a unified whole. Since by inference we construct a vision of what the world beyond our own imme-

26. Copernicus, *De Revolutionibus*, Bk. I, chap. 10, cited in E. A. Burtt, *The Metaphysical Foundations of Modern Science*, 56.

27. And not, as the related mistake has it, William Shakespeare.

diate experience is like, it is important that we be able to distinguish good from poor inferences.

If (*per impossibile*) inference were a purely ideal activity unconnected with the physical, then there would be no need to evaluate it. We could appreciate the flow of one idea into another on aesthetic or even entertainment grounds; it does not matter what one thinks, as long as it is interesting or results in agreeable feelings. But the mental life is not such. Our mental lives are a constant flux and flow of thoughts, perceptions, impressions, feelings, actions, and reactions. A philosopher wise and sober reflects on Kant's antinomies of pure reason, when a stray thought—perhaps a fresh pun on the Transcendental Idealist's name—sets him to chuckling. Then it occurs to him that the quantum theory may significantly relate to Kant's arguments. We move from thought to thought in a way that our wills only partially control. (Why did Kasparov lose to Big Blue, if not because—unlike the machine, which had only to calculate its next move—the World Chess Champion saw himself playing for the honor of the human race? He was rattled by the responsibility.) Hume identifies three principles of connection among ideas: "Resemblance, Contiguity in time or place, and Cause or Effect." He continues:

That these principles serve to connect ideas will not, I believe, be much doubted. A picture naturally leads our thoughts to the original. The mention of one apartment in a building naturally introduces an inquiry or discourse concerning the others; and if we think of a wound, we can scarcely forbear reflecting on the pain which follows it.[28]

That is, one thought can recall another as an image, an icon. Another may be an index that points beyond itself to what comes next or after, and a third refers to what habitually follows, to a general law. "Mother" can lead one to the memory of that woman who bore and raised him, to the thought of "father," or to reflections of gestation and reproductions—or, by a more complex path, to the 1989 Gulf War, in which Saddam Hussein promised the "mother of all battles." Hume's argument was right, but only so far as it goes. Perceptions trigger thoughts, thoughts trigger more thoughts, and thoughts influence perceptions. Where Hume falls short is that he does not account

28. Hume, *An Inquiry Concerning Human Understanding* (Indianapolis and New York: Bobbs Merrill, 1955), Section III, 32.

for how the human intelligence can monitor and control this flow of mental activity.[29] Every "thought" or mental event is a sign, which requires some sense or meaning. What harm is there if a child refers to a spider as a "bug"? Minor a point as it is, parents or teachers will carefully explain the difference between spiders and insects, so that the child will use the word according to its meaning. Since there is no perception without interpretation and no action without purpose (as the next chapter will make clear), everything in the mental life is a sign and can be related to other experiences as interpretive. The task of logic is to evaluate the sign according to whether it interprets the other signs and the world accurately.

Because logic can be formalized, it is possible to reduce it to a kind of algebra. Further, a machine operates according to well-defined and determined mechanical procedures, and these can be designed to function as logical operators, which enable machines to mimic logical inferences. The Aristotelian syllogism, "B is C; A is B; therefore, A is C," can readily be stated in a logical calculus. Knowing the appropriate rules, one can infer "$\sim P \wedge \sim Q$" from the formula, "$\sim(P \vee Q)$," without even knowing what P and Q mean. This suggests that logic may be simply a kind of calculus, whose formulae enable one to reproduce rational thought mechanically. But how does such a system apply to reality? Let us begin by noting that there is no reason one cannot construct a consistent logical system in which all values are "true": "p" is true for all "p." Therefore, "not-p" is true, even if "p" is true. This is comparable to an arithmetic in which the sum of every two numbers is 1. In such an arithmetic, there would, of course, be only one number, namely 1. Such an arithmetic theory is consistent; within it, we can derive theorems and state general laws (not very interesting ones, of course). It is also completely useless, except perhaps to a Sisyphus. The only number in the system, 1, cannot apply to anything real. Similarly, in a logical system in which everything is true, no proposition can apply to anything. If "p" and "not-p" are both true, then "p" can represent any state of affairs. If a proposition is to mean anything, it must admit of falsity; that is, one must be able to differentiate states of affairs that it repre-

<hr />

29. The same objection can be brought up against Dennett's proposal, "A scholar is just a library's making another library" (*Consciousness Explained*, p. 202). Dennett appeals to a mechanical evolution of *memes* (units of mental activity) but without showing how this could result in a new library that makes sense.

sents from those that it does not. A univalent logic is trivial, meaningless. A simple proposition consists in the ascription of a predicate to a subject, which may be an individual, a group of individuals or a class. Therefore, as Aristotle says, "to say that what is, is, or that what is not, is not, is true." If the predicate does not apply as stated in the proposition, then the proposition is false. Should it apply, then the proposition is true. If all propositions are held to be true, then every predicate applies (and does not apply) to every subject. Like the univalent arithmetic, such a symbolism reduces all words to one, which means nothing and everything at once, a word which is predicated of itself alone.

By destroying truth we destroy meaning, and this point is key. What the mechanical procedure can do is to trace the steps of an algorithm and, as a result, produce an expression, whether this be a dollar amount, a chess move, the addition of a measured amount of chemical to the solution, or a statement. What the algorithm does is to provide us with a diagrammatic way to move through the steps of an argument quickly. To say "$p \leftrightarrow q$" means simply that wherever p appears, one can substitute q. Whether the algorithm itself is logically useful depends on the logic inherent in the meaningfulness of language. Searle approaches this point in his *Minds, Brains and Science*, where he argues precisely this point, that the capacity of the computer is only syntactical; it cannot deal with meanings.[30] However, Searle goes on to characterize meaning (or intentionality) as a biological phenomenon, a kind of mental event caused by the brain.[31] This account of meaning cannot be adequate, because the meaning of a symbol appearing in an argument does not depend on its being a mental event as such, but on its interpretive relationship with other signs (including images) symbols and things (which may include mental events). That is, "man" in the textbook syllogism about Socrates' mortality has meaning, not because of the state of the speaker or anyone else's brain, but because of its relationship with other terms in the English language, particular sorts of organic entities (including Socrates, St. Peter's mother-in-law, my insurance agent, and Mary Queen of Scots), and the images and associations called up in the minds of English-speakers when they encounter it. The

30. Searle, *Minds, Brains and Science*, chap. 2, especially 39 ff.
31. Ibid., 41.

plantation owner who denied that the slave is a man or the witness in Poe's "Murders in the Rue Morgue" who identified the orangutan as a man were wrong because their uses of the term "man" were not in accord with the logical demands of that sign. A language-using bipedal animal who can carry out plans is a man, skin color notwithstanding, but a large primate acting on instinct is not, regardless of the state of the speaker's brain. The slaveholder needs not only to change his attitude, but also to understand the full significance of the term "man," while Poe's witness needs further information about the creature he saw. The reason that language cannot reduce to syntax is that the term is related not only to other symbols in the system, but also to the worlds of perception and action. (One shakes hands with a man, but not with an orangutan.) In fact, in many spheres of activity we distinguish those who simply know the right words from those who really understand.

The Humean account suggests a kind of physics of the mind, a set of three laws of association. The house cat's stalking a mouse calls to mind the panther's stalking the gazelle. The resemblance of the one image to the other evokes the recollection. The sense of strengthening and replenishment that follows upon eating bread leads the mind to expect such experiences in the future. The life of the mind becomes, for Hume, a sequence of triggered associations. As a psychologist, Hume was an astute amateur, and his successors have significantly developed his simple model. Freud found complex subconscious mechanisms that also determine the perception and interpretation of experience. Contemporary neuroscience and psychology locate different mental activities in different parts of the brain, and they trace the neural pathways that connect them. In a way, however, these contemporary professional models are variations on Hume's simple laws of association. This model, however, is inadequate, and its inadequacy has nothing to do with its simplicity. What Hume's principles of association do not account for at all is that each idea,[32] each mental event represents and interprets other ideas. In virtue of what does the picture lead our minds to the original? Animals, who have senses comparable to ours (often better), seldom show interest in pictures; the dog does not gaze wist-

---

32. Here I use the term *idea* in Hume's sense, as a perception of the mind, an image of some sense impression (*An Inquiry concerning Human Understanding*, Section II).

fully at the photo of his absent master. The picture is usually smaller than its object, and it is two-dimensional. It does not move and emits neither smell nor sound. We connect the picture with its original because we know that this is what a picture is intended to do. The picture represents according to certain particular rules and is interpreted according to those rules. The monochrome photo reproduces shape and shading, but not color. A picture recalls its original because the human person can abstract some features (shape, color, spatial arrangement) from others. Even an unintended image (such as a rock outcropping that resembles an old man or a potato that looks like Abraham Lincoln) triggers a connection only when one has learned how to decipher it, to see how it could be an image. The "Resemblance" of which Hume speaks is not that obvious. The cat owner may marvel at Fuffy T.'s predatory resemblance to the panther, but the gazelles of the Serengeti would not deign to notice the little pet. The operation of the mind depends not on observable laws of interaction, but upon the propensity of human persons to interpret what they experience.

Inference is the process by which one thought gives rise to another in order to represent truth. The mind notices a resemblance, sees a connection, expects a cause or explanation, and therefore it connects two thoughts.[33] So far goes Hume, but the mind carries the matter a step further. The mind does not simply observe as a train of random, somehow interconnected thoughts pass by; it uses those thoughts to understand. Not only does the mind notice the resemblance, but it can also examine its basis. Those stars resemble the figure of Taurus, a bull; does this constellation have other noble taurine qualities? From this kind of question arose the science of astrology—and from that, astronomy. Is there a common predicate that we can attach only to Aldebaran, the Pleiades, and the rest of Taurus's stars? Is there some common relationship among them? Astrology arose not simply from patterns that shepherds and sailors picked out during boring nights, but from the impulse to find what general conception applies to them. Although astrology failed to find such conceptions, they were there to be found by astronomers, who asked what kinds of things these stars and planets are. The human acts of perceiving, working in the

---

33. By *thought* here I mean, of course, any mental event, whether a perception, a feeling, the experience of exertion, or what we ordinarily call thought.

world, and thinking symbolically are all formed by general conceptions. The mind does not simply receive and process images, like a video processor, but it relates to them ideally, as general conceptions, according to which further conceptions will be received and integrated.

Forms of inference. Reasoning or inference takes three general forms. Taking the syllogism as the fundamental form of inference, Peirce shows the relationships among deduction, induction and hypothesis (or abduction).[34]

	Deduction	Induction	Hypothesis
Premise 1	A is B (Minor)	a_i is B (Minor)	A is c_i (Conclusion)
		(i = 1, 2, <ell>., n)	(i = 1, 2, <ell>., n)
Premise 2	B is C (Major)	a_i is C (Conclusion)	B is c_i (Major)
Conclusion	A is C (Conclusion)	B is C (Major)	A is B (Minor)

In the following sections we develop Peirce's understanding of these three forms of inference.

Deduction. Deduction is the logic of applying a habit to action in a particular case. Let *B* be "occasions when I am thirsty" and *C* be "I will drink water"; if *A* is "now," then my habit is triggered and I drink. Deduction is, in this respect, quasi-mechanical, developing the implications of a general conception in a particular circumstance. Indeed, deduction is the kind of reasoning operation a machine can do particularly well. It enables us to apply the knowledge we already have to particular situations. If the motorist is told to get onto I-465 around Indianapolis, then (assuming he knows the Interstate numbering system) he knows already that the road will be multi-lane with limited access and heavily traveled by local drivers during rush hours. By knowing that I-465 is an urban interstate highway loop, he knows, in general, what to expect while driving there, because he knows what class of things "I-465" belongs to. If the instructions for repairing the

34. Peirce, "Some Consequences of Four Incapacities," in *Collected Papers*, 5.264 ff., and "The Law of Mind," in *Collected Papers*, 6.102 ff.

lawn mower refer to a set-screw, then the homeowner recognizes the part when he sees it. Deduction is the kind of inference operating when reality presents no surprises but shows itself as expected.

Because it moves from the general to the particular, or from the generic to the specific, deductive reasoning delivers no new truth but rather applies truth already known to things unknown or, at least, formerly unconsidered. Therefore, in the thinker's life deductive reasoning is ordered to the future. By reasoning deductively one knows, in virtue of its essence or general nature, the characteristics of a being one has not before encountered. Thus deduction has a twofold value. For the acting person engaged with the world, deduction has the practical benefit that it enables one to use knowledge already acquired to make his way through situations as yet uncharted. For the scientist deduction serves to confirm truths genuinely had and to expose falsity in his general conceptions. The "crucial experiment" is such precisely because it tests the deductions made from the theory under consideration. By deducing particular consequences, we refine our general conceptions, discovering their inadequacies and uncovering their strengths. Deductive reasoning enables us to compare the truth we have imprecisely with reality.

Induction.   Induction is the logic of learning by experience. Again let a_i be a series of "occasions when I walked down the stairs," B be "occasion when I walked upright," and C be "occasion when I have bumped my head on the transom." The conclusion is "when I walk down the stairs upright I bump my head on the transom." Since I do not want this to be the major premise governing my habits, I cease walking upright and make a habit of ducking as I walk down the stairs or forgo using that staircase. Through induction things in the world impress their forms upon the subject by fostering behavior that coordinates his nature with theirs. The training of animals is by induction; the dog learns that the leash "means" going out for a walk. The sharp jerk on the line as his master says, "heel!" forms a connection in his canine mind, so that eventually he learns to "heel" when commanded. Hume's laws of association are inductive. The empiricist's point was precisely that the repetitious triggering of one thought by another establishes an inference in the mind. Significantly, Hume allows the validity of such inferences, even as he rejects the notion of causality that is intended to undergird them.[35] The involuntary associations our minds make of one idea with another constitute a kind of inductive inference. Inductive reasoning proper reflects, but also makes explicit the associations by which we learn from experience.

As a mode of inference, induction intends to attain the truth. However, the "training" that we receive from the "school of hard knocks" is imprecise and often misleading. More to the point, however, is that experience alone cannot answer the question, "Is it true?" Experience "teaches" that a man's shoelaces break only when he's in a hurry. More often than not if you forget your umbrella, it will rain. More serious is the police officer's growing conviction—based on seventeen years patrolling the worst areas of town—that most Hispanic men spend their evenings drinking and starting fights. And he knows that when he sees a group of black youths gathered there will be trouble. Parents of children with autism point to the fact that many of their children first displayed symptoms of the condition only after their childhood vaccinations. In addition, many women who had received silicone breast implants suffered serious health problems. In all these cases, from the trivially annoying to the most serious, experience teaches a lesson, but the task remains of evaluating the lesson. Is it true?

To ask the question of truth requires that the question be formulated, that the pattern of experience be represented symbolically and then the argument constructed. We recall that the structure of the inductive argument is as follows.

a_i is B (Minor) $(i = 1, 2, \ldots, n)$
a_i is C (Conclusion)
B is C (Major)

It is immediately clear, of course, that such an inference is not necessary (for one thing, the middle term is undistributed), but with an inductive argument we are looking for truth, not simple validity. We have to use inductive arguments for the simple reason that they are, in a sense, written into our nature and experience; we notice patterns and respond accordingly to them. In this argument, the a's, as the middle term, are crucial. If it could be established that the entire class of B is accounted for by $a_1, a_2, \ldots,$

35. Hume, *An Inquiry Concerning Human Understanding*, Section IV.

a_n, then the conclusion would follow necessarily (since B would then be distributed). Ordinarily we cannot list all the children who have been vaccinated, occasions of tying shoes in a hurry, and so on. Therefore it is necessary to insure somehow that the a's are representative of B. Are the men a policeman encounters while patrolling during third shift representative of their ethnic group? Are women with post-implant health problems representative of all who have received the implants? (It turned out that they were not.) The principles and rules for sampling can be found in any good statistics textbook. What is important for our present discussion is that by reducing a pattern to a symbolic representation, the truth of an implicit inference can be evaluated. That is, by symbolically representing the experienced pattern it is possible to determine whether the conclusion fostered by the pattern is true. It is possible to establish rational—indeed, mathematical—criteria for evaluating inductive inferences, and in this way reason can transcend the practical habits fostered by repeated experience.

Hypothesis.   The third form, the hypothetical (or to use Peirce's term, *abductive*), entails the application of an idea, that what I have experienced can by unified under the predicate B, that it shares a common nature with B. In Arthur Conan Doyle's "The Speckled Band," Sherlock Holmes concludes that the murder is committed by using a poisonous snake, a swamp adder.[36] If A is the nexus of events surrounding the dead sister's murder, we find within it the victim's final words ("The speckled band!"), a bed bolted to the floor, a dummy bell rope reaching almost to the pillow, a vent between the bedroom and the uncle's study, and in his study a dish of milk, as well as a safe with small holes drilled in it.[37] Holmes's reasoning here was not deductive but hypothetical. Let B represent the swamp adder as a murder weapon. The species in question was speckled; it could be kept in a safe and fed milk from a saucer, and induced to slither down the bell rope into the bed of a sleeping heiress. All the relevant predicates applicable to the murder and its scene are unified by positing a swamp adder as the murder weapon. Let us consider another example. Quite by accident, the amateur player strikes the ball weakly but with backspin and in doing so scores a

36. Arthur Conan Doyle, "The Adventure of the Speckled Band." In *The Complete Adventures of Sherlock Holmes.* New York: Bramhall House, 1975, 98-113.

37. I am leaving out many additional clues, of course.

point. The same tennis player notices that Steffi Graf's backhand, in which the racquet travels in a downward motion, disconcerts her opponents. Reflecting on these and other experiences—perhaps on the behavior of the ball when he just bounces it with the racquet into the air—our player hypothesizes that controlled backspin will sometimes give him an advantage and that such and such a racket motion will impart the spin. He practices and incorporates backspin into his game. The behavior of the thinker trying to come up with an explanation is remarkably similar to that of the novice trying to work out a new skill. Hypothetical thinking and behavior is not just thrashing about until something works. It is a directed thrashing about, which is based on some model or observation from which an idea was drawn.

Here we have a form of inference that is distinctively and characteristically human: the ability to recognize new ideas, to bring a variety of experiences under one head—in short, to use general or universal concepts. This is a kind of reasoning most clearly dependent on ideas. Although a human being or an animal may indeed discover something by accident—perhaps that beehives contain honey or that a hollowed rock can catch rain—the human mind has the capacity to leap to a hypothesis, a subject that unifies disparate predicates. Here we touch on the most intractable problem of psychology and the practice of science: How is it that the human mind comes up with its ideas? Johannes Kepler proposed that planetary orbits are elliptical, and that in any given period of time the arc from the focus to the ellipse will always sweep the same area. What made him come up with this? Why did he, but no one else, see his laws of planetary motion? Einstein proposed that in place of the laws of conservation of matter and energy the velocity of light be the fundamental invariant for physics. He traced the consequences of this proposal and developed the Special Theory of Relativity. After the fact, the hypothesis makes perfect sense. Like Dr. Watson, we slap our heads and ask why we did not see what was so evident to Holmes. However, our embarrassment is misplaced. The logic of the hypothesis is this.

A is c_i (Conclusion) ($i = 1, 2, \ldots, n$)
B is c_i (Major)
A is B (Minor)

We know that A has properties $c_1, c_2, \ldots, c_n$, and we ask why. What accounts for those characteristics? The trick is to come up with the major premise, to find some B that has all the same characteristics. There is, however, no rule, no procedure for discovering the right B. That we can do this testifies to the operation of ideas that underlie our thinking. The inference is possible because an idea common to A and B is identified, a principle in virtue of which the two are alike or behave the same—in virtue of which the predicates "c_i" can be applied to them. And this is verified by the fact that ordinarily it is the scientist or the expert who comes up with the right hypothesis, the one that, in retrospect, anyone could have thought of it. It is the one who has devoted his mind to understanding a particular kind of thing who sees the idea. It is he who makes good use of the accidental or "chance" discovery. The same applies to art, where so often it takes the genius to discover the richness of even the simple idea. Concerning the first movement of Beethoven's *Fifth Symphony*, Leonard Bernstein said, "Three Gs and an E-flat. Nothing more. Anybody could have thought of them—maybe."[38] Bernstein's point is that precisely from this simple theme—perhaps reflecting fate knocking at the door, or maybe just a friend knocking—Beethoven could develop one of the world's great musical masterpieces. The mind of a Beethoven is, in a sense, musical, able to make musical connections among sounds and to discover the ideal possibilities latent in them, just as an Einstein has a "physical" (in the sense of physics) mind.

In discussing these three forms of inference we have considered not only verbal behavior but action as well. The relationships and connections between the two will be further developed in the next chapter. It is important at this point to stress also the importance of ideas. We may describe inference as the unification of many predicates in relation to one other. But this bringing into unity is precisely the effect of ideas. The argument for the reality of the soul as something in some respect immaterial comes down ultimately to the fact that human rationality cannot reduce to a physical or mechanical procedure. From the foregoing it is clear that in some ways inference can be regarded as physical processes. Deduction comes down to the application of habit; a thing does what it always does in this situation. And induction is a principle by which habits are modified by

38. Leonard Bernstein, "Beethoven's Fifth Symphony," in Bernstein, *The Joy of Music* (New York: Simon and Schuster, 1959), 73–93.

experience. One eventually learns to duck beneath the low transom, just as the squirrel learns to access the bird feeder. Induction provides us with one way in which habits are modified. However, it is also clear, especially when we consider hypothetic reasoning, that physical factors alone cannot account for all inference. Recent developments in logic make this clear, as the next section will show.

Reason's scope and mechanical process

According to evolutionary materialism, the human power to reason and to know is an organic adaptation by which human beings survive successfully in their physical environment. The power to reason and establish beliefs is nothing else than the ability to determine accurately the present and probable future dangers and opportunities for life in a variety of environments and to devise ways to confront and adapt to them. It is the power to predict destructive weather, plan ambushes, and air-condition Phoenix. We have argued that the human power to know and understand far exceeds such adaptations and, indeed, is fundamentally different from them. Human understanding extends in principle to anything that may in any way be considered to be, including not only the conditions of life in France, but the nature of the universe as a whole, the possible structure of alternative universes, and the relationship of the world to its Author. In Thomas Aquinas's terms, the object of the human intellect is the essence of the thing. The primary object, to which the human intellect is most naturally fitted, is the essence of the material substance, since all human knowledge is mediated through the body.[39] To limit the range of human intellect to the material alone, however, is not only counter to human experience but also constitutes an arbitrary and logically unjustified constraint on the operation of human reason.

A being subject to the laws of nature, the human being also transcends the nexus of relationships into which his roots are sunk.[40] To be human is

---

39. Aquinas, *Summa Theologiae,* Ia q. 84, a. 7; q. 85, a. 8; q. 87, a. 2, r. 2, q. 88, a. 3; *In De Anima,* Book III, Lec. 7, §681. On the importance and implications of this principle, that the natural object of the human intellect is the material substance, see Fulvio Di Blasi, *God and the Natural Law,* chapter 2, "The Presupposition of Lex Naturalis: Man as *Capox Dei,*" 73–152.

40. The remaining paragraphs of this section are adapted from Reimers, "Truth and the

to be part of the natural order, while at the same time transcending it in a certain way. If nature, or the natural order, be conceived as the totality of existing entities, mutually interacting according to knowable laws (habits), then it manifests a curious open-endedness. So long as human beings are part of it, nature cannot be a closed, self-contained, fully explainable system. To see why this is, it is helpful to consider the works of Kurt Gödel and Alan Turing.

In 1931 Gödel showed that in any formal axiomatic system there are true, knowable statements which cannot be derived from the axioms that found the system.[41] No finite set of laws or principles is sufficient to derive every true statement, even in so simple a system as arithmetic. It follows *a fortiori* that the totality of scientific laws and principles can never capture all the truths that there are to be known. The implications of this are sharpened by the work of Alan Turing on artificial intelligence. Turing proposed the concept of the universal machine, which can, by iterated manipulations of symbol-tokens (for instance 1s and 0s), generate a required set of symbols or stop itself if the required series cannot be generated.[42] The Turing machine represents mechanically what the axiomatic system does symbolically. It turns out, however, that a truly universal Turing machine is not possible. There can be no universal algorithm to decide when the Turing machine is to stop, that is, to recognize that every truthful conclusion has been reached. Neither can it generate an algorithm to instruct itself when to stop.[43] No physical mechanism, no matter how large or complex, can mechanically generate all true symbolic representations of the truth on the basis of finite truthful information.[44] To complete an

Open-Endedness of the Natural Order," in N. H. Gregersen and W. Parsons, eds., *The Concept of Nature in Science and Theology*, Part I (Geneva: Labor et Fides, 1995).

41. Angelo Margaris, *First Order Mathematical Logic* (Waltham MA, Toronto, London: Ginn and Company, 1967), 187 ff.; Earnest Nagel and James R. Newman, "Goedel's Proof," in James R. Newman, ed., *The World of Mathematics* (New York: Simon & Schuster, 1956), 1668–1695.

42. Alan Turing, "Can a Machine Think?," *Mind* 1950, repr. in James R. Newman, ed., *The World of Mathematics*, 2099–2123.

43. David Braine, *The Human Person*, 468; see also Roger Penrose, *The Emperor's New Mind* (New York, Oxford: Oxford University Press, 1989), 63.

44. On this see also John Lucas, "Minds, Machines and Gödel," in K. Sayre and F. Crosson, *The Modeling of Mind: Computers and Intelligence* (New York: Simon & Schuster, 1963), 255–261.

axiomatic system—indeed, to formulate the meaning of its axioms in the first place—there is needed an insight into a truth that stands outside and "above" the system. A "Gödel Proposition" is one known to be true, independent of the system's axioms. It is above the system in the sense that it derives its truth not from the system but from the intelligence that is using the system. Furthermore, on the basis of its own intellectual insight, human intelligence is able to judge that the iterations of the algorithm should stop, that pursuing them further is futile. Intelligence can grasp conclusions that iterated calculations cannot attain to. These considerations from mathematical logic and artificial intelligence theory show that even to attain to all the truths within an axiomatic system, more is needed than the logical manipulation of symbols or the mechanical and electronic operations of a calculator. Some power beyond axiomatic deduction is needed to attain to every knowable truth. We recall, however, that action resulting simply from the application of a habit is essentially deductive. Therefore more must be at work in the reasoning human mind than simple obedience to law, that is, behavior according to established habit.

The impossibility of stopping the Turing machine and of establishing the validity of inferences by syntax alone points to a more fundamental reality, the existential relationship with truth. The logic of the axiom is to posit: "All A are B." The logic of the theorem is to be deduced: "F_1 and F_2; therefore, F_3." Neither the axiom nor the theorem asserts a truth concerning existence. To assert the existence of something as true is to transcend the deductive logic of the axiomatic system. To assert the truth of something real is to unify under one demonstrative predicate (such as "this," "my new car," or "Bob") whatever descriptive predicates apply to that thing. Logically considered, the assertion of real existence has the character of a hypothetical conclusion; it proposes some reality whose existence explains or accounts for the predicates.[45] The ability to assert the truth requires more than the bare mechanisms of material interaction. By asserting truth one joins to his naturally conditioned experience the general conception of the intellect and unifies these in an existential affirmation, one not compelled by strict deductive necessity.

If logic has for its purpose the evaluation of judgments in relation to

---

45. Peirce, "Pragmatism and Abduction," in Peirce, *Collected Papers*, 5.181.

truth, this goal of necessity lies beyond the inner framework of deductive logic itself. The work of intelligence is not simply to replicate computationally the mechanisms of nature and their workings, but rather to grasp what nature is. Intelligence seeks to understand nature in such a way that the knower can represent symbolically the truth of the world he encounters. His goal is not simply to carry through a sequence of mental operations, possibly with a practical outcome, but so to conceive an idea that he may reproduce logically that which really exists. To know the truth is to 'have' reality in mind according to its essential features.[46]

The unfolding of nature is an operation of nonreflective habit. Among animals these habits are governed by instinctive values, toward which the animals are ordered teleologically. However, because even the highest of these animals lack the ability to know other beings save in relation to their own needs and instinctive desires, they cannot develop new habits based on revised or new desires.[47] The animal cognizes other beings only in relation to its instinctive habits. To be sure, the animal is not a machine, for unlike machines, animals have an internalized teleology. The animal needs no algorithm to determine when to stop pursuing a line of activity. Its appetites and awareness of its own body enable it to recognize when further activity is pointless. We may almost say that the animal has a kind of Turing intelligence, a pre-Gödelian wisdom. It perceives and processes the information received according to the algorithms of its animal logic, a logic that does not allow it to make the leap to a new idea, a new hypothesis. The child, who may fear and dislike the doctor with his cold instruments and sharp hypodermic needle, accepts the need to visit the clinic to get healthy. The house cat—one of nature's most intelligent beasts—never connects the trip to the veterinarian with the cessation of itching skin. The beaver builds a dam to provide himself a home. Human intelligence conceives the possibility of digging artificial rivers—and eventually viaducts—to irrigate gardens and farms far from the pond.

In the human being habit can be reflective, formed according to one's judgment concerning truth. The human person can govern the develop-

46. Pierre Rousselot, S.J., *L'intellectualism de St. Thomas* (Paris: Gabriel Beauchesne, Éditeur, 1936), 41.

47. Ibid., 14–15.

ment of his own habits according to ideas and beliefs about what is true.[48]
But the mind's grasp of the truth always has the character of a leap, an
ascent—logically a hypothesis. Physical interaction can only evoke a response. Hypothesis suggests experiment, and this not only in science.
Even in practical problem solving, as when building or repairing or moving something heavy, we propose hypotheses. A worker proposes that, although they cannot see it, the workers' progress is being hindered by a part
that is hooked onto the concealed framework. When the workers act on
the hypothesis, the piece remains stuck, but its pattern of movement suggests a modification of the hypothesis. That is, the workers form a mental
model of the situation, including those aspects that they cannot see, and
act on the basis of that model and its unseen properties. This is more than
simply responding to the situation as perceived. Furthermore, the proposition that something is true is tantamount to positing a thing as being, as
having existence and essence of its own. Therefore, it follows that the development of human habits transcends the processes of the natural order.
Indeed, by his relation to the truth, the human person is in principle capable of attaining to the truth that lies beyond the interactions of nature and
which explains them.

The very existence of the scientific enterprise follows from this unique
character of human intelligence. The scientist stands not as within nature,
but above and outside it. He conceives nature's structures, as it were, in his
own mind, and by symbolic representations he recreates an aspect of the
natural order. The scientist replicates conceptually the works of the Creator.

The role of ideas

To be a scientist (broadly conceived as one who thoroughly understands
some realm of being) is to form one's mind according to ideas that represent
certain kinds of things. Aquinas aptly characterizes the scientific mind.

When the mind reaches the degree of actual apprehension of intelligibles that
is found in the knowledge habitually possessed by a man of science, then it can
already be called an intellect in act; and that degree is reached as soon as one is

48. Peirce, "Ideals of Conduct," in *Collected Papers*, 1.602.

capable of producing, on one's own initiative, the intellectual activity called understanding. For the actual possession of any form is coincident with the ability to act accordingly.[49]

Thomas's point here is that to be a scientist, it is necessary that one's intellect be actualized, informed according to the "intelligibles," the ideas governing the objects of the study. To be a scientist is to have a certain cast of mind, to have one's mind formed in a particular way. The test of this is whether one can actually do the science: "For the actual possession of any form is coincident with the ability to act accordingly." Thus, the task of the university's science faculty is not simply to teach students all the facts about a branch of science, facts many of which they will forget and others of which will be disproved or superseded. To be a biologist is to think biologically, and this is different than to think mathematically or chemically. Arthur Conan Doyle has his celebrated detective express this quite admirably. Riding a train with Sherlock Holmes, Dr. Watson admires the freshness and beauty of the countryside. But Holmes will have none of it.

"Do you know, Watson," said he, "that it is one of the curses of a mind with a turn like mine that I must look at everything with reference to my own special subject. You look at these scattered houses, and you are impressed by their beauty. I look at them, and the only thought which comes to me is a feeling of their isolation, and of the impunity with which crime may be committed there."[50]

The difference between Holmes and Watson is not that the detective is so much more clever, but rather that he has formed his mind criminologically, subsuming his experiences and observations under the category of *crime*. He habitually recognizes the ways, opportunities, traces, and motivations of crime. The mind of the knower is formed by ideas, and the process of developing these ideas and relating them to subjects of consideration is inference or thinking.

To have an idea is a personal thing. Ideas, if they are to be located anywhere, must lie in the intellects of individual persons. It is in the mind of the

49. Aquinas, *In De Anima*, §700.

50. Arthur Conan Doyle, "The Adventure of the Copper Beeches," in *The Complete Adventures and Memoirs of Sherlock Holmes* (New York: Bramhall House, 1975), 161.

individual thinker that an idea develops, alters, grows and relates to other ideas. This does not mean, however, that ideas are either essentially private or incommunicable. We know from the experiences of communication, the art of teaching and the practice of science, that the use of ideas is public. Teachers regularly challenge their students' ideas, and parents teach their children ideas by means of example, correction and varied application. The activity of using ideas—thinking—has both an active and a passive aspect. The learner's mind receives images and signs from the environment and others who communicate with it, images and signs which may be recognized and remembered. In doing so, the mind recognizes these as meaningful, that is, as standing in relationship with other signs. This response is characteristic of the human being as rational; the mind works by thinking. The language student, for example, memorizes words and phrases. Actually to learn the language, however, one must learn the logic, the structure of the meanings as expressed in the foreign tongue. The student has to go beyond correlating Spanish words with English to being able to think in a Spanish way, that is, to use Spanish language to express ideas. The use of "story problems" in teaching mathematics serves a similar role. The student may well be able to solve the equation "$60t = 300 - 50t$" without much trouble, following memorized rules for manipulating the symbols. However, when the question is posed in terms of the point at which two trains traveling at different speeds will pass, the student is challenged to interpret the numbers and their relationships in connection with objects of experience. The teacher uses the story problem to help the students to grasp mathematical ideas more fully than is possible with simple manipulation. The introduction of new ideas makes this process especially clear.

The processes of teaching and learning reflect what we have observed about inference. The teacher (or parent or colleague) presents the images, symbols and things, saying that *A* always refers to or means *B*. ("This is a monthly report, which contains all the data you need for planning your sales activity.") That is, the learner acquires new general terms for interpreting data and experiences. The teacher also drills information into the learner. Elementary school pupils must repeat their "math facts" or respond appropriately in the vocabulary drill. This is inductive learning. The true test and challenge of education, however, is in the grasping of new ideas, where the student relates things formerly disparate under the new idea. This relating, however, is voluntary and, to an extent, unpredictable. The student must want to learn and must of his own come to see the connections between the ideas. Aquinas observes this same dynamic, writing, "anyone can experience this of himself, that when he tries to understand something, he forms certain phantasms to serve him by way of examples, in which as it were he examines what he is striving to understand. It is for this reason that when we wish to make someone understand something, we lay examples before him from which he can form phantasms for the purpose of understanding."[51]

It is not only human teachers who present ideas to the mind. Nature also presents ideas to us through our bodies and the things we experience in our environment. The object of experience makes its impression on the mind through the senses, and the mind can relate this impression to others in virtue of its ideas. The question arises immediately whether there corresponds anything in reality—in the thing—to the idea in the mind of the thinker. A man looks into the water and sees a white figure swimming. Relating it to other, similar things of comparable behavior and shape, he identifies it as "fish," more specifically (since he is a whaler) as "whale," a fish of direct commercial value, from which are derived important oils. Since the man's name is Ahab,[52] the whale also represents nature's intransigent defiance to the will of man and personal insult to his own dignity. It demands a response.

In this example we find several ideas differently rooted in the object of experience. The object is identified as real, and not a phantom or apparition, and a member of a class of animals, namely whales, which is further identified as a subclass of fish. The idea *whale* does apply to the object, but that of *fish* does not. That the object is real can be verified by taking action—giving chase and attempting to harpoon it—and drawing others (the crew) into one's activity. If the whale is Ahab's perceptual illusion, then his harpoon will not stick nor will his crew respond to it. Similarly, all will identify this physical object (known to be physical because of its relation-

---

51. Aquinas, *Summa Theologiae*, Ia, 84, 7.

52. I beg the reader's indulgence as I take a fictional tale as my example. The reference, of course, is to Melville's *Moby Dick*, in which novel is also expressed the notion that a whale is a kind of fish. My interpretation of the whale's significance to Ahab is obviously simplified and should not be taken as an original analysis of the novel.

ship with harpoons and water) as a whale, because it looks and responds as whales are understood to respond. The essence of this being, which is the basis of its regular behavior, is the basis for Ahab's and the crew's understanding it under the idea *whale*. Contrary to what the whalers thought, however, Moby Dick is not a fish. They understand *fish* to mean a streamlined aquatic animal with fins. On the basis of other facts, the zoologist classifies them as mammals. The attribution of the idea *mammal* and denial of *fish* to whales is not arbitrary, for in virtue of this attribution the scientist is able to predict whale behavior more accurately and account for its greater intelligence than fish and its skeletal similarities with land-based mammals. In short, it is possible to ascribe predicates to the thing, confident that some aspects of the thing will correspond to some of the predicates. Ahab also identifies the whale as a sign of nature's intransigence to his will. To this one may well respond that the Captain is projecting his own ideas onto a dumb beast, that the whale is but a whale, doing what whales do. Nevertheless, we do not dismiss Melville's novel as a curious tale of a neurotically metaphysical sea captain. Even if most of us do not attribute malice to whales, we can recognize a cold, at times almost perverse indifference of nature to our needs and our projects, to our humanity. The idea applies *somewhere,* and Melville's task as an artist was to bring it to light through a work of fiction, through an extended representation of what could be and one kind of response to it. In short, the answer to the question whether ideas correspond or apply to anything in reality is answered by our engagement in the world as beings at once material and spiritual.

TWO SENSES OF TRUTH

The investigation thus far indicates that we may speak of truth in two closely related ways. First, a proposition may be true indexically when the things its terms refer to stand to each other as the proposition represents. Insofar as a belief is indexical, it admits of two mutually exclusive values: *true* and *false.* Either Faithless Frank was in another woman's arms cheating on Polly, or he was not. Second, one's understanding is said to be true to the extent that it represents a state of affairs both as it actually exists and

in the possible relationships that it—or states of affairs like it—or its constituents may have with other things. The theoretical truth of a belief is
thus related logically to the truths of other propositions about beings that
are or might be somehow related to the kinds of being referred to in the
original proposition. In this sense, the belief constitutes a more or less satisfactory understanding of things. That is, understanding admits of varying degrees of truth. Consider the following statements.

1. The sun rose at seven a.m.
2. The sun began its diurnal orbit of the earth at seven a.m.
3. At seven a.m. the earth's rotation brought the sun into view.

Indexically the first and third are true, but only the third expresses accurately the relevant known truths about the relationship between earth and sun.
We now regard the first expression as metaphorical and the second as false,
because it expresses a relationship that does not obtain. Let us note, however, that if the third expression specified the time as eight p.m., it would be
false in a way that the first and second expressions would not. Anyone with
a train to catch would prefer the metaphor or the false cosmology.

What is really at stake here? True understanding is founded on the
knowledge of what things really are. Who believes that the sun is a light
placed on an inverted bowl or, like Aristotle, that it is an eternal substance
of incorruptible matter, does not really know what kind of thing that heav-
enly body is. Knowing that it is a Main Sequence star, about one-third of
its way through its life span, and fueled (as such stars are) by nuclear fusion of its hydrogen, not only provides us with a much better knowledge of
the sun and what to expect concerning it, but it also helps to structure our
knowledge of the rest of the solar system, other stars, and the universe as
a whole. The progress of the sciences in the past century ought to alert us
that even the advanced understanding we have today of the physical universe will probably be replaced within the century. Our understanding is
always partial and deficient, admitting of growth. This truth can blind us,
however, to the validity of much understanding that we have attained so
far. Our ancient and medieval colleagues had no conception of neutrinos,
DNA, galaxies, or prehistoric animal species.

Can one say, therefore, that their knowledge of human nature will be
similarly superseded, that it was as primitive as the knowledge of the sun

and planets? Certainly there are those in our day who urge precisely this point, that what we know of human nature now is mostly metaphor. Dennett, for example, dismisses non-mechanistic accounts of learning as "simply loony."[53] Francis Crick speaks of the "fuzzy folk notions we have today" about human perception and consciousness.[54] Crick and Dennett, as well as Patricia Churchland and others, are convinced that our knowledge of human nature is in a relative infancy, comparable to the common conceptions of the universe at the dawn of the modern age. Scientists and most scientific-minded philosophers confidently predict that a proper understanding of human nature can be had only in terms of empirical science. Armstrong justifies this conception by pointing to the distinctive characteristics of the empirical mathematical sciences: "Historically, scientific investigation has proved to be the only way that a *consensus* of opinion about disputed matters of theory has ever been achieved among those who have given the matters serious and intelligent attention. Only science has settled disputed questions."[55]

I propose that this perspective is mistaken. Indeed, it is a serious error, for if we are ignorant and in such a way as proposed by these thinkers, then our understanding of love, marriage, parenthood, society, government, education and a host of other topics is not simply incomplete, but indeed primitive and misleading. It means that to relate to one another according to principles found in the *Nicomachean Ethics,* the United States Constitution, or the Bible is to fail to relate according to the truth. If the understanding of human nature inherited from the classical humanist tradition combined with Jewish and Christian revelation, founded as these are on teleological principles and an understanding of human nature as (in some sense, at least) spiritual, is false, then our most sophisticated and effective understandings of the organization of business, government, and education, as well as our cultural insights into the human heart, should be seriously misleading in some important respects.

It is clear, however, that the understanding we have of human nature (among other things) is already mature, well-developed, and fairly accurate in many respects. To put it more simply, the overthrow of Newtonian

---

53. Daniel Dennett, *Consciousness Explained,* 183.
54. Francis Crick, *The Astonishing Hypothesis,* 256.
55. D. M. Armstrong, *A Materialist Theory of the Mind,* p. 52.

science does not call into question everything that we think we know or understand. The revolutions in scientific understanding are, in one sense, very limited in scope. The impressive results of the empirical sciences are in reality the working out of a handful of fundamental ideas about matter. Materiality is reactivity; therefore, the properties of a thing insofar as it is material (and thus the properties of matter) are its reactive properties. The empirical sciences have therefore restricted their investigations to essentially dyadic relations, to reactions between physical things. The Galilean hope was to account for matter in terms of size and shape—that is, in geometric terms. Newton amplified and, in a way, completed that project by introducing the concept of *mass* and showing that quadratic, rather than linear, equations were required to account for the behavior of matter. Today, the mathematics is much more complex and the notion of matter more sophisticated. The goal, however, is still that of Galileo: to characterize fundamental physical structures in terms of mathematics. This project has born immense fruit, both in terms of the speculative understanding of the material universe and in its technological results. Among these fruits is a deepened understanding of the human organism, understood as a material entity. Does our newfound comprehension of such sciences as human genetics and neurology mean, however, that we have superseded our forebears' understanding of what a human being is? Can we say that only now do we understand what it means to live as a human person? This is so only if the human being is nothing other than material system.

Underlying the modern physical sciences are two notions: first, that every material entity, insofar as it is material, can be adequately characterized in mathematical terms (such as values for mass, charge, spin, momentum, and so on), and second, that the interaction of material entities admits of adequate characterization in terms of mathematical laws (which may be statistical). Thus the formula for habits, "When Z obtains, a occurs," becomes an equation or perhaps a schematic. Although Aristotle and his heirs, including Aquinas, speak much of essences, they do not actually analyze too many specific essences. Aristotelian science with its division of forms according to genus and specific differences lacked the flexibility and precision to define and differentiate the variety of material things in the world. The genius of the early modern philosophers was that they looked for properties that could be measured and controlled and then characterized material things in terms of these. Such properties essentially entail the notion of continuity. This is fundamentally where the Aristotelian method proved clumsy and ultimately unproductive. Aristotle distinguishes between sentient and non-sentient living beings and the rational from the merely sentient, but to distinguish the essence of lion from that of a panther proved more difficult. (The essence of the lion is to be "animal with superabundance of courage" or something like that.) The modern scientist, on the other hand, can allow for gradations, gradually transforming from one kind to another. For example, the organic chemist does not see any point to finding the *specific difference* (in the Aristotelian sense) between, say, polystyrene and nylon within the genus of plastics. He needs simply to know the chemical formula and physical structure of their respective molecules. Similarly, the zoologist is no longer concerned about the *specific differences* among lions, panthers, and cheetahs, because these can be accounted for in terms of DNA.

What the Aristotelian tradition did very well, however, was to distinguish the specific differences between living and nonliving, rational and nonrational, and therefore between the human and the nonhuman. They did this in terms of ideas that lie outside the scope of the modern physical sciences—specifically, the ideas of teleology (and the good) and form (or formal cause). It is not necessarily true that because we have learned about the existence of other galaxies only within the last century, we may really know next to nothing about our own nature, the relationship between the sexes, human community, and the sense we have had throughout our history that there exists a higher being or realm of beings, to which we are in some way responsible. To be sure, there remains much to learn about the inner structure of the human organism, its genetic code and nervous system. The promise of this new knowledge does not, however, invalidate the concepts in terms of which we can even now understand ourselves as rational, loving beings. The sciences can doubtless delve more thoroughly into the physical structure of the human being, but its discoveries alone cannot explain his rational self-governance. A vision of reality may more accurately express the truth of things, even if heavily influenced by myth and metaphor, than a purely scientific cosmology, simply because the former avails itself of a richer store of fundamental ideas for understanding the whole.

This second sense of truth is the fundamental one. It is the conformity of the living intellect (or intelligent being) with reality. Truth is a characteristic of the mind itself as it understands the world. It is the adequacy of the ideas by which one grasps the essences of things in the world and their interrelationships. Because ideas are not static images but principles of the living intelligence, truth itself is a principle of intelligent life. In this context we may speak also of the truth of circumscribed realms of understanding. One may understand physics well and economics badly. And the scientific community as a whole will certainly grow in its understanding. Ultimately the truth of propositions derives from truth in this primary sense. To judge truly that the ball is on the table is to express confidence in the adequacy of a current (or recent) perceptual image, which is a kind of mini-understanding. The finite individual knower grasps the universal truth, understands the order of things in his (admittedly fallible) knowledge of individual facts. It is precisely this notion of truth as the truth of understanding that makes human communication and relationships possible. To communicate with another is seldom, if ever, to signal the existence of isolated facts. Rather, any communication depends on shared understanding of how things stand and what the world as a whole (in respect, at least, to the subject at hand, whether business or building construction or music-making or family management) is like. This becomes especially clear in those situations where there is little disagreement about the facts, but a fundamental misunderstanding about their larger context. The intelligence officer and his superior both know that villagers have been restive, demonstrating against government policies on pricing and transportation tariffs. If the agent sees fairly normal agitation for better opportunities to market their goods but his superior sees the unfolding of a broad Communist strategy, they may well find themselves speaking at cross-purposes, hardly communicating at all. Comedic writers often use misunderstanding in their work, presenting two people, perhaps in love, who see the same facts but interpret them in opposite ways. At the basis of human relating must be a shared understanding of the truth. Kierkegaard stated that the world is a system only for God,[56] whose understanding includes all particular facts.[57] And so it is that the individual human knower stands in a

---

56. Søren Kierkegaard, *Concluding Unscientific Postscript* (Princeton, NJ: Princeton University Press, 1941), 107.

57. Aquinas, *Summa Theologiae*, Ia, q. 14, a 11.

dialectical relationship with the universe and therefore with its Author, grasping its general principles and structure as these are instantiated by particular facts. Metaphysical knowledge is in this sense knowledge of—or desire for knowledge of—God.

THE MIND AS A SIGN

Every mental conception embodies some general conception and is therefore a kind of sign. Because these conceptions develop as inferences, Peirce says, "The mind is a sign, developing according to the laws of inference."[58] By his life in the world, in all its aspects, the human person is a sign, representative of reality.

How the mind represents

If the mind is a sign, we must ask *how* this sign represents and, indeed, *what* it represents. A sign is some physical or perceptible being that represents or stands for some other thing in some respect. For Pierce, a sign is something that stands for a second thing in relation to some third thing.[59] The human being is an existing thing, a body alive in the world, and it is as such that he is a sign. This body, as it is lived and experienced in the world represents. As we showed in chapter 2, it is through the body that materiality is known and grasped intellectually. The body shares with the stars and the planets the subjection to the laws of gravity (experienced as weight), and with rocks and rivers the characteristics of shape and fluidity. As Plato's *Timaeus* mythically represents, it is a kind of model for the universe as a whole. Similarly the body is a sign of every living body. One recognizes in the cat's unexpected lethargy the signs of illness and in the mother bear's ferocity an instinct similar to that in oneself when loved ones are threatened. We learn about our own nature from the animals, because we first learned about them through our experiences of our own animal nature. In perceiving the world, we reduplicate it according to certain of its properties. The landscape and the starry heavens, as well as the layout of the living room,

58. Peirce, *Collected Papers*, 5.313.
59. Ibid., 2.228 ff.

exist in the image one has formed and preserved in memory, so that the human being can make his way through the world according to that image.

Furthermore, every act one does, every work he undertakes interprets the world. The human act, precisely as act, is not only a physical interaction with the environment, but also an exercise of the intelligence, manifesting one's understanding of the natures of things. The farmer intends to grow crops for food and by doing so he expresses his beliefs concerning the fertility of the soil, the likelihood of rain, the value of his produce, the length of the growing season, and so on. Precisely in virtue of this, the science of archeology is possible, for archeologists examine the artifacts and activities of a people precisely in order to learn how they understood the world, what they valued, sought, feared, and fled. So the discovery of spearheads in an archeological site may indicate that the people who occupied it hunted large game, which implies that the area was, at that time, populated by such animals. Grandma's abhorrence of waste is one sign of the Great Depression's effect on the working classes. The point of work is to meet human needs by reforming things in the environment, and this reformation reflects one's understanding of them.

Human significance is most evident in our sign-making and sign-using activities. As producers and users of signs by which we represent the world, we are ourselves signs. Just as much as the farmer who spreads lime on his fields, the agricultural agent who says, "The soil in this county is highly acidic," is a sign of a belief about the soil. Not only do we construct buildings to protect us from hostile aspects of the environment, but we also erect statues to commemorate heroes, gods, and ideals. One knows something about American ideals from the Statue of Liberty, just as Trajan's column manifests the Imperial Roman conception of glory. The point of writing biographies and memoirs—and of funereal eulogies—is to represent to others the significance of one person's life. (Whether that significance is rightly construed is, of course, another question.) We can and do represent symbolically a person's significance. Even that conniving, ambitious, and manipulative accessory to murder, Lady Macbeth, was, to her husband, a sign representing the futility of life as a "tale / Told by an idiot, full of sound and fury, / Signifying nothing."[60]

60. Shakespeare, *Macbeth*, Act V, scene v.

Whatever is expressed or interpreted through perception and work can be expressed symbolically, through language. There are no surds in human experience. Although there may well be that which one cannot express adequately, no human experience or act is *in principle* incapable of expression. In other words, there is nothing unknowable within the range of human experience. If one has experienced something, then his body has responded to that thing. Knowing how he has responded, the human subject can begin to name, that is, to subsume what has been experienced under general categories. We do not at all assert that one's knowledge of the thing is complete. Indeed, the category may be very general and thus relatively indefinite. Is any reality unknowable? The only such reality would have to be completely outside of possible human experience. The inner life of God is one such reality, and this is why such doctrines as the Trinity must be a matter for divine revelation. To know that God is Father, Son, and Holy Spirit, three in person but one in substance, one needs to take God's word for it.

If the human person is a sign, then ought not this sign be univocal and integrated? Yet, no living person's life is so integrated that it can be readily subsumed under one idea. We live in uncertainty and—our best efforts notwithstanding—in contradiction and dissembling. Henry Higgins, in the Lerner and Lowe musical *My Fair Lady*, describes himself as "an ordinary man," a scholar and lover of the arts, fair and even-handed, but Eliza Doolittle, who lived in his house and learned under him, saw him as a tyrant, a domineering bully.[61] The same is true of peoples. The Statue of Liberty with its stirring inscription, "Give me your tired, your poor, your huddled masses yearning to breathe free," stands across the harbor from Ellis Island, where arriving immigrants were examined and evaluated, reviewed and even renamed before being admitted to the country—assuming they were found acceptable. And it is the rare human being whose life displays transparent, indubitable significance. The reality of inconsistency does not, however, prove that various kinds of habits are essentially unrelated, that symbol-making and using activities—thought and understanding—are absolutely independent of work and perception. What makes perception and physical activity (work), *as well as mental activity*, rational is that they

61. Alan Jay Lerner, "Ordinary Man," *My Fair Lady*. New York: Hal Leonard Co., 1981.

are governed by ideas. An idea brings diverse signs or representations into unity. Insofar as an action or thought is one, it expresses an idea, and the ideas by which one lives and acts admit of logical interrelationships. The problem of one's lived incoherence, that is, the inconsistency of one's behavior and even perception of the world, is exactly parallel to the logical inconsistencies of symbolic expression. The quantum theory is ultimately inconsistent with General Relativity, but physics cannot yet resolve the inconsistency, and there is (as yet) no experiment that brings the opposing propositions to the test. And so for the time being, scientists live with the tension, expecting further inquiries to resolve them. The import of human inconsistency is not that human lives are insignificant, directionless, or random, but that they are finite and incomplete. One reason the unexamined life is not worth living is simply that if one lives without intellectually considering his life, he lives at cross purposes with himself and with others.

The object of belief is the truth. If, as Peirce says, man is a sign, he is a sign ordered to truth, and, indeed, here is a key. For no one wants to be ignorant of the truth, to be deceived. Those who lie want to deceive others, but not themselves. Even those who refuse to "accept the truth" do not want to be deceived. The distraught parents who will not accept the pediatrician's diagnosis of leukemia do not reject truth as such. They do not want to believe a lie. Rather, they cannot accept that this diagnosis is true. They want the truth, but not the disease in their child. To be sure, different persons may quite differently conceive this relationship with truth. One may well consider himself the master of truth, capable of determining it by his own will; Josef Stalin was apparently such a one. One person may believe that truth comes only from sense experience and another only from the Bible. There are those whose concern for truth extends only to what directly touches them. Although the notion of truth may be in one respect invariant (as the agreement of thought and reality), we nevertheless choose how we shall determine truth and what we shall recognize as criteria for truth. In other words, how an individual conceives truth depends on his conception of reality. Indeed, the individual decides on his or her own principles of thought, which reflect an underlying conception of reality. At the beginning of Robert Bolt's A Man for All Seasons, Richard Rich tries to convince Thomas More that every man has his price, whether to be bought or to be impelled by pain.[62] By the end of the play we realize that Rich has so embraced this principle that it is almost inconceivable to him that one could do something for any other reason than to enhance one's own career or standing. We choose where to find truth and how. Although truth, coherently understood, must be independent of any individual thinker and in that respect above him, one can embrace another conception of truth, another standard. People often do.

This fundamental orientation toward truth extends to the practical order. Work, or practical activity, is ordered to results, to success. In an obvious sense, the worker does not care for right answers or clear thoughts; he wants the project to come out right. It is not hard, however, to see this as fundamentally related to the question of truth. The worker whose efforts have failed will eventually ask, "What has gone wrong? What could I do differently?" He will "go back to the drawing board" and think. Success and failure in work point to truth and falsity in the mind. If "the mind is a sign, developing according to the laws of inference," then that sign ought to represent in virtue of some general idea. In its most abstract sense, that idea is the idea of truth. For the individual person, this idea is further specified by an underlying conception of reality. In this sense, the human person, the mind, is a sign of the world or of reality as a whole.

Just as the question of truth creates a distance between perception and reality, that the human person is a sign creates a certain distance between him and the world. The ability to represent conceptually, according to ideas, extends the mind's scope beyond the qualities of perception and the experiences of working with the world. The human mind, whose first conception is *being*,[63] is able to conceive of nonbeing, of nothingness—to which nothing in his environment corresponds. This mind is able to juxtapose itself over against the world as a whole, in order to understand it. Whether the conception, *world as a whole,* can function effectively as an element of thought may remain to be seen, but the idea is there in the human mind. As a result, the human mind can conceive of the world as not existing at all. To be sure, one can object (and it has been objected) that if one truly negates the world, he has to negate himself with it, that having

62. Robert Bolt, *A Man for All Seasons* (New York: Vintage Books, 1962), 1–2.
63. Aquinas, *De Veritate,* 1, 1.

denied the world its existence, he is left with nowhere to stand. But this objection is not to the point. Even if one cannot *imagine* a totally empty universe, one can *think* it. The words make sense. And the conceivability of the world's nonexistence suggests Heidegger's famous question, "Why is there any being at all and not rather Nothing?"[64] The contingency of the world suggests the question of its cause. These are, of course, all questions, not answers, but they are questions that arise from the stance of the human being vis-à-vis the world, the stance of a knower concerned for the truth. The range of ideas by which the human mind operates extends beyond the realm of the material and the sensible. The human person, a sign, constitutes himself as a sign of the world, of reality as a whole, in terms of or in rejection of these ideas. As a sign, he is perforce a metaphysical being.

64. Cited in Walter Kaufmann, *Existentialism from Dostoevsky to Sartre* (New York, London, Scarborough Ontario: New American Library, 1975), 277.

CHAPTER 5

Love, Consciousness, and the Power to Choose

Because the behaviors of things are rooted in their natures, we expect that characteristic human behaviors will be rooted in human nature. To the extent that there is such an essence, these distinctively human behaviors point to the essence of the human being. The thesis of this chapter is that the distinctive characteristic of human behavior is that the human being transcends habit through rational self-governance, that the human being differs from animals and other living things in that he rationally forms his actions and habits. To some extent, therefore, the human person authors his own inner governing principles. It remains, then, to specify what this self-governance consists in.

VALUES AND ACTION

When Karl Marx wrote, "The chief defect of all previous materialism (including Feuerbach's) is that the object, reality, what we apprehend through our senses, is understood only in the form of *object* or *contemplation;* but not as *sensuous human activity,* as *practice,* not subjectively,"[1]

1. Marx, "Theses on Feuerbach," in Eugene Kamenka, ed., trans., *The Portable Karl Marx* (New York: Penguin Books, 1983), Thesis I, 155.

he intended not only a call to revolutionary action but also a fundamental critique of modern philosophy. Ironically, although modern philosophy has deliberately sought to avoid the speculative, it has driven such a sharp wedge between thought and action that philosophers today may question whether there is any relationship at all between the two. Francis Bacon's dictum, "Knowledge and human power are synonymous . . . and that which in contemplative philosophy corresponds with the cause in practical science becomes the rule,"[2] suggests that a philosophy in tune with the empirical sciences would itself be practical. What resulted, however, was a widening gulf between the contemplative and the practical. In order to attain to certainty of knowledge, Descartes famously doubted everything, even his own existence as a bodily being. Then, while explaining and defending his method, he remarks: "For I am assured that there can be neither peril nor error in this course, and that I cannot at present yield too much to distrust, since I am not considering the question of action, but only of knowledge."[3] He thus reassures his readers that he will not be incapacitated in a practical way until these doubts are resolved. In other words, Descartes' intellect has a kind of double life: on the one hand enabling him to get around, get his supper, visit with friends and so on, and on the other giving him access to certainty and truth. Kant established a gulf between the scientific knowledge of phenomena and the rational principles of moral action. The knowledge of the physical world is not of things in themselves but only their appearances. The world known by science is a world contemplated but not engaged by human action. The result of this disjuncture is a serious problem of reconciling the life of the mind with the practical life in the world. It is the root of the fact-value distinction that crippled ethics for so much of the twentieth century, as well as of phenomenology's concerns to connect the world of consciousness to the world of things. Today, scientific materialism presumes that a sufficiently detailed account of the operations of the brain will explain all aspects of human behavior, thus rendering irrelevant the contemplative aspect of human being.

This disjuncture between the contemplative and the practical is false, artificial. Even at this point of our investigations it is clear that everything

2. Francis Bacon, *Novum Organum*, First Book, 3.
3. Descartes, *Meditations*, Meditation I.

a human being does is mental, rational (in the sense of subject to reason). In this chapter we shall look at the rational structure of human acts in relation to values and consciousness. We shall argue that human habits are to be understood in terms of practical syllogisms, which have ultimate reference to values that the rational person has adopted, and that habits develop ideally; that is, they manifest the person as spiritual.

Innate goods

In chapter 3 we noted that the human being comes into the world valuing particular goods as innate, and of these life is first. But life is not the only such innate good. When we compare human behavior with that of animals, we find remarkable similarities, along with important differences, that indicate additional goods that can be called innate. The systems of animal bodies are effectively ordered to growth and the preservation of both the individual and the species. They are teleologically ordered. The digestive system craves food that the animal needs to grow and continues living. The reproductive system is oriented toward the generation of young by mating with animals of the opposite sex. The respiratory system takes in oxygen. We may say then, that the animal (and I am thinking here primarily of the higher animals) is subject to natural appetites, whose cumulative effect is to promote the individual's survival and the continuation of the species. Indeed, their teleology becomes manifest especially as we consider two aspects of their government of the animal's behavior. First, animal instincts are limited. For example, in most species the appetite for food "turns off" when the animal has eaten enough. This appetite seems to be for somewhat more food than the animal actually needs, probably because moderate overeating at one point offsets the loss of nutrition during times of shortage. (Animal obesity is a problem primarily among animals under human care, where they reliably receive ample supplies of food every day.) In general, animal instincts seem admirably geared to meet the organism's needs but not exceed them. Second, we notice natural priorities among animal appetites. A hungry animal in danger from an enemy will flee (or fight), although that response to danger is closely calibrated. The zebra or wildebeest herd will continue grazing as the lion stalks, taking evasive action only when the predator is close enough to constitute an immediate danger. Animals are not paralyzed by conflicts among their appetites, but ordinarily and under natural conditions respond according to the most urgent need. Among animals, we see a balance and order among appetites such that the animal's survival is fostered in a way consonant with the continuation of the species.

The human organism has organic systems similar to those in the higher mammals, and the appetites associated with them are remarkably similar to animal appetites. Our bodies are oriented so as to direct us to preserve our lives and foster the continuation of the human race. As with our animal cousins, our human appetites naturally cease when they are satisfied. After a meal one feels "full" and inclined to stop eating. Each of these organ systems has its own teleology, in virtue of which the human person experiences a "vector of aspiration,"[4] an inclination toward the sort of activity associated with that system. Thus, we find in human beings an innate valuing of food, drink, sex, respiration, and rest. Furthermore, human beings are differentiated sexually, with different reproductive systems corresponding to the maternal and paternal roles in procreation and nurture of the infant. These complex systems, with their associated external manifestations, hormonal relationships, and so on, create respective vectors of interest for the female and male human persons. The female body "wants" to conceive; the male, to beget. The sexual difference divides humanity into two broad classes with two complementary forms of interest. Other differences result in other kinds of interest. Whether one is tall or short, physically strong or frail, mentally acute or slow, and other such accidents of birth all affect what one will tend to value. It is not by accident that Ted Williams, with his extraordinarily acute vision and sharp reflexes, should have become an athlete, while Mozart, with his unusual sensitivity to sound and his digital dexterity, should have become a musician. We may observe something similar in dogs, that different breeds have different vectors of interest, whether for hunting, herding, digging and sniffing, or fighting. The disposition of the body constitutes a disposition toward valuing certain things and kinds of activities as goods to pursue.[5]

4. Wojtyła uses this phrase in his discussion of the difference between animal instinct and human urges in his *Love and Responsibility* (New York: Farrar, Straus, Giroux, 1981), 46, from which much of the current argument is drawn.

5. See Aquinas, *Summa Theologiae*, Ia, IIae, q. 63, a. 1. Thus Aquinas argues that in one

Beyond these innate goods, which our bodily systems and predispositions crave, human persons desire cultural goods, which are, as it were, inherited values. The child learns from parents that certain words are "bad"
and that fishing is fun, that turkey is what we *always* have on Thanksgiving,
and that the Christmas decorating is not finished until the crèche is set up.
Indeed, before he is five years old, he learns the right way to express desires
and beliefs, not only the importance of saying "please" and "thank you" but
also the right words for things in his environment. We could go on to list
the influences of playmates, relatives, television, teachers, and others. The
point is clear that the human being is disposed to value a wide range of
things, even before attaining the maturity to recognize moral good and evil.
Not only does the body come into this world disposed toward particular
values, but the family and cultural environments impress a disposition of
their own on the child. The human being finds himself in a life with a wide
range of different kinds of goods to integrate into his system of values.

Animals come into the world with appetites integrated and therefore
governed by instinct. Because human government of appetites does not
function in the same way as the animal, unregulated human appetites can
become excessive and even dangerous to the individual. Parents watch that
their children not overeat, knowing that those who do not control their
food intake actually train their bodies to desire ever-greater amounts of
food. We hear psychologists and popular writers today talking about problems with sex addiction, a condition that arises among those who exercise no restraint of their sexual activity and then experience a compelling,
promiscuous need for sex. In short, human appetites are not entirely self-
regulating, as animal appetites seem to be. We may note a further aspect
of human appetite that is different from the animal. Human beings can
seek to satisfy appetites only for the pleasure involved. In the orgies of the
ancient Roman aristocracy, the partygoers would feast until they were full
and then induce themselves to vomit so as to continue feasting. Less dramatically, we today will finish a large meal with a dessert, a food that is
not needed but desired only for its sweetness. Much sexual activity today
is described as "recreational," that is, simply for pleasure. Human beings

---

sense some virtues can be natural to a particular person, depending on the conditions of his
body.

regularly enhance the satisfaction of their appetites such that the pleasure gained from them is increased. We add sweetening and spices to our foods, taking care that our meals are varied and interesting. We flavor water and find tasty combinations of juices for drinking. Sex between humans is ordinarily far more than simply mating, involving as it does romantic or seductive rituals, the enhancement of physical beauty, and physical techniques of increasing pleasure. It is common now for couples to engage in sexual intercourse exclusively for the sake of pleasure, having insured that conception will not take place and with no further commitment pledged to each other. A human being can indeed live for the sake of pleasure. Aristotle acknowledged this,[6] and Mill made it the principle of his ethics.[7]

It is a matter of experience that, unlike the animal, the human person needs to govern his own behavior. We do not have an instinct or a predetermined balance of appetites such that simply by "doing what comes naturally" we can attain what is best. Natural as it is, for example, to crave carbohydrates when one's blood sugar is low (surely a natural need, known by the body), one feels the same sort of craving for refined sugar or fats after having consumed sugar or fats. One may have a strong desire for homosexual sexual contact, but this contact cannot result in the good of progeny. Animal instincts are balanced such that, at least within its own appropriate environment, the animal seeks what serves its good as a living organism. In other words, animals do not have moral problems. They do not have to choose what is best to do. We want what is good, but what is genuinely good is not immediately manifest to us. One may say that it consists in continued biological life, but another requires that that life be comfortable and pleasant. Some value pleasure and sense stimulation as the highest good, while others focus their lives on gaining power and controlling persons and things. Some value the love and friendship of other persons; others devote themselves entirely to the love of God. In Book I of his *Nicomachean Ethics* Aristotle argued that the one thing that all men desire is happiness, but it is not until Book X that he can fully explain what happiness is. It remains a task for rational investigation to determine what that happiness must be, for the truth about the good is not immediately evident

6. Aristotle, *Nicomachean Ethics*, I, v 1095b 17.

7. John Stuart Mill, *Utilitarianism*, in *Great Books of the Western World*, vol. 43, Robert M. Hutchins and Mortimer J. Adler, eds. (Chicago: Encyclopedia Britannica, Inc., 1952), 448.

to human beings. Neither is it written into our natures, as it seems to be in the case of animals. To understand the good better, we turn our attention to the structure of human acts and habits, by which human goods are attained.

The will and its freedom

One of the great and ongoing controversies of the modern era is the question of freedom of the will. Materialist philosophers and scientists argue that whatever sense we may have that we are free in our choices is illusion.[8] Before entering into our analysis of act and habit proper, we shall clarify what we mean by freedom and how this relates to the power to know.

Abstractly regarded, the freedom of the will is absolute. The will can choose to affirm and pursue anything as a value and, indeed, to affirm any ultimate value. This absolute freedom and universal capacity is a direct consequence of reason's universal scope. There is no restriction on what the mind can conceive, and in this one is free. To put it starkly and extremely, one can determine as his purpose to walk alone and barefoot to northernmost Greenland in search of the Mystical Walrus of the Golden Tusk (for only one who journeys on unshod foot is able to find this walrus), a tuft of whose fur will bring astonishing riches. Because one can think of this, he can conceive of doing it. To be sure, there is no reason to believe such a beast exists, and the promised benefits befit a fairy tale. The journey is almost impossible. What is significant for our purposes here is that such an ideal is conceivable. To conceive this ideal all I had to do was manipulate a few mental signs and type them into a computer, a task no more difficult than describing my home. Having formulated this ideal, I am in a position to propose it as a choice to make.

What this illustrates is an aspect of the reciprocal, almost dialectical, relationship between particular goods and the good in general, a relationship that Thomas Aquinas relies on. On the one hand, the human person naturally experiences and recognizes certain things as good. On the

8. See, for instance, Roger Wolcoll Sperry, "Consciousness and Causality," 164; Searle, *Minds, Brains, and Science,* 13 and especially chap. 6, and D. M. Armstrong, *A Materialist Theory of the Mind,* 137.

other hand, as we have already argued, the human intellect can abstract the notion of *good in general*, raising the question whether this particular good in experience is *really* good. On the face of it, this *good in general* is an abstract term, possibly empty and without referent, if considered only from the logical point of view. This dialectic of good, however, is based on the will's relationship with the good, and not simply on the logical relationships among ideas. The questions, "Is this really good?" or "Is this the highest good?" or "In virtue of what is this good?" are not simply the curious constructions of an idle intellect. They arise, rather, from the experience of each good's limitation. Experienced goods do not fill up our desires.[9] No matter how rich the experience, the satisfaction of enjoying the good fades, and there always remains some need or yearning that the experienced good does not fill. The genius of Kierkegaard's "Diary of the Seducer" is that the seducer recognizes that having enjoyed the night of erotic love, he cannot extend or maintain that enjoyment. "I have loved her, but from now on she can no longer engross my soul."[10] Therefore what reason identifies as the inquiry after the good in general is identical with the heart's yearning for the perfect good, the highest and best good that will satisfy every longing.

The choice of the will—we might even say, the will itself—is infinite in its scope. One can will anything conceivable. This is the basis for the freedom of the will. The form of the understanding of the ideals, however, has to be brought into relation with the nature of things—including oneself—as they are. The free choice of the will is therefore related to truth. The attempt to live by willpower "against all odds" often amounts to an effort to live according to what is false. If one is short and slow, his competitive spirit will not make him a professional basketball player. The celibate cannot ignore the natural teleology of the reproductive organs, but must manage their insistent demands. Furthermore, what a person has adopted as values conditions what habits he can adopt in the future. An example: To play classical guitar properly, the fingernails on the right (plucking) hand

---

9. Aquinas, *Summa Theologiae*, Ia, IIae, q. 2, a. 8. See also Ia, q. 54, a. 2; q. 77, a. 2; q. 82, a. 5, and especially Ia, IIae, q. 105, a. 4: "Now the passive power of the will extends to the universal good, just as the object of the intellect is universal being."

10. Søren Kierkegaard, *Either/Or* (Garden City, N.Y.: Anchor Books, 1959), 1, 440.

must not be too short, but for piano-playing, fingernails must be trimmed close. The serious musician has eventually to decide which instrument to play. Much more significant, however, is a decision's effect on one's capacity to embrace other values. If the acquiring of power or the enjoyment of pleasure is the highest good for one's own life, it becomes difficult even to conceive how others can adopt some other value. The reason for this is precisely because a person's values are what he or she *wants*. Having settled on what one wants, the human person cannot easily want something else, because the person is formed by his values. Values structure habits.

The challenge of freedom, both logically and existentially, is to bring one's drives, urges and desires into harmony. So it is that we rationally govern our desires. The coach's pre-game pep talk tells the players nothing they do not already know. Rather it reminds them of how much they want victory and why. The limitations on what one can effectively will are the limitations of truth and reason, not only those of physical nature. Working with nature, we can overcome disease, fly, travel to the moon, and transform much of the earth, provided we learn the truth and work according to the understanding formed by truth.

Habits and self-determination

The critical issue is the formation and modification of habits. Implicit in our discussion so far has been that rational activities can be governed according to rational criteria. Therefore, since human habits are rational, then human behavior is (or can be) rationally governed. This, of course, seems to imply that human beings are free in relation to the causal order of the physical world. By what warrant, however, do we assert that the human being enjoys some kind of exemption from normal physical laws? The simple answer is that we assert no such exemption. In the first place, there can be no question of a nonphysical cause of bodily motion. That is, every motion of the body, from stroking one's cat to swinging a tennis racket to uttering objections against scientific materialism, originates in nervous impulses communicated from the brain to the muscles, which derive energy from the nutrients in the bloodstream. The brain, prior to having signaled for the motion of the muscles, had, for its part, received signals from the perceptual organs and other systems in the body, signals which cause the muscle-moving signals. In short, the body is entirely physical and behaves as a physical entity. In the organic causal chains are no uncaused causes. Nevertheless, we can confidently assert that the human being can exercise rational control of his behavior. This is perhaps most evident in the control we can and do exercise over verbal behavior. When one uses the wrong word or expresses himself illogically, he corrects the error and strives to avoid it in the future. It is precisely for this reason that we teach logic and critical thinking to undergraduates.

In chapter 2 we characterized physical laws in terms of habit, "When Z obtains, a occurs." What a physical thing is can be defined by how it interacts with other things. If a substance interacts with alkali such that it forms a salt, that substance is an acid. A thing is material inasmuch as it interacts with other material things. *What it is* is determined by its regular behavior. By scientific investigation, especially in physics, we can determine what the fundamental forms of matter there might be, or better, what basic material objects there are. What we find concerning the human person is that his essence does not completely determine him to pre-established ways of behavior. In a sense, the human person has an open-ended essence; *what he is* is not fully determined. Certainly, the dynamics of the various organ systems within the human body dispose the human being toward specific ways of behaving, as we noted above. The human being is, as it were, naturally fitted to live in a world in which the atmosphere is about 80 percent nitrogen and almost 20 percent oxygen, with plentiful water, and a wide variety of fauna and flora. The male human being has a reproductive system that complements and corresponds to the female, such that both male and female can mate and produce offspring. There is, in other words, a kind of natural conformity of the human being with its environment, just as there is a natural conformity of the electron to its environment. With the human being, however, this conformity is neither complete nor decisive. Let us consider ritual behavior. Upon entering a very warm building during winter, one removes his overcoat. This action is "natural" because being too warm is uncomfortable for the human body. The overcoat wearer conforms to the warm environment. On the other hand, when the Catholic enters a church, he genuflects, a ritual behavior. There is nothing about the environment physically to compel or influence him so to behave. The act of genuflecting is a ritual, not like the practical act of reaching out for a railing to steady oneself or ducking under a low transom. The Catholic genuflects because he believes that God is present in the church's tabernacle, and the genuflection is an act of homage. By his ritual action he conforms himself to the reality that he believes to be present, a conformity that is strengthened by other ritual and devotional acts, such as prayer and participation in liturgical celebrations. It is not only in religion that we do this. The point of military drill and ceremonies is to form among soldiers an awareness of unit cohesiveness and responsiveness to commands. What ritualistic behavior does is to conform the person artificially, as it were, to an object that is not given to immediate experience. We may also note how the serious athlete does something similar, quite literally tailoring his (or her) own body for the sport. The tennis player avoids becoming muscle-bound, while the football lineman "bulks up." Champion athletes drill themselves to ingrain proper form into their bodies, so that the correct backswing or follow-through becomes instinctive. Athletes will speak of becoming a "machine" at the sport. We find much the same sort of behavior with virtuoso musicians and practitioners of other highly skilled professions.

The rational modification of habit requires its symbolic representation and formulation. One represents the habit to himself in order to change it. Because symbolic representation is so malleable, the person can represent to himself all the changes that need to occur in his movements in order to realize the habit. C. S. Peirce tells the story[11] of his younger brother, who was deeply impressed by newspaper accounts of a woman burning to death from a splash of burning alcohol on her dress. The boy rehearsed in his mind what he should do, should something of the sort happen in his presence. Eventually, precisely such a thing did happen in the Peirce home. Before anyone else at the dinner could react, young Peirce snatched up a napkin and smothered the flames on his mother's dress. Charles S. Peirce credits his brother's quick and expert response in this emergency situation to his earlier mental rehearsal. Safe driving pamphlets and videos rely on much the same premise. If one is mentally prepared, then he will respond more appropriately to a rare and unexpected emergency, such as a tire blowout or skid on "black ice." Our habits can be formed non-reflectively by the influence of the environment; rational manipulation of representa-

11. Peirce, *Collected Papers,* 5.487n and 5.538.

tions makes possible the formation of habits independently of such pressures. But let us consider this closely and in detail.

HABIT, WILL, AND THE PRACTICAL DIALECTIC

The act and its structure

By *action* we understand a movement or complex of bodily movements directed toward an end.[12] As such, action applies to scratching one's head, the beating of the heart, repeating the words of a song to oneself, constructing a barn, or disciplining a child—anything that the person does, whether consciously or not, whether under explicit control of the will or not, toward the attainment of some end. An action is, by definition, directed to an end. This end may be some external result, such as the erection of a barn, or some state of the person himself, such as comfort, improved health, or intellectual understanding of something. This definition is deliberately broad, including as it does such activities as fidgeting with one's pencil and breathing, for these activities also have ends. Fidgeting, for example, expresses and helps to relieve boredom and may alleviate bodily discomfort.[13] A particular action is constituted, therefore, by two elements or aspects: a bodily motion (or complex of motions) and an end. On the other hand, one's accelerating downward motion after falling from a ladder is not an action; it is the behavior of any unsupported physical body under the influence of gravity.

Like a physical object, each action admits of a general description in terms of the motions of parts of the body. To hammer requires swinging the arm in a simple arc while holding a hammer in the same hand. Because it is an event in the world, the behavior of an existing being, the human action has existential effects. This is the basis for the notion of *efficacy* that is central to Karol Wojtyła's analysis of the human act.[14] The end or purpose

---

12. Aristotle, *Nicomachean Ethics*, I, i, 1094a 1.

13. We may note that although for most of us, such actions are entirely unconscious and therefore not human acts in the Aristotelian-Thomistic sense (see *Summa Theologiae* Ia, IIae, q. 1, a. 1), there are those—for example guards at Buckingham Palace and professional poker players—who exercise great control of such actions.

14. Wojtyła, *The Acting Person*, Part I, chap. 2.

of the act is one of these effects, and the agent evaluates his act according to its success in realizing that end. This efficacy is the link between the bodily motions of the action and the end or purpose for which it is done. Beyond the intended effect, of course, there may well be other effects. The criminal intends that his act will leave the victim dead, but in carrying out his action he leaves footprints and other clues behind. The homeowner intends to mow his lawn, but in doing so he wakes the neighbor's child. Not only will the human act result in unintended effects, but also the intended effect may remain unrealized and the act thus fail of its purpose. As an engagement in the world, an interaction with the environment, the act encounters resistance. This may result from the brute inertia of things, such as one encounters when trying to force open a heavy door that is jammed shut, or from their complex or unpredictable behavior, as when naturalists attempt to lure a frightened animal into a cage. In acting, the human person experiences the environment reacting upon him as he acts upon it. The physical objects upon which one acts resist the human act and in this respect form it. The agent changes the manner of moving in order to accommodate the end or goal of his act.

As things falling under a general description, acts can differ in their performance while remaining acts of a particular kind. Most acts are a complex of motions, coordinated into one. Swimming involves not only moving the arms, but also kicking the legs and controlling breathing. Although we do not pretend that there are fundamental or "atomic" acts, an act can be broken down into its constituent motions or acts. To serve a tennis ball is a single act. The player seeking to improve his serve, however, will break the act down into its constituents—the toss, backswing, shift of weight, and so on. Each of these sub-acts has its own purpose or end. The purpose of the toss, for instance, is to get the ball into a place where it can be struck with maximum power and control. This means further that there can variations within one kind of act. To serve is an act, but one can vary his service among the slice, twist, and cannonball (or flat) serve, depending on how he varies the elements of the act of serving.

In virtue of the foregoing, we can state clearly what constitutes an event as an act of a particular kind, as act *a*. First, the act has an end or purpose that the agent intends. Two identical motions constitute different acts if they have different ends. One man holds up a lighter to his cigarette to have a smoke, while a spy does the same motion to signal his contact. That the acts are different is clear from the prior and subsequent behavior of the two men. The one smokes a cigarette roughly once an hour and is careful to insure that he always has a pack with him. He will smoke his cigarette to the end. The spy may never smoke for pleasure and carries a pack only when planning to meet a contact. He may not completely smoke the cigarette he lit on the corner. His act was one of signaling. Later, in the police station, the smoker will be released and the spy detained. To perform act *a* is to act for one particular end. Second, the motions that constitute the act fit a general description. To hammer is not simply to fasten one piece of wood to another. Gluing or stapling will also accomplish this end. To hammer is to fasten with a nail, driven by a hammer in the hand. (Of course, both the hammering and the stapling can be subsumed under the common act of building.) To perform act *a*, then, is to engage in physical activity falling under a general description and to do so for a particular end. To intend to perform *a* is to intend both its end and a specific kind of physical motion to attain it.

Because the act falls under a general description, it admits of development into or subsumption under a habit. We may say that every act, every purposeful motion is at least a nascent habit. It is precisely because of this that the development of habits is even possible. Having once or twice found his mouth with his thumb, the infant quickly learns to duplicate the feat. And indeed so it is through adulthood. Having successfully attained a desirable end, perhaps haphazardly or even by accident, one makes a note of how it was done and tries the motion again, refining it and practicing, until a certain facility and consistent effectiveness has been achieved. As Aristotle noted in his *Ethics*, habits are formed by repetition, which is the point of practice, fostering and facilitating the disposition to behave in a regular way so that the act feels natural and "comes automatically."

At this point I can address a concern that has surely crossed the reader's mind (at least that of the Thomistic reader). The discussion fails to address Aquinas's distinction between "acts of a man" and "human acts," the latter of which are characterized by deliberate intent. The beating of one's heart is something that goes on in every human being, but it is not under rational control. I may flex my muscles, but I do not beat my heart. The distinction is both right and valuable; it is not, however, appropriate to our present stage of analysis. The problem we face is the status of human habits. In virtue of what can they change? If a man runs, his heart rate increases. We call that an involuntary consequence of his action. But what is it that makes his running voluntary? Is it a consequence of something further, just as his heart-rate increase was the consequence of the running? That is, our endeavor now is to account for the development of habit, which I maintain can be explained only in terms of a spiritual factor, the soul. What we see with the example of the infant or even the novice golfer is that a kind action becomes a kind of human act gradually, as one learns to control it. I suggest that the line between human acts and the acts of a man, though clear, need not be sharp. Indeed one fruit of these analyses should be to account for the distinction and the evolution of the one into the other (when that occurs).

Habits and representation

Peirce argues that a habit is a kind of universal sign. He writes, "A sign, or Representamen, is something which stands to somebody for something in some respect or capacity."[15] Anything whatsoever—an individual object, a feeling, a general law or pattern—can serve as a sign for something, as long as there is a principle or rule of interpretation by which the signifying thing (the sign) can be applied to that which is signified. As a general law of behavior, a habit is a sign that can represent something to someone in some respect. Archeologists collect artifacts on the basis of which they identify the habits of ancient peoples. Certain kinds of artifacts in a burial site imply that the people believed in an afterlife. The habit represents a connection between some kind of state of affairs and a value. Jones' habit of putting on galoshes in snowy weather represents the value he places on supple shoes and dry feet. Criminal investigators and psychotherapists "read" the habits of others to determine what they really value. A value (or a good) is a state of affairs whose realization or preservation is desired and intended by a person. (At this point, we do not address the question of whether every value a person may value is truly worth valuing.) A habit is a kind of general law that determines how a person will behave in the fu-

---

15. Peirce, "Division of Signs," *Collected Papers*, 2.228. See also 1.541.

ture, and this general law is instantiated by individual acts. As something general, the habit represents something general.

We have distinguished three fundamental kinds of human habit: (1) perception or habits of imaging the world; (2) habits of work or effective interaction with the world, and (3) reasoning or habits of representing the world according to its general characters.[16] Every habit expresses a potential or implicit belief.[17] Even perceptions express the belief that unified sense can be made of one's feelings. Taking *knowledge* in the broadest sense as cognition, the application of a habit is at the same time an application of some knowledge to the act. In stating this, I clearly reject a strong demarcation between mental and physical acts of habits, as though some acts of a human being might be purely physical or others purely mental. Inasmuch as it is formed by an idea, every physical act expresses a thought and every thought involves some physical activity. Every mental act (that is, every "thinking of something") is bodily and every bodily act is act is also an act of mind. An act of thinking is a bodily act intended to represent something as true to someone (if only oneself) and not necessarily to rearrange the world. Every physical act represents a thought, even if the intention is not to represent but to change the way things are.

The practical syllogism

In virtue of his abilities to reason and to know how things are, the human person can govern his behavior. Because by the rational power he can interpret his needs in a variety of ways or represent other goods to himself, he is free of the constraints of instinct to which the animal (not to mention the plant) is subject. The human appetite is rational because human desire is not limited to what is sensibly perceived. Human beings can desire whatever their imaginations, guided by reason, can present to them.[18] Therefore, we can expect human desire and action to manifest a logical

16. For a further discussion of this classification, see chapter 4 of the present work, as well as Adrian J. Reimers, *An Analysis of the Concepts of Self-Fulfillment and Self-Realization in the Thought of Karol Wojtyła/John Paul II* (Lewiston, NY: The Mellen Press, 2001), 122 ff. Also Peirce, "Phenomenology," in Peirce, *Collected Papers*, 1.284ff.

17. Peirce, "A Survey of Pragmatism," in Peirce, *Collected Papers*, 5, especially paragraphs 470 ff.

18. Aquinas, *Summa Theologiae*, Ia, q. 83, a. 1.

structure. Precisely such a structure arises in the application of knowledge through habit to act in a particular situation. Willed human behavior is syllogistic. In the practical syllogism, the habit serves as the major premise, the cognition of a particular kind of situation the minor. The conclusion is the act to be done. Aquinas writes:

> The mind's universal judgment about things to be done cannot be applied to a particular act except through the mediation of some intermediate power which perceives the singular. In this way there is framed a kind of syllogism whose major premise is the universal, the decision of the mind, and whose minor premise is the singular, a perception of the particular reason. The conclusion is the choice of the singular work, as is clear in *The Soul*.[19]

Since habits express beliefs, we can identify the "universal, the decision of the mind" as a habit. The "singular, a perception of the particular reason" is a perceived situation or state of affairs. Let us then recall Peirce's characterization of habit as "a specialization, original or acquired, of the nature of a man . . . that he or it will behave, or always tend to behave, in a way describable in general terms upon every occasion . . . that may present itself of a general describable character." Because such a habit is a sign of a general law,[20] it can serve as the premise in a syllogism, *even if this remain unexpressed in a symbolic proposition*. The practical syllogism then takes this form:

> Major premise: When Z obtains, a occurs.
> Minor premise Z is perceived to obtain.
> _____
>
> Conclusion a occurs.

This syllogism need not be explicitly expressed in a proposition nor otherwise envisioned, because the practical syllogism is not a mental event that occurs prior to the act, somehow exerting an influence over it. Indeed, we know well enough from experience that mental acts ("Tomorrow I am going to stick to my diet.") may have no influence at all on one's be-

___

19. Aquinas, *De Veritate*, q. 10, a. His reference is to Aristotle, *On the Soul*, Book. III, xi, 434^{b}16.

20. Peirce, "A Survey of Pragmatism," cited in note 17 above, and "Some Consequences of Four Incapacities," in *Collected Papers*, 5, para. 310 ff.

havior. However, in developing a habit, the human subject will often represent the major premise to himself. The novice golfer repeats to himself, "Head down, eye on the ball, left arm straight," until he forms the habit; the professional does all these things without thinking about them. The habit, which the professional can certainly express (and does express when teaching), is—as it were—written into his body. The practical syllogism is the dynamic of habitual action, not a theoretical superstructure.[21]

We characterize the structure of the human act in relation to habits and values as follows: Let Z be a situation perceived as existing, a be an act, and V a value. Then the act presupposes (at least implicitly) a belief, B: "If Z obtains and a is done, then V results." This is expressed by the habit H: "When Z obtains, a occurs." Consequently, if the belief is true, the following holds:

> If Z obtains and a is done, then V results.
> Z obtains. a is done.
> _____
> V results.

The value can be anything that is good or desirable, from arriving at work on time to speaking French to playing a well-tuned guitar. Likewise a habit can be anything from the complex nexus of habits that constitute driving a car to memorizing the French word for the day. It is not necessary to specify that a habit be consciously adopted or under rational control. In this respect the "a" in "a occurs" is weak; it does not require conscious decision.

A caveat is in order here. This analysis considers habits abstractly. In any of life's activities an entire array of habits is called into play, habits that interact with each other to a greater or lesser degree. The habit of driving a car consists of many constituent habits involving use of the pedals, manipulating the steering wheel, watching the road, and so on, as well as an intellectual knowledge of traffic laws. Just as the physicist may consider the law of gravity independently of other forces, so too do we isolate habits

21. On Aristotle and the practical syllogism, see the excellent article by Fulvio Di Blasi: "Practical syllogism, *Proairesis,* and the Virtues: Interpreting the *Nicomachean Ethics,*" *Nova et Vetera* 2, no. 1 (2004): 21–42. Particularly noteworthy is Di Blasi's argument that for Aristotle *nous* and appetite work together in a unity, that the soul's understanding forms not just thinking, but action as well.

here in order to grasp their fundamental structure. We no more pretend that any human behavior can be reduced to a simple formula than does the physicist pretend to reduce a tornado to an equation.

Because of the syllogistic relationship among habits, states of affairs and acts, as well as the character of habits as signs, a dialectical relationship obtains among these factors. As we investigate this dialectic, we shall find the ideal principles that must underlie human behavior. Let us turn to the practical syllogism based on value V.

> B: If Z obtains and a is done, then V results.
> H: When Z obtains, a occurs.
> Z is perceived to obtain.
> ___
> a occurs.

If all goes well, then from the performance of a in situation Z, the value V is realized. It may occur, however, that the smooth progression from perception and belief to the realization of the value is impeded by a contradiction of some sort. The dialectic ought to take the following form.

> B: If Z obtains and a is done, then V results.
> H: When Z obtains, a occurs.
> Z obtains.
> a is done.
> ___
> V results.

However, the act may fail of its goal. The value represented by the term V may not be realized. In this case, the syllogism suffers an internal contradiction. One of the premises must be false. Specifically, any of the following may hold.

- Performance of a in situation Z does not effect V. The agent is wrong about how to attain his goal.
- Z does not actually obtain. The agent's perception that Z obtains is false.
- The action a has been performed improperly. The agent did not form his motions appropriately.

This failure of the practical syllogism has repercussions on two levels. First, the acting person is frustrated in that he fails to realize the value for which he acted. Second, his rationality requires that the contradiction within the syllogism be resolved. A premise has to change. Since the syllogism is practical, however, this means that his actions must also change.

PRACTICAL SYLLOGISM: CONSCIOUSNESS AND THE SPIRITUAL[22]

From the structure of the practical syllogism, it is possible to discover the structure of the human person's consciousness of and relation to the true and the good. In other words, we discover the fundamental structure of the human mind. More important, at least for the purposes of the present study, we are able to discern more precisely what we mean by soul, and why this soul must be something immaterial. Let us begin with Thomas Aquinas's definition of "*conscientia*":

> For the name 'conscience' [*conscientia*] means the application of knowledge to something. Hence to be conscious [*conscire*] means to know together. . . . Hence conscience cannot denote a special habit or power, but designates the act itself, which is the application of any habit or of any act to some particular act.[23]

Although Aquinas's primary concern in this text is to characterize moral conscience, he distinguishes two applications of the term *conscientia*, corresponding respectively to consciousness and conscience. He distinguishes consciousness from conscience (that is, the two senses of *conscientia*) by noting that this knowledge can be applied in two ways, according to whether the act exists (consciousness) or whether it is or is not correct (conscience).[24] The *conscientia* that the act is not correct is the warning sign from conscience not to perform the act or, if after the fact, is the "pang

---

22. This section is an adaptation and correction of Adrian J. Reimers, "A Definition of Consciousness," *Gregorianum*, 76:3, 1995.

23. Aquinas, *De Veritate*, q. 17, a. 1.

24. We may note that the parallel passage at Aquinas, *Summa Theologiae*, Ia, 79, 13, treats only of moral consciousness, or conscience.

of conscience" one experiences after doing wrong. Specifically at issue in Aquinas's text is whether "*conscientia* [is] a power, a habit or an act." In responding to the first two "Objections" of the article, Aquinas intends to show that *conscientia* is neither.[25] Rather, *conscientia* (as both consciousness and conscience) is the agent's application of his knowledge to the act.

Although most today hold that consciousness is a kind of property or power (indeed, for some it is the foundational power), Aquinas holds that consciousness is not an abiding condition, neither an inherent property nor a power. Commenting on Aquinas's personalism, Karol Wojtyła writes: "According to St. Thomas, consciousness and self-consciousness are something derivative, a kind of fruit of the rational nature that subsists in the person, a nature crystallized in a unitary rational and free being, and not as something subsistent in themselves. . . . The person acts consciously because the person is rational."[26] This analysis is important to the contemporary discussion, in which the characteristically human is identified with this mysterious power or property we all have and call "consciousness." As noted earlier, for Descartes and his successors, the phenomenologists, consciousness is the foundational reality within which knowledge and the world as experienced are constituted. The problematic for such thinkers is to recover reality and the objectivity of scientific knowledge within the structure of consciousness. For those, on the other hand, who accept the empirical sciences and the scientific way of knowing, consciousness appears as an inexplicable surd, a property that is important to us who are conscious but which appears to explain nothing about our behavior. John Searle writes, "We think of ourselves as *conscious, free, mindful, rational* agents in a world that science tells us consists entirely of mindless, meaningless physical particles. . . . How, for example, can it be the case that the world contains nothing but unconscious physical particles, and yet that it also contains consciousness?"[27] [emphasis in original] His answer is that consciousness is a biological feature or state of the brain, just as liquidity is a state of water.[28] This biological feature of the brain is not itself causal; that

---

25. See Wojtyła, *The Acting Person*, 33. Wojtyła makes a similar point in his response to the Husserlian school, arguing that consciousness is neither a habit nor a faculty.

26. Wojtyła, "Thomistic Personalism," in Wojtyła, *Person and Community*, 170.

27. Searle, *Minds, Brains, and Science*, 13.

28. Searle, *The Rediscovery of the Mind*, 13–14.

is, consciousness does not affect the brain. Indeed, according to Searle, we can conceive of a silicon brain doing everything our brains do but without being conscious.[29] I use Searle here by way of example, although other philosophers and scientists have posed similar problems. David Chalmers calls this "the hard problem": How do physical processes in the brain give rise to subjective experience? "The ineffable sound of a distant oboe, the agony of intense pain, the sparkle of happiness . . . All are part of what I am calling consciousness. It is these phenomena that pose the real mystery of the mind."[30] These difficulties are transformed and—I argue—become manageable if we cease regarding consciousness as a distinct property or power, but instead follow Aquinas's direction. The mind is a mystery only if we insist that the laws governing the human being and his behavior are exclusively physical, material.

Because belief—and therefore knowledge—takes the form of habits, we can summarize Aquinas's definition of consciousness as follows: *Consciousness is the application or invocation of a habit in a concrete situation.* Therefore, the form or kind of consciousness one has at any particular time depends on the kind of habits being applied. Furthermore, in tying consciousness to act, Aquinas implies a direct relationship between consciousness and the will. One is conscious not simply in virtue of being a knower, but rather in virtue of his willing and acting on the basis of his knowledge. As Aquinas says, consciousness "designates the act itself." The act is conscious, and as we shall show, the kind of consciousness one has depends on the relationship of the act with the will.

The following corollary of Aquinas's characterization of *conscientia* will be the key to understanding the conception to be developed in this analy-

29. "It is perfectly conceivable for you to imagine that your external behavior remains the same, but that your internal conscious thought process gradually shrinks to zero." Ibid., 67.

30. David Chalmers, "The Puzzle of Conscious Experience," *Scientific American*, (December 1995), 81. See also Roger Wolcoll Sperry, "Consciousness and Causality," Daniel Dennett, "Consciousness Explained," and Dennett "Consciousness," in *The Oxford Companion to the Mind*, Richard L. Gregory, ed.; Bruce Bower, "Consciousness Raising—Part I," *Science News* 142, no. 15 (October 10, 1992): 232; Francis Crick and Christof Koch, "The Problem of Consciousness," *Scientific American* 267, no. 3 (September 1992): 152–159; Margaret Wertheim, "After the Double Helix: Unraveling the Mysteries of the State of Being," *New York Times*, April 13, 2004; and Antonio Damasio, "How the Brain Creates the Mind," *Scientific American*, December 1999, 114–115.

sis: *Since consciousness is the application of knowledge or a cognition to an act, an act is conscious to the extent that it cognitive consideration invokes a habit or modifies the habitual response. Consciousness arises from cognitive change of the terms in the practical syllogism.*[31] The evidence for this is both abundant and varied. For example, although perception seems to amount to little more than the passive reception of sense data, ordinary experience discloses that, to remain in consciousness, perceptions require some change in the pattern of sense stimuli. One commonly loses consciousness of the feel of the armrest under his elbow, regaining it only when he moves. Uniform sensation eventually becomes no sensation. The habit of imaging proceeds automatically as long as input is constant (or rendered irrelevant by the subject, as when students tune out the droning professor). The reason we develop habits is precisely to be able to do things without having to be aware of every move we make. The good driver is precisely the one who does not normally have to think about how hard to turn the wheel at a curve or when to start slowing for stopped traffic ahead. The beginner has to pay attention to all these things. In our daily lives we perform a wide variety of complex tasks without *thinking about* them, that is, without bringing our actions to the forefront of consciousness. This is why we put radios in our cars and enjoy having company to talk with as we work—to have something to focus attention on. Even mental activities can recede from consciousness under the operation of habit. The rapid patter of the sports play-by-play announcer is an excellent example. The narration of unfolding events fairly falls from the experienced announcer's tongue without his thinking or even being fully conscious of what he is saying.

The converse of our corollary is that action governed by the ongoing action of habit is, to that extent, unconscious. Consciousness arises when a new habit must be invoked by a change in situation (or the cognition of it) or when the operation of the practical syllogism breaks down. The reduction of this habit to act presupposes his perception of the environment, so that he can recognize that Z obtains. He must be capable of consciousness of his environment. Such consciousness can be rudimentary, as when one simply feels cold and reacts with a shiver or by holding the arms close to the body. More characteristically, Z is recognized to be a state of affairs

---

31. See Peirce, *Collected Papers,* 5.235, 237.

among objects in the world: "There is a lion nearby. I must escape!" It may also be a mental or spiritual context, as the atmosphere in a home during a serious marital spat. The unannounced visitor notices the tension and adjusts his behavior accordingly. Z is that in the world to which one is predisposed to act on or in, in virtue of his having a particular habit. It is a state of affairs falling under some general description.

The act of perceiving—let us take seeing as an example—is a complex set of actions. We know now that different parts of the brain respond to color, patterns, and motion. The act of actually seeing an object is one's representation to himself based on this complex of information received by the brain. The pattern of visual stimuli entering the eye is constantly varying, forcing the brain continually to adapt to new data. Therefore the subject can never be content that what he has seen is what he continues to see. In other words, we see (and hear and feel and smell) because our environment is continually surprising us. Taking Z to be the visual field, we see that it is constantly changing. Hence we are constantly aware (conscious) to a greater or lesser extent of our sensory environment. Because consciousness is filled with perceptions, we can, in one sense, identify consciousness with the totality of perceptions. Even during sleep, the human person is constantly alert to changes in his environment that impinge on his values. This is why alarm clocks work and mother hears the baby's whimper. Therefore, even sleep is a state of consciousness, albeit diminished. During wakefulness perception is constant, as the person negotiates his way through tasks and responds to environmental changes and threats to his values. The impression we have that consciousness is a continuous and abiding state or quality arises largely from the simple fact that we are constantly confronted with situations that we can, might or must respond to. The power we have to focus on some particular thing, to concentrate attention to the point of being comparatively unconscious of most other things, attests to the same fact. The subject's entire attention is dedicated to fulfilling some one particular value to the point that habits fulfilling other (perhaps for the time being lesser) values recede, and he does not notice the situations to which these other values respond. Ordinarily, however, a variety of values present themselves to be realized in a continual flux of situations in which one finds himself. It is this continual awakening of consciousness of unfolding existential situations, that forms the apparent continuum that we call the stream of consciousness.[32] Such consciousness of the environment does not necessarily involve thinking explicitly about it. Environmental consciousness is usually of the sense-and-do sort. It is not at all necessary to posit an explicit thinking-about to account for the reduction of habit to act. In baseball the good batter swings when the pitch is in the strike zone. He does not need a mental act—"Now swing!"—to precede or accompany his muscular act.[33]

Forms of consciousness

We turn now to unfold the implications of this analysis by analyzing the ways in which the practical dialectic "fails" by coming up with a false or contradictory result and tracing the consequent development of habit in relation to the true and the good. (We recall that to be spiritual is to be related to the true and the good.) Let us consider the following possibility.

> B: If Z obtains and a is done, then V results.
> H: When Z obtains, a occurs.
> Z obtains.
>
> a is done.
> _____
> V fails to result.

Something is wrong. The expected good is missing, and the agent experiences this as an evil. The conclusion is false, which means that one of the premises must be false. Therefore, something must come to consciousness, according to our principle that consciousness arises when knowledge is applied to the act, when a new habit is invoked. The different manners of dealing with this contradiction give rise to different forms of consciousness.

---

32. Daniel C. Dennett, *Consciousness Explained,* chap. 11, 12.

33. The story is that New York Yankees manager Casey Stengel once admonished catcher Yogi Berra to think while at bat and not swing at so many bad pitches. The next day, Berra was unable to hit anything. When Stengel brought this up, Berra exclaimed, "Think! How the hell are you gonna think and hit at the same time?"

Consciousness of environment.   The habit has apparently failed and the subject is frustrated in his desire. It may be that a mistake was made, that Z_1, contrary in some essential respect to Z, obtained, and the desired value was therefore not attained. The truth of the perception that Z obtained is called into question. Here either the agent becomes aware of Z_1 as different from Z and does not do *a,* or he will notice the difference between situations and reality itself trains him to adopt a new or revised habit of acting to cope with Z_1.[34] The failure to attain V brings his perception of situation Z to consciousness, demanding the agent to pay closer attention and even reflect intellectually on the environment. The subject may then realize that he mistook Z_1 for Z or discover a previously unrecognized but important factor in or aspect of Z. He may then refine his habits of perception so that he can notice the distinguishing factor between Z and Z_1. For instance, the tennis player learns to observe the topspin on his opponent's shots, in order to avoid hitting his return into the net.

In passing we note that we must explicitly reject the notion that one sees what he did not see, that is, that one could see without having noticed at all. Consider a situation of perceptual difficulty: a soldier-trainee must find the "enemy" soldiers hiding in the underbrush. The soldier scans the field and picks out four helmets, their even, curved shape distinguishing them from the brush, but when the sergeant orders the "enemies" to stand, there are seven. The trainee had missed three. If a photographer had been on hand next to the trainee, he could show him a photo where the "enemies" would all be seen. The fact that this image was caught on film does not mean that the trainee had seen the other three "enemies." Even though one can argue that light reflected from the missing three had certainly struck the trainee's retina, it cannot be held that he *saw* them, for his visual apparatus did not respond to them. We think he must have seen them, because we know that they were there and could even be photographed. But the untrained soldier was capable of seeing only the bushes.

There are, therefore, two ways in which the failure of the practical syllogism can be resolved. The first is by sharpening one's habits of perception. After repeated frustrations, the agent, having picked up on some feature

---

34. See Peirce, "Some Consequences of Four Incapacities," on the process of induction by which the mind adopts new habits.

of the perceptual field, eventually takes attentive note of it and adapts. By a dynamic analogous to inductive reasoning, the agent is trained to perceive something new within the perceptual field (such as the topspin on the tennis ball or the telltale knock in the engine). It seems that animals experience such refinement of their own perceptions. The second way is by expressly calling into question the truth of one's perceptions. As we have already noted, perception does not carry its own truth-warrant. The failure of the habit, the contradiction of the syllogism can occasion a questioning of the truth of the matter. Is what I saw what was really there? In order to refine the habit and more accurately judge when to apply it, the agent studies the issue, to learn how more accurately to discern how things really stand. Here then we discover two ways in which habit is modified. The perception on the basis of which the act is selected and initiated is refined, either through inductive repetition (trial and error) or by explicit reflection. Perceiving the world more accurately, the agent acts differently in it.

Sharpened consciousness of the environment is not forced on the agent, nor is the explicit questioning of the truth of the matter. He may instead bring the act, *a,* to consciousness and seek to refine it. The golfer may adjust his stance to correct a hook, not realizing that it is was the wind, an environmental factor, that pushed his ball to the left. He may also call into question his belief, "If Z obtains and *a* is done, then V results." It is even possible to decide that V does not matter any more, that it is of indifferent value to him. We will be able to note, as we examine each of these cases, that the failure of the practical syllogism entails only that the subject become conscious of some aspect of it. It does not absolutely determine which aspect the subject will focus on.

Interlude: Animal Consciousness.   Animals act on the basis of perceptual knowledge to attain their purposes.[35] Unlike the photographic paper, which darkens immediately and always upon exposure to light, the leopard does not attack until it has seen its prey and determined that an attack can succeed. Led to water, a wild horse will drink, but a sound may induce

---

35. Of course, there is a wide range of animal behaviors, from the almost mechanical behavior of some insects to the sophisticated hunting and social behaviors of the higher animals. For our purposes here, it will suffice to examine the characteristics of higher animal behavior.

him to stop and evaluate the possibility that danger lurks nearby. The animal perceives those things in his environment that he needs to survive and perpetuate the species, and he responds with appropriate actions. It is important to note that such action need not be automatic, the blind response to stimuli, as though the animal's behavior is a result of the various forces impinging on it. Animals can use problem-solving strategies and deceit to resolve dilemmas. In the worst case, an animal will give up on the food and go elsewhere. In the higher animals we see gradations of intelligence. Some predatory cats are bunglers in their attacks, while others are patient and cagey. The higher animals manifest a capacity to make quasi-prudential judgments as they search for food or seek to evade capture.

In the light of this we must further develop our understanding of the formula for habit: "When Z obtains, a occurs." First, the state of affairs Z must contain within it not only the objective lay of the land about the animal, but also the animal's perception of its needs and what in the environment will meet those needs. The hawk will not dive unless he is hungry and until he sees the rabbit. Furthermore, the act a is not always a simple motion, like the response of the compass needle to electricity passing through a nearby wire. The hungry animal will forage or hunt until it finds food, which it then eats. Monkeys will peel bananas, and chimpanzees will fashion simple tools to capture termites to eat. In other words, the act a is a complex of motions with a purpose, namely to attain or realize a value V. Implicit in the animal behavior is that the performance of a in situation Z will realize V. When the act a is frustrated in its effect, the animal will repeat the act (with variations if the animal is intelligent) until V is realized. In this respect, the animal has a subjective aspect. He is conscious of the world around him, at least insofar as it can provide for his needs. (And so my cat is oblivious to Respighi playing on the stereo, but is promptly at the bedroom door when the alarm clock sounds; she knows that breakfast will follow soon.) In short, animals differ from inanimate things first in that their response to the world around them depends on their having an awareness of the situation and not of simply being in the presence of other things, and second in that their actions are clearly directed toward the realization of certain goods or goals.

Consciousness of one's act.   The failure of the syllogism may also result in consciousness of one's performance of the act. If, instead of a, the agent had performed a similar but in some respect different act a_1, then the failure to attain the value can bring to awareness the inadequacy of one's performance of the act. Sport provides abundant examples of this sort of consciousness. Failing to hit well, the batter may correct his swing. He has been, in effect, not performing the act as he proposed—swinging smoothly and powerfully at the ball—but has changed it, perhaps by backing away and chopping at the ball. The failure of his habit makes him conscious of his act; he tries to refine it by seeking coaching and taking more practice time. In identifying the flaw in the act and taking responsibility to correct the habit, the person becomes conscious of himself as actor or agent. Thus consciousness of the act leads to a moment of self-consciousness. It is possible, of course, for the agent to fail to take such responsibility, to direct his attention to the environment. The batter may blame better pitching, or poor officiating by the umpires, or even "bad luck" for his failure to hit. In doing so, he fails to accept responsibility and to that extent remains unconscious of himself as an efficacious agent. One may also deliberately bring the act to consciousness in order to improve it. Athletes and musicians periodically analyze the movements they employ in their professional activities in order to perform at a higher level of excellence.

Difficulty in execution of the act is a second way in which the consciousness of the act comes to the fore. Arthritis, prolonged inactivity, or aging can render one unable to carry out some acts with the facility he had previously enjoyed. Such failure of the act can result in a consciousness of one's own body and its systems. The failure to act well according to an established habit can amount to a symptom of a disease or physical deterioration. It then becomes necessary either to correct the problem with one's body (perhaps by therapeutic exercise or medication) or to adapt the environment (by removing barriers, installing a chair lift, or otherwise allowing for the incapacity). Such consciousness of act thus becomes a consciousness of one's own body—another kind of self-consciousness. (Of course, it can also be that one denies the difficulty, as with one whose hearing is deteriorating and who insists that others speak too softly or indistinctly.) Such a difficulty tends also to call the habit itself into question. If the imperative, "do a," becomes difficult or impossible to execute, then the habit must be modified or dispensed with, which entails that the value served by that habit will either remain unrealized or will have to be attained in another way.

As the person becomes conscious of his act, the physical structure of his body in relation to the things in the world comes to the fore. The agent pays attention to his hands, his legs, his head, and other members of his body and how these interact with the world. This constitutes again an intervention of intelligence. The human agent does not simply repeat a failed act or continue to exert efforts with a damaged limb, but instead seeks to understand what has gone wrong. This is precisely what athletes do when they seek coaching or instruction to improve weak aspects of their performance. This endeavor is a matter of understanding the body, its properties, and causal powers in relation to things in the environment in order to determine how the proposed ends can be attained. By means of a mental representation or even a diagrammatic model, the person can understand more clearly the principles on which his body is structured and can incorporate those principles into his future performance. This is a point to which we will return throughout and especially at the end of this section. Symbolically the agent recreates a model of his body and the things around it in order to modify his use of his body. What this symbolic model shares in common with the body and its "effect" on behavior, however, is not physical. We note further that this understanding is not directly induced by the environment, whose direct message is "success" or "failure." The habit is modified according to a symbolic representation.

Consciousness of belief. Beliefs can be—and frequently are—accepted and acted upon without express intellectual consideration. Furthermore every habit is potentially a belief and can be articulated to express a belief. (If Z obtains and a is done, then V results.) Therefore the agent may consider the failure to be in the very first line of the practical syllogism; it may be that if Z obtains and a is done, V does not result. Having performed the act in the situation as understood and not realized the desired good, the subject can blame the failure on the implicit belief that founds his habit. The forms of this reflection can range from the momentary reflection, "Is this really true?" to a full-fledged scientific investigation.[36] In attributing

36. Let us note that this is not the next step in a kind of pre-ordained or natural sequence, as though first one questions the cognition of Z, then the performance of the act, and then the belief. One may from the start call cognition, act, or habit into question. The point of this

his failure to erroneous belief or unquestioned assumptions, the subject becomes conscious of himself as a knower. In recognizing that the belief, "If Z obtains and a is done, then V results," may be false, he locates the mistake in himself; it is *his* mistake. To be sure, one can do otherwise, as when a child complains to his mother that the teacher gave the wrong instructions. The agent is not forced to accept responsibility for his own error or ignorance. Nevertheless, he becomes conscious of the possibility that he may be in error, that his beliefs about the world can differ from the world he encounters experientially. The encounter with the "real world" is thus a strong impetus toward consciousness of oneself as a knower.

To call a habit into question is to make explicit one's assumptions or implicit beliefs. That is, he must formulate and express them symbolically, if only to himself. One can express consciousness of the environment by looking more closely and attentively to see if Z really obtains and of the act by repeating it with more care. The belief, however, cannot be brought to consciousness except through explicit intellectual formulation. A man who habitually uses temper outbursts to get others to do his will, often to find that they still do not obey, may reflect on the adage about catching more flies with honey and conclude that his habitual act of temperamental display is counterproductive. He resolves to try a new approach. This consciousness must involve explicit formulation, because at stake is a different understanding of the relationship among things. To question the belief, it is necessary to look at the effective relationship among the act a, the situation Z that it addresses, and the value V it is intended to realize. A belief may also be called into question when its conflict or inconsistency with other beliefs becomes apparent. For instance, one who uses appropriate forms of motivation with his employees may realize that his temper outbursts at home are the cause of sullen uncooperativeness from his teenage children. In this, another's formulation may trigger the awareness; the father's wife may ask if he relates to his children the same way he relates to his work subordinates. As beliefs become intellectually explicit, their mutual coherence and consistency—or lack thereof—can become evident.

This process is so ordinary, so normal and natural, that we may miss its

---

analysis is to characterize different forms of consciousness and not to find a kind of law or natural pattern of consciousness development.

significance. The consciousness of error is a consciousness that something has gone wrong *with me*—but in a non-pathological way. The agent's problem is not that a part of him has malfunctioned. His problem is that he has, apparently, adopted a false belief. His understanding of the situation is faulty. Now a philosopher can find this peculiar, because it entails an apparent connection between some mental fact (a belief) and the physical world. Having this mental fact renders him incapable of attaining his chosen ends. Were a belief nothing more than the mental adoption of a proposition as true, then we would indeed have a mystery. As we have seen, however, a belief consists in a habit (which may be more or less strong), and a habit is a disposition or a specialization of a something to behave in a certain way in a certain kind of situation. That is, by taking a habit, the agent conforms himself to the situation. The ideas that logically structure the expressed belief correspond (or fail to correspond) to the structure in reality concerned. The ideas by which one's habits are structured reflect the natures of the things about which he holds the belief. Therefore in an ideal way the agent takes into himself the forms or natures of the state of affairs he is addressing, to conform himself to things as they are. This is the reason that, while animals simply search for food, human beings take soil samples to the agricultural agent for testing, to determine how to make crops grow more abundantly.

This bringing of beliefs into consciousness by explicit formulation means that such consciousness has an aspect that is in principle public. Because the belief is formulated in language, it can be criticized by oneself and others. In the example of the temperamental boss, I cited the adage about catching more flies with honey. Precisely such an adage—a cultural belief—may enable one to bring his own belief into consciousness. It may well be that other persons bring one's belief to consciousness. Observing someone's behavior and knowing his goals, they may bring the implicit belief to expression. Seeing the homeowner preparing to fertilize his dying lawn for a third week in a row, the neighbor calls out, "Too much lawn food will kill your grass," calling into question the homeowner's implicit belief that additional lawn food will always help his grass to thrive. Precisely this is how social reformers, revolutionaries, environmental activists and others change or foster social consciousness. Parents in a town are concerned that their children seem not to be healthy. The activist proposes that chemicals being dumped in the groundwater are slowly poisoning them. By proposing a new belief connecting their values with their situation and acts, the activist or revolutionary fosters the development of new habits. The consciousness-raising is in fact the proposal of new beliefs to replace the unquestioned assumptions about important aspects of a group's life.

Human rationality is most manifest when our behavior is changed not on the basis of perception or interactive experience alone, but on the basis of understanding, when we draw up maps and schemata and set out plans and timetables to meet goals. It is precisely in this that consciousness of our beliefs comes to the fore. In the sales meeting or the planning session, the family discussion or team meeting, implicit beliefs, hitherto manifest only in habits and predispositions, become consciously known.

Consciousness of values.   In a similar way one's values may be brought to consciousness. Let V and W be desired values, and H and G, respectively, the habits determined by them. Let a and b be mutually incompatible acts. What results are the following two schemata.

1) If Z obtains and a is done, then V results. Therefore
   H: When Z obtains, a occurs.
   Z obtains.
   _____

   a occurs (and not b).

2) If Z obtains and b is done, then W results. Therefore
   G: When Z obtains, b occurs.
   Z obtains.
   _____

   b occurs (and not a).

W may be a newly adopted value. The young man has fallen in love, and W represents "pleasing the beloved." Z may represent "Friday after work" when he is accustomed to having a drink with his friends in a bar (a). It turns out, however, that the beloved expects that this time be spent with her (b). The importance of V ("fellowship with the guys") is thus brought into focus and is questioned. Or it may be the case that either Z or a (or both) is more complex than originally understood. Killing off coyotes saves livestock from attack, but also allows jackrabbits to multiply exces-sively, devouring crops and vegetation needed for grazing. Such a dilemma brings to consciousness the agent's freedom or self-determination as he is forced to choose between two values.

In his discussion of the question whether a person can sin from weak-ness, Thomas Aquinas notes that, even though one may have knowledge of the universal (*scientia*), he need not apply that knowledge to a particu-lar act. He may instead yield to the demands of passion with respect to the particular.[37] In his response to objections Aquinas is even more specific:

Consequently, each [i.e. the continent and the incontinent man] uses a syllo-gism having four propositions, but for contrary conclusions. For the continent man syllogizes in this manner: No sin is to be committed. And this he propos-es in accordance with the judgment of reason, yet according to the movement of concupiscence he turns over and over in his mind that everything pleasur-able is to be pursued; but because in him the judgment of reason prevails he adopts the first proposition and concludes under it: this act is a sin, therefore it is not to be done. However, the incontinent man, in whom the movement of concupiscence prevails, adopts the second proposition and concludes under it: this is pleasurable, therefore it is to be pursued. And such is properly the man who sins from weakness.[38]

When distinct habits will result in incompatible actions in the same situ-ation, then neither habit is of itself sufficient to effect the action. In such a case there is clearly no question of the two habits interacting in such a way that the act is ultimately a kind of resultant, similar to the behavior of a physical body moving along the boundaries of equilibrium between the gravitational and magnetic forces that affect it. The end of such a body is to move according to the laws (habits) of gravitation and magnetism, not to arrive at a particular position or state. Such a body is, in fact, behaving according to both habits. Furthermore, the very fact of a conscious choice distinguishes the situation of a human being from that of a brute ani-mal. The animal behaves according to habits that are mutually ordered to individual and specific survival. The hungry animal ceases eating when the

37. Aquinas, *On Evil* (Notre Dame, IN: University of Notre Dame Press, 1995), q. 3, a. 9 response.

38. Ibid., q. 3, a. 9 ad 7.

enemy appears. The person confronted with an existential decision, such as Sartre's young man who must choose between going off to war and caring for his mother,[39] has no "resultant" third path between the two alternatives, nor does he find the choice made for him instinctively. Rather, he becomes conscious of himself as having to decide between alternative values. To his self-consciousness as knower and agent is added his moral self-consciousness, as one who must choose between competing values. This is, in effect, consciousness of one's freedom of choice. Concerning both acts *a* and *b* he has the awareness, "I can, but I do not have to," which Wojtyła identifies as the consciousness of freedom.[40]

Such reflection is not forced. The decision concerning the act to be performed may be made impulsively and thoughtlessly, as when one simply performs an act to get through the dilemma. Even here, however, the values are brought to consciousness. The agent is aware of an inconsistency, of a conflict between values. Furthermore, the act chosen—even if only to get past the conflict—is de facto a choice of one of the values at stake. (Avoiding "hassle" is also a value—for many people an important one.) Because habits are formed by repetition of acts, the habit represented by that act is strengthened and the other weakened. One can, however, act reflectively, deliberately choosing one value over the other. By thus choosing one value, the person chooses the form of one part of his life. Future acts of a particular kind will be regulated, at least in part, by that value. Thus can the experience of choice become a choice of one's future. With this comes to the fore the possibility of one's consciousness of self-determination.[41] The consciousness of freedom is written into the logical dialectic of acting. The very fact that the person must choose, that his future behavior *cannot* be determined by the habits on which he had hitherto relied, yields for him the awareness of freedom, the consciousness of himself as a free agent.

The practical dialectic also brings to consciousness hierarchies of values and consequently the reality of higher values. If act *a*, consequent upon *H*, violates *W*, which is judged to be higher than *V*, then the subject be-

39. Jean Paul Sartre, "Existentialism Is a Humanism," in Walter Kaufmann, *Existentialism from Dostoevsky to Sartre*, 354–355.

40. Wojtyła, *The Acting Person*, 105.

41. Ibid., 150, 170.

comes conscious of his need to break habit *H* and replace it with another. For instance, one may have a habit of comforting a child with a piece
of candy. When the doctor diagnoses the child as diabetic, however, the
pleasure value of the candy is superseded by the value of health and continued life. The parent, who normally did not reflect on the mortality of
his or her child, must find another way to comfort the child as the higher
value is brought to consciousness. He becomes aware of the requirement
to conform his acts to reason, to the truth. A conflict has arisen between
his habits, his regular behavior, and the truth or a deeper understanding of
his principles. In other words, the person in such a dilemma may become
conscious of duty, the consciousness that in the light of some higher value
he must act contrary to established habit. By the very nature of habit, this
is disagreeable and uncomfortable, since, as Aristotle notes, conforming to
habit is what comes naturally or easily. On the other hand, to violate duty
by performing *a* anyway is consciously to reject the higher value.

Here we have an expression of what Karol Wojtyła calls "vertical transcendence." Wojtyła defines "horizontal transcendence" as "Transgressing
the subject's limits in the direction of an object—and this is intentionality in the 'external' perception or volition of external objects."[42] By this he
refers to the conscious subject's transcending the bounds of his own consciousness. (We may remark that one of the points that *The Acting Person*
aims implicitly to settle is the phenomenological problem of the existence
of the world external to consciousness.) But this horizontal transcendence
is not significant for understanding the person in his freedom. For Wojtyła
freedom is founded not on indeterminacy but on self-determination.[43] He
continues: "The transcendence we are now considering is the fruit of self-
determination; the person transcends his structural boundaries through
the capacity to exercise freedom; of being free in the process of *acting*, and
not only in the intentional direction of willings toward an external object.
This kind of transcendence we shall call 'vertical transcendence.'"[44] Wojtyła
goes on to argue that this transcendence can be based only in the acting

42. Ibid., 119.
43. Ibid., 117.
44. Wojtyła, *The Acting Person*, 119. Cf. Wojtyła, *Person und Tat* (Freiburg i. Br., Basel, Vienna: Herder, 1981), 135.

person's knowledge of the truth about the good, for the will can act freely only in reference to truth. "Choices and decisions, which take as their object what is not a "real good"—especially when contrary to what has been recognized as a real good—lead to the experience of "guilt," or "sin." But it is the reality of guilt—of sin or moral evil—known from the moral experience that brings to light explicitly the fact that the reference to truth and the inner dependence on truth is rooted in the human will."[45] The act—and with it the person performing the act—has reference not simply to the environmental factors with which the agent is engaged, but also to truth, which, as we have noted, transcends the material order.

Our thesis, then, is that the development of habit can be understood only in spiritual terms, and the choice of values under the guidance of reason is a decisive element of this dynamic. The material resists efforts and impacts other material things, effecting change through the brute reality of interaction. The spiritual, however, is governed by the relationship with truth and the good, especially as these are experienced in beauty. The argument here is that the dynamic of choice among values is governed by the aspiration for the good. Let us note that the consideration of a choice among values is not determined by material factors. Why? The person confronted with such a choice represents to himself (more or less adequately and accurately, to be sure) the ideals represented by his values. His situation, regarded in respect to the choice as such, is one of freedom, constrained only by his own imagination and powers of ratiocination. Material factors may influence how he *feels* about these ideals. Nonetheless, as representations they are subject to him. On what basis does he decide, then, between them? His decision, no matter what direction it takes, is tantamount to deciding to recognize that *this* is good and better than *that*. To be sure, he may choose the lesser value, perhaps despairing of his own ability to attain the greater or succumbing to some sort of pressure. As we shall show shortly, this ultimate or determining good is not arbitrary but must somehow be appropriate, fitting. However, we need to carry our analysis of the practical syllogism further before we can address this.

45. Wojtyła, *The Acting Person*, 139.

Consciousness of self

Like consciousness in general, self-consciousness is not some one state or thing. In its common usage, the term refers to the discomfort one feels when he fears he may not fit into a particular social situation. One is self-conscious when playing a role or trying to make a favorable impression. Such self-consciousness is a form of embarrassment and is not so much consciousness of one's self (in the sense of the ego or "innermost me") as of one's appearance and bearing. In such a situation, a person is conscious of his clothes, accent, lack of family background, or the like. To a certain extent, animals manifest such self-consciousness, as when a lion skulks around in another's territory, aware that if discovered he will be attacked. Such is not the self-consciousness that philosophers ordinarily understand as distinctively human self-consciousness. On the other hand, there is no direct consciousness of the self as self. Indeed, by raising the apparently innocent question of self-consciousness, we find ourselves in the thicket of conceptual puzzles surrounding the very notion of self. In this context we can find the analysis of the practical dialectic especially helpful.

As mentioned above, *self-consciousness* ordinarily refers to a sense of awkwardness or embarrassment one feels in front of others, especially where one is afraid that he might not fit in. Expressed more generally, self-consciousness is a kind of discomfort at finding oneself an object of others' evaluation. The premise of our current analysis is that the practical syllogism has failed; the act flowing from the habit directed toward the value has failed to realize the value. Such a failure can result in one's becoming aware of his own defective perception, action, or knowledge, as well as of hierarchical relationships among his values. The question arises: In what subject do these failures inhere? Clearly in some cases one can identify the body itself as that subject. Tired muscles can result in poor task performance. In unusual lighting conditions or when one is tired, his eyes can "play tricks on him." However, the failure may also be one of knowledge. The general failed because he was wrong about how the enemy's troop disposition. He did not know how things really stood. But *where* is the general's ignorance? We may place it in his mind, of course, by which he represents to himself how the enemy troops are disposed. We may also place it in maps and plans which he drew up according to his understanding. The same general who, because of an old war wound, may limp slightly is he who misunderstood the battlefield situation. The young wastrel is filled with regret, having squandered his educational opportunities and the goodwill of his benefactors. He foolishly pursued lesser values and lost what was better. Clearly the ignorance belongs to the general; it is he who is ignorant. And the folly belongs to the wastrel. Indeed the self-consciousness of each is analogous to that of the man with a spot on his tie. He is an object for evaluation by others. The general knows he must render account to the review board, which will evaluate him. The wastrel must answer to his father.

There are two things to note here. First, the self of which one is conscious when one is self-conscious is not something elusive and subjective. It is one's whole being, in its bodily and spiritual manifestations, that one is conscious of. Although the expression "self-conscious" in ordinary parlance may sometimes refer superficially to the self ("I feel self-conscious at my father-in-law's place if my shoes are not shined."), the reference is always to one as a whole being. Second, this self has aspects that are immaterial, spiritual. The point of the examples of the general and the wastrel is that failure in relation to the truth and the good pertain to the person just as really as physical characteristics. But what is the self? For Peter Singer it is precisely the awareness of self that constitutes an animal as a person deserving of rights.[46] This self, however, is not founded directly in the organism, but rather in its consciousness. Along much the same lines, Dennett—who, like Singer, is a scientific materialist—argues that the self is "an abstraction defined by the myriads of attributions and interpretations (including self-attributions and self-interpretations) that have composed the biography of the living body whose Center of Narrative Gravity it is."[47] The self is, therefore a kind of fiction, a construct of human consciousness, that cannot be rooted in the being of the thing that has a self.

It is precisely in the context of this difficulty that Karol Wojtyła invokes the concept of *suppositum*, by which he means the subject of experience and activity.[48] As such, this suppositum must be something transphenom-

---

46. Peter Singer, *Practical Ethics,* 86–87.

47. Daniel Dennett, *Consciousness Explained,* 426.

48. Wojtyła, "The Person: Subject and Community," in Wojtyła, *Person and Community,* 222.

enal, a metaphysical reality. Wojtyła continues: "The *suppositum humanum* must somehow manifest itself as a human self: metaphysical subjectivity must manifest itself as personal subjectivity. This *must* is the strongest argument for the metaphysical conception of human nature."[49] Personal subjectivity is constituted precisely by the person's capacity to know the truth and to desire the good, that is, by his spiritual character. The *suppositum*, therefore, is not simply the physical human organism, but rather the human being in the fullness of its (his) being.

Let us return to the consideration of the practical dialectic and its implications concerning the consciousness of self. Our analyses thus far have shown how the person can become conscious of himself as knower, as well as of his relationship to values.

Habits of knowing.   As noted earlier, the dialectic that arises from the failure of the practical syllogism (we may call this the "practical dialectic") can bring to awareness an error in the agent's beliefs. As our discussions in chapter 4 showed, a belief does not stand alone as a bare fact, but is held by a living intelligence within a nexus of logically interrelated beliefs. It is the intellect, and not just the one symbolic representation, that corresponds to things. But let us trace this in relation to the practical syllogism.

The belief is constituted by the habit and (when it comes to consciousness) in mental activity can be represented: "If Z obtains and a is done, then V results." This belief involves an understanding of relationships among Z, a, and V, which can itself find expression in more general beliefs, beliefs that can form the bases of a science. So if Z is "springtime," a, is "planting seeds," and V is "a crop," this belief is related to a whole nexus of other beliefs concerning agriculture and plant fertility. Or, if the terms are respectively "ladder leaning against a wall," "walking under it," and "misfortune" then the belief finds its context in the nexus of more general beliefs about occult forces and superstitions. What I want to draw attention to here is that this more general nexus is presupposed as soon as the belief comes to consciousness. In formulating or somehow expressing the belief one implicitly places it in a broader conceptual context, and this for the simple reason that the terms in which the belief is expressed are themselves gen-

---

49. Ibid., 225.

eral. There is something about springtime in general and about seed planting in general that makes planting worthwhile for someone who wants a
crop. Of course, this general knowledge is not directly given to the one
who believes "If Z obtains and a is done, then V results." Rather, having
expressed the belief, he *wonders*[50] about it. Why is this so? What does this
have to do with other beliefs I hold to be true? The person can and often
does seek to know more, to increase his knowledge and understanding.

In chapter 4 we considered the implications of Gödel's work for deductive logic, showing that even a deductive system has an open-ended
character, requiring a further intellectual operation. In truth, the project
that Gödel addressed was unreal. At stake was the notion that all human
knowledge might be syntactical, that all truth ultimately reduces to the implications of fundamental, primordial axioms of some sort. Whatever may
have been the merits of this project, it does not reflect common human
experience, which is not deductive. We start with experience of the world
around us, not with universal axioms. The truly great mystery of human
intelligence is not the descent from the general to the specific or particular,
but the ascent from the specific to the general. This is the process that Plato
illustrates in his metaphor of the Cave but which Socrates professes himself unable to explain.[51] This is the intellectual operation by which we recognize what is universal in the particular, what Aquinas calls "abstraction."
It is the operation by which one is able to recognize the general character
governing several concepts and the signs that represent them. What I contend here is that this operation cannot reduce to a material interaction or a
complex of such interactions.

By means of repeated interactions of a particular sort, an organism can
be induced to adopt a habit. Pavlov's dog salivated at the sound of the bell.
Indeed, even an inorganic thing can, in a sense, be so "trained," as can happen with self-correcting computer programs. (A sufficiently sophisticated
chess-playing machine will not fall for the same trap twice.) The abstraction of a more general form is not a matter of response to repeated interactions. Let us consider the matter. One holds a belief, "If Z obtains and a
is done, then V results," but notices an anomaly. This anomaly might be

---

50. The allusion to Aristotle's *Metaphysics* I, 2, 982b12, is intentional.
51. Plato, *The Republic*, VII, 533b.

the discovery that if Z^* obtains and a is performed, V results. Or it might be that V results from a^*, which is different from a. Either way, it appears that a more general conception of the state of affairs or of the required act will realize the value. One asks what this more general conception might be. In chemistry burning is understood as oxidation; a burning substance undergoes a chemical reaction in which the atoms of the burning substance bond with oxygen atoms. As chemists investigated the dynamics of chemical bonding, however, they discovered that the oxidation of a chemical substance always involves the loss of electrons and that this was, in fact, the more important conception. Thus oxidation is now defined more broadly in terms of the loss of electrons rather than simply in terms of loss of electrons by bonding with oxygen. Now, to be sure, the individual steps from watching paper burn to determining that any transfer of electrons (in what we now call an oxidation reaction) releases energy all seemed "perfectly logical" to the scientists developing them, but this is so because they had already begun to develop models for reflecting chemically on things. Toward the end of the nineteenth century chemists were getting into the habit of looking for explanations at the atomic level, particularly in reference to electron levels. Now the point here for us is that the inference, the growth in knowledge and understanding, results not directly from the impact of the environment upon the human subject, but upon the construction of an ideal representation to explain the particular experience one has had. The parameter here is true understanding of things. The result is not to establish the truth of the belief held all along, but rather to determine the truth about the more general realities (essences and principles, if you will) that govern the original belief.

What we are talking about here, in a sense, is the genesis of what Aristotle called intellectual virtues, the habits of mind by which one may understand reality. Now whether he does this poorly or well, the individual person structures a worldview, a conceptual framework based on the beliefs and conceptions that he has received or originated. (I say "whether one does this poorly" advisedly, for one may certainly elect to structure one's beliefs according to some criterion other than truth properly understood by, for example, taking one's own perceptions, experiences, or received tradition as the criterion of truth or by refusing to accept knowledge one does not find congenial. As I have mentioned earlier in this section, the practical dialectic does not force the correct inference or form of consciousness on the person.) On the basis of one's interests and environment and more importantly based on one's habits of mind—whether he is a businessperson, a scientist, an artist, or a farmer, for instance—his mind is formed by certain guiding conceptions, whose expression will develop in characteristic ways. This frame of mind will, to be sure, be shared with others to an extent. In some ways, all engineers, French persons, Thai villagers, rabbis, and New York socialites think like others in their respective classes. The reflective person, at least, is conscious of self in this respect, therefore, that he has a cast of mind, that the world he experiences, of which he is a part, has certain universal characters and is best understood conceptually in terms of certain general ideas. In this respect the person has a "cast of mind" that constitutes an aspect of his self. Or to put the matter in more traditional terms, the "who I am" is defined in part by one's intellectual virtues. And these virtues are spiritual, because they are habits of representation governed by the principles of reason—laws of logic—for the end of truth. But the laws of logic are nonmechanical and the relationship that is truth is nonmaterial.

Habits and Values.   Just as the natural dynamic of believing is toward more general ideas, so too does valuing naturally lead to a general conception of good. The earlier discussion of consciousness of values centered around conflicts that arise when the habits that realize one value conflict with those fostering another. The young man must choose between "good times with the guys" and spending time with his fiancée after work. The consciousness of value, however, is deeper than this and the dynamics governing it parallel those governing understanding. We must acknowledge first that one is not forced to become conscious of any obligation to any value or structure of good. (This is why misfortune embitters one person and strengthens another toward moral heroism.) This is in itself an indirect indication of the spiritual character of the human person. There are more direct indications, however, and they have to do with the inherent tension between the material and spiritual aspects of human being.

Earlier we discussed certain innate goods that we are born desiring and which, because of the nature of our organic constitution, we cannot help wanting. In that context we observed that a significant challenge that the human person faces is the integration of these innate desires, from the fundamental desire for life to the cravings of the reproductive and digestive systems, the inclinations toward comfort and pleasure, and so on. Let us note now that in the section just concluded we identified a further good that human beings are naturally drawn to—the good of understanding. This wonder, of which Aristotle and Aquinas spoke, is the natural desire that we have for understanding truth.[52] Understanding of the truth is a value that human beings pursue. Furthermore, it is a spiritual value, one that can be opposed to a value pertaining to the physical order. (Simple example: Because overeating makes one sleepy and unreflective, it interferes with study.) Whether, as James would have it, truth is pursued only for material advantage as a kind of useful mental "tool," or for itself, is irrelevant to the current discussion. Truth, a nonphysical relationship, is desirable and valued. If truth is a good, then we may expect that it, like other values, determines habits, and to be sure, the previous section indicated what some of these (intellectual) habits might be. However, it is also the case that the inquiry for truth relates to other values and their corresponding habits. And the most important issue is that if truth is a value, a good, then our lives are governed not only by material considerations. In at least one respect the human person desires a spiritual good.

This natural desire for truth casts a new light on the question of value itself. It does not suffice to order values according to physical considerations, such as survival and comfort, alone. The question of what it means to be *good* takes on a new depth, if truth is a good. The good of truth constitutes a serious challenge to the materialist notion that good can be reduced to—or indeed explained away as—the effect of material interactions. The materialist can respond only by denying the reality of the desire for truth and, indeed, by denying that truth is the sort of thing that can even be desired. In the final analysis, this must amount to a reduction of the concept *truth* to something else. While such a reduction may be accomplished, it suffers several significant, and in my view fatal weaknesses. First is the well-known *ad hominem* argument that whoever poses such an account poses it as true, investing time and significant intellectual effort into his theory, seeking to produce a convincing theory that others may embrace in their own understanding. Such an *ad hominem* argument is important because

52. Aquinas, *Summa Theologiae*, Ia, IIae, q. 3, a. 8.

it is structural and not personal. Unlike the personal (and fallacious) *ad hominem* argument—"Of course, Jones believes tax cuts are good for the economy. He's an investment banker, who has gotten rich through tax loopholes."—the materialist, no matter who he is, undercuts the ground of his own deeds precisely by the acts of advocating his materialist position. He may, like Wittgenstein, have used the ideas as a ladder which he may discard after climbing it,[53] but there remains the unanswerable question why anyone else should ascend this same ladder. The second weakness is that this experience of wonder is a matter of common human experience. Even if it may be argued that the attainment of truth is impossible and irrelevant to other human concerns, it is nevertheless the case that human beings do desire to know how things really stand, to bring their own conceptions into agreement with what they purport to represent. In short, the conception of truth is a vital part of human being and the desire for it is real. Third, this striving to understand truth is rewarded by growth in human understanding. Not only do scientists and, indeed, ordinary persons experience the satisfaction of having adequately represented things to themselves and others, but, further, these representations, based on their understanding, give rise to practical applications of technologies and the development of further understanding of related matters. If the conception of truth is an illusion, it is indeed a most remarkable one. Finally we must observe that the desire for understanding of truth is universal. Whether we consider ancient myths and legends or modern sciences and humane letters, whether we regard the adolescent's reflections on authentic friendship or the scholar's inquiry into Renaissance politics, we find human beings concerned to know how things really are. Human beings value truth, and that means that some spiritual condition or relationship is a value. If this is so, then the criteria in virtue of which values may be judged to be authentic goods must refer to the spiritual as well as the material, for truth is a condition of the human intellect, not of the body.

From this it follows that as one forms his habits, the higher values under which the values represented by various beliefs ("If Z obtains and a is done, then V results.") are to be subsumed must be, in some sense, spiritual. Were this not the case, then by arguing deductively, the V of a "lower-

---

53. Ludwig Wittgenstein, *Tractatus Logico-Philosophicus*, 6.54.

level" belief could not be "understanding the truth about *X*." To make this clear, let us first look at the case of animals. Maintenance of individual life is one of the highest governing values among the higher animals. A cat will do what it needs to in order to stay alive. This governing value is manifest in many lower-order habits. In particular, when threatened by a stronger enemy, the animal will flee. But if the situation is changed, so that the animal is cornered, it will fight. In a sense, these habits—flight or fight—are deduced from the governing habit: when life is threatened, protect it. Of course, the animal does not carry out this deduction ratiocinatively; we do not attribute beliefs to the animal, as we do to human beings. (Of course this is precisely the point.) The real issue before us here is whether this animal "deduction" is what really occurs with humans. If this is so, if human habits are governed only by material values, such as physical survival and comfort, then it is indeed true, as some have argued, that our reasons for acting as we do are only rationalizations, that what actually governs our behavior is "the law of nature," the instincts for survival and reproduction, the desire for comfort, and so on. Ratiocination could follow from such ultimate values only to the extent that it affects survival of self and species. This is, however, contrary to our experience. We wonder because we need to understand how things are. Survival may demand maps of the Mississippi Delta but not of the solar system. The highest governing values for the human person must, therefore, be spiritual. Whatever the good is, it cannot be simply a physical state or condition.

This is further evident from the fact that human beings are concerned for morality, for an ordered understanding of right and wrong, good and evil. Because the good has a spiritual aspect, we distinguish between "successful" and "good." In the forest and field, there is no justice, no mercy. Not only do animals not practice these, but they do not even care about them. Human beings do. Even those among us who insist that there is no transcendent good, that we are of a kind with the other animals—even they continue to *argue* their thesis, to give good reasons why it is true and worthy of our acceptance. More generally, we human beings put order into our moral conceptions. The values governing our beliefs and habits are judged, as it were, by higher values, which bring them into harmony. Most persons will acknowledge that there are values worth sacrificing and even dying for, whether these values be family, country, or God.

"A SIGN DEVELOPING" AND "THE MEANING OF LIFE"

Consciousness of self arises from the practical dialectic, from the person's experience governing his own acts according to his values, knowledge, and understanding of the environment and not from a kind of privileged introspective awareness of his own mind.[54] From this conscious experience one can arrive at a knowledge of self, which is different from self-consciousness. The preceding analysis of the habits of knowing and the structure among values points this discussion in a different direction than philosophers customarily take. The modern philosopher characteristically focuses on the self as a kind of possession and object of awareness that is somehow constituted of memories and conscious states. Although this focus is reflected somewhat in common parlance (especially in discussions of Alzheimer's patients), there is another concern, equally if not more important. This is the concern for meaning, for principles or values in terms of which one can live and interpret his life. The analysis of habit, belief, and the practical dialectic finds its completion in the conception of the meaning of life.

To understand this, let us recall Peirce's saying, quoted several times already: "The mind is a sign, developing according to the laws of inference." The foregoing discussion of the practical dialectic, in which we sketched the relationships among habits as representative of beliefs, is a development of Peirce's conception. From it two further questions arise, questions that directly address the question of the meaning of life, of personal identity. First, if the human being is a sign (and Peirce argues precisely this),[55] then what does it represent? What is the human being a sign of? Second, if this sign is "*developing* according to the laws of inference," then we may ask, what is it developing toward or into? As far as Peirce was concerned, the answers to these questions were pretty straightforward. Peirce was concerned for science and scientific knowing, and although he does not directly answer the questions as we have put them, it is clear that the man is a sign of the order of nature, and the mind that is developing is actually

---

54. See Peirce, "Questions concerning Certain Faculties Claimed for Man," in *Collected Papers*, 5, especially 5.225 ff.

55. Peirce, "Consequences of Four Incapacities," in *Collected Papers*, 5, especially 5.310–317.

that of the scientific community as it approaches the truth of the order of the universe. And surely this must be at least part of the answer.

Every animal can be taken as a sign of the world around it. One does not need to see the Siberian tiger in its natural habitat or know its name to know from its coat and coloring, as well as its claws and fangs, that this animal lives in a cold and snowy region where there is large game. The animal is a sign of the region it inhabits, and in this sense the human being is also a sign. However, the tiger does not at all intend to represent Siberia. Human beings, however, do interpret the world through our sciences and by our work. We may fairly say that the human person is a sign of the world in which he lives, not only in virtue of the indications his behavior yields about his environment, but more specifically in virtue of his representation of the world. Indeed, we may appropriately state that the human person is a kind of ongoing and as-yet-incomplete argument, a series of mutually interrelated beliefs tending toward and supporting a conclusion. As one integrates his beliefs, both in action and by symbolic representation, he interprets them as the (perhaps provisional) conclusion interprets the premises. By the way he lives, then, the human person expresses and affirms his belief that reality is of such-and-such a character. Unlike the Siberian tiger, however, this significance is neither determined nor limited by the conditions of the physical world around him. One person can live a life of complete trust in a loving God, while another steels himself against implacable, cruel fate. One lives optimistically in a world where everything turns out for the best, while another dreads the occult powers of black cats, spilled salt, and planetary alignments. To be sure, the impact of the real world requires that one adjust his beliefs and understanding, but the physical alone cannot determine what one believes to be real. In this respect, one might say that the human person is an artist, by his life representing the world as it might be, as he himself sees it. As such he is a kind of witness, proposing to others how the world is.

The second question—towards or into what is this sign developing?—takes us to the heart of human morality and meaning. Peirce considered that question (to the extent that he did consider it) in terms of the development of scientific knowledge. It is a matter of common human experience that human beings have goals and expectations, which can differ from person to person. Even two persons who may have similar goals or destinies will usually differ somewhat in how they structure their paths to the goal. To say that the sign that one is develops "according to the laws of inference" does not determine the direction of that development, for a sign develops not deductively but inductively and hypothetically. The logic of hypothesis is particularly important, for it is by hypothetical reasoning that one posits guiding principles and ideas. No one knows from experience that he is the man of destiny to lead the nation to freedom. Moses heard the voice of God from the burning bush (Exodus 3), but what does this mean except that God proposed the hypothesis to him? And proposing to the U.S. Congress to emancipate the slaves, this is what Abraham Lincoln said: "Fellow-citizens, we cannot escape history. We of this Congress and this administration, will be remembered in spite of ourselves. . . . We know how to save the Union. The world knows we do know how to save it. We— even we here—hold the power, and bear the responsibility. In giving freedom to the slave, we assure freedom to the free—honorable alike in what we give, and what we preserve. We shall nobly save, or meanly lose, the last best hope of earth. Other means may succeed; this could not fail."[56] The logical character of Lincoln's belief that the Emancipation Proclamation would help save the Union was hypothetical, and the judgment of its truth was only after the fact, just as Moses had no experiential warrant for believing he could lead the Children of Israel out of Egypt. Now, most of our principles are well founded in the experience of others—that, for instance, firm discipline tempered with kindness will foster strong moral character in children or that reading to children fosters lifelong learning habits. What is important for our present purposes is that the conclusion, the direction of development is not uniquely determined by the premises (that is, one's beliefs). Any number of general principles or theses may serve to interpret one's current life experiences and beliefs.

What, then, determines these beliefs, these principles by which one governs his life? The answer is that nothing *determines* them, but many things can influence them. Certainly, one can simply note that what is pleasant is desirable and what is unpleasant is not and determine that he will live his life for pleasure and the avoidance of pain. This is a governing principle

---

56. Abraham Lincoln, *Annual Message to Congress*, December 1, 1862, accessed from http://showcase.netins.net/web/creative/lincoln/speeches/congress.htm.

that one can adopt and which many certainly have. From traumatic experiences in youth one may conclude that the world is cruel and that no authority figure can be trusted. Or he may conclude that with fortitude, endurance, and patience he can overcome anything. Sitting in the ashes by the hearth Cinderella may dream of the prince, but she may also plot revenge on her stepsisters . . . or simply eat chocolates and grow fat. The story of Cinderella, of course, points to one of the most important sources of ideals: tradition. The point of the fairy tale is that in the end goodness and kindness win ("So you, little girl, should do the same"). Myths and legends, historical figures, heroes and saints all present ideals of life. So too do cultural, moral, and religious teachings. Mom and dad, the teacher, the governor, and the priest all teach what is worth seeking and living up to. All this is common knowledge. Its importance for our present investigation is the logical role of such proposed value structures.

As we said earlier, the governing value is adopted hypothetically. That is, it is posited as true and as the interpretive principle of the beliefs one holds to be true. As the person adopts principles, those principles work deductively to form future behavior. Because the role of ultimate values is logically analogous to that of fundamental theoretical principles in science, the hermeneutic circle functions in real life. Just as the scientific theory suggests experiments that test it, so do a person's ultimate values entail lower values and beliefs based on them that may conflict with those one actually holds. And just as experiment may result in the refinement of the theory, so does experience result in refinement of a person's conception of his higher values. It is common enough to realize as one grows up that real Cinderellas do not get the prince. The shortcomings of a life devoted to pleasure become clear with the first childhood stomachache or adolescent hangover. When Job has lost everything, his wife urges him to abandon his fidelity to God and his law: "Curse God, and die" (Job 2:9 RSV). And if Job remained faithful, there are others in similar circumstances who have indeed ceased believing in a loving God. Given the logical structure of the practical dialectic, two conclusions follow. First, it is impossible to attain either deductive or experiential certainty concerning one's highest values. A child can taste the value of candy, and the mechanic can experience the value of hardened steel tools. There is no such experience, however, of the ideals that govern all the beliefs one holds and values he desires. Second, no single factor can determine a person's governing values. To be sure, many things may serve strongly to influence them. A person may be gifted with acute senses or physical abilities or may have strong sex drives. The culture in which one is raised may be so all encompassing that few options other than its ideals may be presented. The decisive point, however, is that not even the strongest physical or environmental factor is logically compelling. At the very least, the human person can raise the questions, "Is this really worth living for? Is this truly good?" Not only that, but he can take steps to conform his life and behavior to his ideal. The slave shuffles in silent rebellion, and the political prisoner scribbles his memoirs in secret. Therefore, to say of someone that he lives as he does because his father was weak and his mother domineering, or that he is a member of the aristocracy, or that he has a sensitive temperament, can be only a partial explanation. These factors serve to propose—perhaps very forcefully—a way of life. However, the subject has the power to relate the proposed ideals to his other beliefs and values (and to other ideals that may have been proposed), and to accept or reject or relativize those proposed ideals.

The point here is that the question of the consciousness of self is secondary. This notion of self as that which answers the question, "Who are you, really?" is secondary to the issue of one's governing values, the meaning he finds for his life. Louis Rivera, the washed-up boxer in the 1962 film *Requiem for a Heavyweight*, knew who he was: "I fought 111 fights and never took a dive."[57] We identify things by their properties, but ourselves in terms of our ideals and accomplishments in service of those ideals. These ideals are spiritually determined, which is to say that they are inextricably related to the conceptions of good and truth, by which they are evaluated. In virtue of these ideals does the person evaluate his life, whether it is good or going badly.

57. Rod Serling, *Requiem for a Heavyweight*, directed by Ralph Nelson, 1962. The tragedy of the film is that having failed to achieve his goal of a boxing championship, Rivera ends the film as a professional wrestler, paid for "taking dives." He is, in his own eyes at least, reduced to being a nobody.

CONSCIOUSNESS PUZZLES

It is, therefore, the power to know and to choose that makes one conscious, and not consciousness that makes possible reason and choice. By mistaking consciousness for a particular power or habit, philosophers and scientists have created intractable puzzles for themselves. The approach presented here enables us to solve and even avoid such puzzles. In particular, this account of consciousness avoids the dilemmas and mysteries that attend materialist and dualist discussions of consciousness. Let us consider some of these.

On the one hand, since consciousness is entirely private and interior to the person, it must be impossible for one person to know what lies in another's consciousness. The possibility of sympathy and true communication seem to be excluded from the outset. On the other hand, consciousness seems to be entirely disconnected from the world, a kind of qualitative inner life that has little—indeed no—relationship with the nervous and muscular interaction of the organism with the outside world. Consciousness provides us with pleasant, colorful inner lives but does nothing to help us get on with living in the world. Both dilemmas rest on false premises. Furthermore, what we call the "colorful" aspect of consciousness—the range of our feelings and emotions—flows directly from the rational person's relationship with truth and the good.

Privacy of consciousness

It is almost axiomatic that one person cannot share another's consciousness. My perceptions and my feelings are inside me, inaccessible to you. Antonio Damasio summarizes it well: "Anyone's body and brain are observable to third parties; the mind, though, is observable only to its owner. . . . The mind is a private, hidden, internal, unequivocally subjective entity."[58] You can measure the light and sound that impact upon another's senses, and you can observe his behavior, but you cannot know directly what is going on in his mind. Indeed, there is no direct way by which one person can observe whether another even has a mind or conscious life. Re-

---

58. Antonio Damasio, "How the Brain Creates the Mind," 114.

call Descartes's concern that the figures passing by his window might well be automatons. This dilemma spells itself out in greater detail as we consider sensation, whether we can know that one person experiences the same sense qualia as others. Some persons, for example, are color-blind, failing to see colors in the same way and with the same distinction as those with normal vision. When such a person testifies that he cannot distinguish red from green, one with full color perception might well ask which of the two he does see. Do all red things look green to him, or vice versa? Or does he see something that most would identify as neither red nor green? If we can ask these questions, we can go further and ask whether even among those with normal vision the experience of, say, red is the same for everyone. The problem is that although we can observe another's behavior (for instance, the color-blind subject is unable to distinguish the number on the optometrist's chart), we cannot get inside his head to see what he sees as he sees it.

This problem of our alleged blindness to other minds is doubly puzzling: first, because we do not see a way around the dilemma, and second, because the one horn is patently false. If we are closed from each others' minds, we cannot know each other as persons. If we cannot share another's consciousness, then how can our experiences of love and communion be anything but fictions? Why then do we read poetry? And perhaps most telling, we recognize that those who have no sympathy for others, who cannot know or care what others think and feel, are seriously deprived. One of the principal characteristics of autism is the inability to read others' minds in the way we all commonly do.[59] Consider a possible scene in a restaurant: a man with hands folded and downcast eyes saying something to a frowning woman at the table as she sits with her arms folded across her chest. After he shakes his head and says something, the woman slaps her napkin onto the table, picks up her purse, and leaves. A normal person can read this situation well enough to know that the man has most likely offended the woman, probably with a confession of infidelity. However, a person with autism (unless he had made special efforts to be trained) would not draw this conclusion, not for lack of cleverness, but because he

---

59. See Uta Frith, "Mind Reading and Mind Blindness," in Frith, *Autism: Explaining the Enigma* (Malden, Mass.: Blackwell, 2003), chap. 5, for an excellent account of mind-blindness, its manifestations, and the experimental basis for it.

could not recognize in the couple's behavior the telltale signs of their mental states. He could not recognize that the woman was angry or that the man was ashamed. The problem with the traditional dilemma of impenetrable minds is that it appears to assume that autism is the norm.

The problem of the privacy of consciousness arises from a faulty metaphor and not from the nature of human experience. We find the metaphor in Locke's *An Essay Concerning Human Understanding*, where he distinguishes the primary, efficacious qualities of things from their secondary qualities, which exist only as ideas in the mind.[60] The primary qualities are those by which a thing physically interacts with the human subject. The secondary qualities are ideas, which have "no similitude" to the motions that cause them. The metaphor is of a mind inside a physical case, rather like a viewer in a theater. The outside of the theater is equipped with a variety of sensors that pick up data from the environment, which data is then processed by a 'black box' that outputs the data in the form of images on the screen. How the viewer sees the world outside depends entirely on how the data is processed by the black box (which he cannot know). All that he can know is that the images seem to be reliable enough to enable him to make appropriate decisions concerning the theater. However—and here we come to the privacy issue—a viewer in another theater would have no way at all of knowing whether his images are at all like those in the first theater. I cannot know what show you are seeing if I am excluded from your theater. The conundrums we confront concerning consciousness arise from this kind of metaphor, the image of the theater of the mind.

Before showing how this metaphor falsifies the actual situation, we should note how our experience contradicts this doctrine of the radical privacy of consciousness. Even though different persons have different acuities of sensation, we can recognize that these differences exist and determine their degree. Some people with normal vision or hearing consistently fail to notice subtle variations that others with especially acute senses can pick up. Nevertheless, human beings are generally successful at communicating about what they see, hear, and feel. When the couple selects carpet for the home, trying to coordinate it with the color of the

60. John Locke, *An Essay Concerning Human Understanding*, Book II, ch. viii. Note, too, that in this paragraph I am using *idea* in Locke's empiricist sense of the term, as a mental event or image of some sort.

walls and to establish a certain atmosphere in the room, they are both talking about the same thing. Even when they disagree, they know what they
are disagreeing about. Both will shudder at the idea of laying mauve carpet
when the walls are a light olive. Those colors do not "go together." Were
consciousness truly private, then their agreement or disagreement would
be as fallacious as disagreeing that Dame Judy gave a fine performance, because one was in another theater watching another show. At a deeper level,
the falsity of the radical privacy of consciousness is evident from the creation and enjoyment of art. The artist works to share a vision of something
with others. That Robert Frost once stopped by woods on a snowy evening
(or imagined himself so doing) is a trivial biographical fact. His poem,[61]
however, conveys an image, a sense of the yearning to rest peacefully, freed
from burdensome responsibility—a sense that many of us have had, but
have not put so well into words. It is not only artists who express how we
feel, but also those in the counseling professions. Frequently it takes an expert to help the client—whether an emotionally disturbed patient, a job-
seeker, a couple facing marital discord, or a youth deciding on a career—to
see what it is he really enjoys, wants, dreams of doing, hates, fears, or wants
to escape. A similar dynamic occurs with those social and political leaders who can articulate the sense of the people, who can communicate a
vision that the people will endorse and accept as their own. Ultimately at
stake is the possibility of personal communication. Without a doubt one
entity, whether living or inanimate, can signal another concerning its state
and operations. The beaver slaps its tail on the water to warn of a predator,
and the gauge on the dashboard indicates that the fuel level is low. Human
communication, however, can and usually does accomplish more, for by
communicating a person lets another into his mind. Through communication two persons can become of one mind.

The flaw in the doctrine of radical privacy is the theater metaphor, the
notion that consciousness is "inside" the mind, while the brain, its activities and the interactions of the body with the world are all "outside." The
problem is seen, therefore, to be how to overcome the barrier between two

<hr>

61. Robert Frost, "Stopping by Woods on a Snowy Evening," in Charles M. Coffin, ed.,
The Major Poets: English and American, (New York, Burlingame: Harcourt Brace and World,
1954) 490.

consciousnesses. But this is a misunderstanding of human subjectivity. Consciousness is not a primary given, our unique or privileged access to the world. Because consciousness is the application of knowledge or cognition to act, it is not a power or condition and as such is not comparable with other consciousnesses. It makes no sense, in other words, to speak of sharing another's consciousness. Two persons in the same situation are ordinarily conscious of the same environment, seeing, hearing, and otherwise sensing the same things. To ask whether they really see the same colors in the same way (or hear the same tones, and so on) is, at bottom, a nonsensical question. The color green is not some third thing, independent of what people see. If it were, then in what would it consist? Is there, then, a standard for what is truly green? The answer to this is yes. Everyone not color-blind (a condition easily tested for) can learn to recognize it. Furthermore, artists and art critics have trained themselves to recognize subtle variations in color, and they can teach to rest of us how to see these. Where consciousnesses differ there is a difference in cognition or action. Misunderstanding or the failure of one person to appreciate another's feelings or experience does not arise from the opacity of personal consciousness or from a fundamental incommunicability of feeling, but from a lack of knowledge or difference in values. To be sure, there are experiences that are very hard to appreciate if one has not experienced them himself, experiences such as the sudden death of one's child or suffering third-degree burns over most of one's body. Even in such cases, though, it is not the case that such experiences are fundamentally private, but that they are extreme in their intensity and (fortunately) not widely shared. This is why support groups are important. Sufferers of a common pain know what others are talking about.

This is not to deny that there is anything irreducibly unique about one person's experience in relation to another's. This uniqueness results, however, not from a privileged status of consciousness, but from one's existence as a singular being in the world. Each human person has a distinctive history, with different interactions with others and experiences of the world. In using general expressions, one relates them to particulars of his own experience by means of ideas. Only Julius Caesar can know *exactly* what it is like to be Julius Caesar deciding to cross the Rubicon with an army ready for battle. But what does this mean? It may be that as a child he had the chance to take a bold (for a child) step and held back (or took it). Perhaps before the campaign his wife had given him a look he knew well and told him, "Don't go wobbly on me, Julius." Because we do not know all the facts of Julius Caesar's biography, we cannot access his whole life in the way he can, and in this respect, we cannot know fully how he experienced the Rubicon event. This does not mean, however, that we cannot gain a fuller understanding of it. It may well happen that the diary of a childhood playmate will surface, in which we will read about the older boys' cruel ridicule of little Julius when he backed away from a dare. Such discoveries happen frequently, and historians delight in using them to fill in the gaps of the historical record. On the other hand, the very fact that "crossing the Rubicon" has made it into our language as a common metaphor shows that we can share Caesar's experience. Everyone who has made an irrevocable decision whose consequences will be decisively good or bad knows more or less exactly what Caesar experienced there at the Rubicon. Indeed, one need not even have had a comparable experience to enter somewhat into Caesar's experience. Through imaginative reconstruction and comparison, one can enter significantly into another's experience. If Mozart creates the music, one need not be an eighteenth-century noblewoman to sympathize with Countess Almaviva's regret for the loss of past happiness: "Where are the lovely moments of sweetness and pleasure?"[62] The uniqueness of one person's experiences, in short, results not from an impenetrable privacy of consciousness, but from the unique vantage point that each person has with respect to his own biography.

It is ultimately one's concern for the good in his life that makes consciousness so personal. Caesar's crossing of the Rubicon had a significance for him that it could have for no one else. With that act, he put his entire future, his life itself in the balance. He staked everything he had on that choice. Even if others face similarly grave consequences as they cross their own Rubicons, for Caesar the act had a personal and incommunicable aspect: for Julius Caesar, this was something "that concerns *me*." A young man in love hates the notion that others have experienced the same thrill and enchantment he does, not because the experience is incomparable, but because *this* falling-in-love is *his,* changing his life. What is unique

62. Wolfgang Amadeus Mozart, "Dove sono" *Le Nozze di Figaro,* Act 2, Scene 2.

and deeply personal is not the content of one's consciousness but rather his life itself, in which he has a deep and ongoing interest. The theatergoer or Shakespeare himself may enter into the mind of the Moor, but neither has actually to face having brutally humiliated and then murdered a loving wife. What is uniquely Othello's is that by his own acts he irrevocably changed his life and all in it for the worse.

The sense of one's own consciousness as private has its roots not in an alleged epistemological privilege or certainty, but in the fact that consciousness itself reflects the subjectivity of the person. In his audiences on the theology of the body,[63] Pope John Paul II analyzes the "solitude" of Adam before the creation of Eve and in doing so relates it to consciousness. John Paul does not find in the solitude a simple lonesomeness, a desire to have someone to talk with, but a fundamental and original anthropological condition. In the Genesis account, Yahweh-God brings to the man all the animals, which the man then names. In so doing, however, he finds none suitable as a companion. John Paul comments, "By means of this test, man becomes aware of his own superiority, that is, he cannot be considered on the same footing as any other species of living beings on the earth."[64] The man is able to name the animals, to fit them into the common genus with himself, but in doing so recognizes that he is different. "For created man finds himself . . . in search of his own entity; it could be said: in search of the definition of himself. . . . The fact that man 'is alone' in the midst of the visible world and, in particular, among living beings, has a negative significance in this search, since it expresses what he 'is not.'"[65] He discovers himself as a knower and—implicitly—defines himself as Aristotle would, as *zoon noetikon,* rational animal. Through his body, the man is a part of the animal world, and yet it is precisely that body which makes him "alone." He is made for relationship with the Creator and—a point that John Paul's analysis is leading up to—with the other, a relation that involves his subjectivity. "The original meaning of man's solitude is based on experience of the existence obtained from the Creator. This human existence is characterized precisely by subjectivity, which includes also the meaning of the

---

63. John Paul II [Karol Wojtyła], *The Theology of the Body: Human Love in the Divine Plan* (Boston: Pauline Books and Media, 1997).

64. Ibid., 36.

65. Ibid., 36–37.

body."[66] Therefore the significance of that first encounter with Eve is that he recognizes another like himself, a personal self: "This one at last is bone of my bones and flesh of my flesh" (Genesis 2:23 RSV). Were Adam simply another animal, not endowed with the capacity for knowing the truth and discerning the good, or were he purely spiritual, he would not experience this solitude. As an embodied subjectivity, he is linked to but also distant from the other bodies around him. In his subjectivity, the human being can always question the world: "Yes, but is it true? Is that really good?"

Quantitative input, but qualitative experience

What is usually the most mysterious aspect of consciousness, especially for the materialist, is its richness, its capacity for color and emotion. Francis Crick, co-discoverer of DNA and a materialist, challenges scientists and philosophers to address the issue scientifically: "The Astonishing Hypothesis is that 'You,' your joys and your sorrows, your memories and your ambitions, your sense of personal identity and free will, are in fact nothing more than the behavior of a vast assembly of nerve cells and their associated molecules."[67] Concerning the subjectivity of consciousness, he admits, "What may prove difficult or impossible to establish is the details of the subjective nature of consciousness, since this may depend on the exact symbolism employed by each conscious organism. This symbolism may be impossible to convey to another organism in a direct manner until and unless we can hook two brains together in a sufficiently precise and detailed way."[68] For Crick the issue of personal experience, of subjectivity reduces entirely to the issue of how the brain and nervous system are wired. But this does not seem to solve David Chalmers' "hard problem": How do physical processes in the brain give rise to subjective experience?[69] Searle writes: "These variable rates of neuron firing in different neuronal circuits and different local conditions in the brain produce all of the variety of our mental life. The smell of a rose, the experience of the blue of the sky, the taste of onions, the thought of a mathematical formula:

66. Ibid., 41.
67. Francis Crick, *The Astonishing Hypothesis*, 3.
68. Ibid., 252.
69. See note 27 above.

all of these are produced by variable rates of neuron firing"[70] So, how can a purely physical system experience things? The robot that can roll about the room, backing off when it bumps into something, does not experience pain or surprise when it hits a chair or is attacked by the cat. When NBC preempted the final minutes of an exciting football game to show a children's movie, fans were frustrated and angry, but their television sets, which received and processed the same information as the human viewers, experienced nothing. Every personal computer user knows that even the most advanced machine lacks good judgment and a desire to get the job done. On a commonsense level, it seems clear that there is a significant difference between the conscious human being (and indeed the animal) and the machine. Some respond that the processing of data in the human brain is not yet well enough understood, that an account that comes to grips with the brain's remarkable complexity will resolve these problems without recourse to nonmaterial factors. There is a simpler and more realistic way through the problem.

If consciousness is neither a state nor a power, but is the application of cognition to act, then it is in these terms that we must account for the subjectively satisfying, the uncanny, and the personal aspects of our experience. We begin by analyzing perception. From a materialist point of view, the function of perception is clear; we perceive in order to meet our survival needs and avoid harm. Refined powers of perception enable the human organism to move about the environment more successfully as it searches for food and avoids its enemies. However, if this were truly the primary function of perception, then it would be hard to understand why some perceptual experiences are pleasant and others not. Human beings appreciate the beauty of what they see and hear in a way that even animals do not. For example, it makes no difference to the dog whether its master's voice is pleasant and lilting, or harsh and grating. What matters is that it is the *master's* voice. Animals can live equally comfortably in attractive or unattractive surroundings. What the human sees as clutter, the cat may see as hiding places. Animals are thoroughly pragmatic and not aesthetic. Their senses serve only their survival and continuation of the species. Because the purpose of human perception is to image a world, its sensitivity

70. Searle, *Minds, Brains, and Science*, 9.

is perforce different from animal sensitivity. Unbound by the requirement that it discriminate only what is vital to self, human perception tends to discriminate whatever it can about the object. Human perception is, in this respect, more objective than animal perception. To be able to do this, however, human perception must be free of the preordained patterns by which the animal perceives, and analyze its perceptions in terms of general ideas.

Because perception and experience in general are governed by ideas, they have an aesthetic aspect. Aquinas argues that the intellect's motivation, its fundamental appetite is wonder: "and this desire (namely, to know the essence of the thing) is one of wonder and causes inquiry."[71] Perception serves this desire by creating images of the world, of reality. The ideas by which the world is to be understood are not written into the perceiving mind as part of its nature or essence. Rather the perceiving mind attempts to discern ideas within the structure of its experience. To the extent that the experience resists subsumption under general ideas, there is puzzlement and discomfort. The intelligent perceiver is spurred to make sense of the image. When, on the other hand, the idea is discerned, the perceiver experiences satisfaction, a sense of complacency and admiration. Recall our earlier characterization: *Beauty is the being grasped as a whole according to a single idea.* One looks at the billboard, power lines, and gaudy fast food restaurants along the urban "strip" and feels a twinge of annoyance at its chaotic ugliness, or he glances out the window and notes with pleasure the pattern of color in the garden. The reason is that the human person, even casually looking at or listening to something, is intellectually engaged with it, is interpreting it. The details, that is, stimuli that may not originally be presented as part of the expected image, become important for the additional light they shed on the image, the perceptual interpretation. In principle, every perceptual detail is important. The field of perception, as a project to be interpreted is, *ipso facto,* a matter of concern, of interest to the human subject. Simply as the object of perception, it is full of opportunities for wonder and admiration.

Precisely because the human subject is rational and therefore rationally engaged with the world, his experience is emotional. The good is attrac-

71. Aquinas, *Summa Theologiae,* Ia, IIae, q. 3, a. 8. For his part, Aquinas refers to Aristotle's *Metaphysics,* I, ii 982b 12.

tive and draws one to it; it is what he *wants*. To value something is to invest oneself in it, by striving for it and organizing one's activities around it. If the failure to attain these values is frustrating, joy and satisfaction accompany success. The realization of a value is to integrate one's life (or an aspect of it) according to an idea or a principle, and in doing so one's own life becomes admirable—rather as a finished work or an artistic piece is admirable—and he experiences this as a satisfaction or, if the value be sufficiently important, as a joy. This is particularly clear from the phenomena of falling in love and courtship. With animals the matter of sexual selection is fairly straightforward. During mating season, the males compete for the females by displays and fighting, and the female mates with the one that is most promising.[72] Much of this certainly survives with human beings; one need only watch adolescent boys showing off in front of the girls. The human response, however, is much more complex than that of the animals, because it is not simply biological or instinctive. It is rational and therefore emotional. John Paul II analyzes this dynamic in his discussion of the first encounter of Adam and Eve, which was for Adam more than the discovery of a mating partner. John Paul makes the point that the elements of this biblical narrative are "always at the root of every human experience."[73] The animal response in the situation would be simply to mate until Eve conceived. The human being, like the animal, has a natural vector of aspiration built into the reproductive system, which results in an innate desire to mate. However, the object of that desire can be known as more than just a mating partner. Adam rejoiced in Eve, according to John Paul's analysis, because he found in her another rational being with whom he could be an equal partner. Thus the significance of nakedness and shame. The human feels shame or embarrassment before the other, not because the naked body is somehow evil or lascivious, but because the other person can refuse to accept one as a person. To be clothed is to be protected. Therefore the human sexual relationship involves far more than

---

72. This is somewhat simplified. Among the higher primates females may sneak off to mate with a male other than the alpha, apparently to create a protective uncertainty about the true paternity of their offspring. Should the alpha be displaced, she does not want her young ones killed. See Craig Stanford, *Significant Others*, chap. 4, "The Handmaid's Tale," especially 72–73. Notice, however, that the female's strategy is to protect her own offspring.

73. John Paul II [Karol Wojtyła], *The Theology of the Body*, 51.

sex. It engages one's sense of self and self-worth, a desire for communion with another person, a desire for meaning, which true love is hoped to give. One who has fallen in love tends to see the beloved at the center of his life, as a kind of organizing principle around which other elements of his life will find their proper places. This vision, which is admittedly inchoate, based as it is around someone much admired and sensually desired, is itself beautiful for its promise of order and harmony. For the young person in love, it is also very precarious and not at all certain of realization. Here we find that the straightforward responses that characterize animal life in the attainment of well-defined animal goals become complicated by the rational structure of human nature. The lion tries to mate with the lioness; if he fails, he goes in search of another lioness. The young lover, however, sees a vision of his entire life and the possibility of genuine personal acceptance by and communion with one who is beautiful and admirable, a vision and possibility that are not yet realized and may not be.

We may also consider the negative example of confronting danger. The beasts can seem to be remarkably sanguine about the danger of death. When the predator stalks the herd, the antelopes become skittish and alert, eventually running off. Yet, when the leopard has made her kill, or perhaps slunk off unsuccessful and hungry, the remainder of the herd get on with their lives. The trauma of being hunted leaves no apparent effect on them. A human being threatened with death will tremble for days—months—afterwards, suffering sleeplessness, anxiety, and stress over the realization of "what could have happened." When the human person encounters an apparent danger, his experience is similar, but not identical to the endangered animal's. The instinct that would lead the animal to avoid the danger or run away survives in him, but it does not govern. Unlike the animal, the human being can ask, "What is this? Is it truly a danger?" The animal instinct to flee is an innate habit, like breathing or seeking the breast. Should it be allowed immediately to govern his acts, the threatened person would flee, and in doing so, he would not be immediately conscious of fear. (Lest this seem unreal, consider the common experience of those in emergency situations that demand immediate response, such as a wartime ambush, automobile accidents, and the like. Those who take the most immediate and vigorous action will often testify that they felt no fear during the emergency, but only afterwards, when the gravity of the situation hit home.)

The endangered human being experiences fear precisely because he does not run away. Fear is, as it were, his animal nature's protest that it is time to run. It is the persistence of the innate habit to flee danger making itself evident.

We may summarize our remarks on the colorfulness of human consciousness more systematically as follows:

- Since each habit is ordered to some value or desired good, the failure of an act according to the habit represents a failure to achieve this value and this is experienced as an evil. Were it not so experienced, the realization of one's values would be matter of indifference, which is plainly false. Success is, of course, experienced as satisfying and a good.

- Each habit, whether innate or acquired, represents a kind of behavioral law, compliance with which results in pleasure or satisfaction and disobedience to which causes discomfort, anxiety, or pain.

- The habits of imaging and reasoning have their own finality, coherence and truth, respectively, the desire for which is wonder and the attainment of which is admiration. This makes the entire perceptual world and, indeed, all reality of interest to the human being, for besides its usefulness for survival and continuation of the human species, it is a source of ideas and understanding.

Understood properly, the subjectivity of human consciousness is not mysterious. The mystery arises when we conceive of the interaction of the human being with his environment in purely material terms, as the behavior of a biological machine within its environmental constraints. As Searle puts it, "How could this grey and white gook inside my skull be conscious?"[74] We cannot so conceive the human being. Rather than such a machine, he is a rational being, that is, one whose habits are guided and formed by the power to reason and understand.

---

74. Searle, *Minds, Brains, and Science*, 15.

UNDERSTANDING, BELIEF, AND PERSONALITY

The existence of a thing consists in its regular behavior. A human being's regular behavior is constituted by his habits, that is, by his beliefs,
which are formed by his understanding. The existence and, consequently,
the essence of a human person therefore depend not only on what is innate or specific, but on that person's individual habits. This brings us to the
heart of the question concerning a human nature. If we ask *what* Socrates,
Teresa of Ávila, Napoleon, and Madame Curie are, the answer is "human
being." They are all the same kind of thing, sharing a common essence,
classically defined as "rational animal." In speaking of human beings, however, we may ask not only *what* but also *who* they are. Socrates and Madame Curie both required food and walked about on two feet. Teresa and
Napoleon both concerned themselves with questions about the weather,
when to expect rain and how best to prepare for storms. All four communicated with colleagues, friends, foes, and those they encountered incidentally. In these things, they manifestly shared a common humanity.
On the other hand, their respective understandings of the truth about the
good distinguish them dramatically from each other and from their fellows. Socrates "busied himself about moral matters"[75] and neglected natural science, while Madame Curie devoted herself to understanding radio-
activity. The Saint from Ávila believed that all things—most especially her
own self—must be subject to the will of God; the French Emperor believed
that all Europe must be subject to his own will. In a sense, the differences
among these four persons are greater than the differences between, say, a
cow and a horse. Each of these persons—and, indeed, each person who
has ever lived—represents an interpretation of the world according to the
truth as understood, and therefore represents an interpretation of the lives
of others in the world. According to the legend, Napoleon could reject a
man for being "unlucky," but Saint Teresa believed that "patience gains all
things."[76] Each interpreted those around him differently.

We may say then that one's understanding of the truth of the world, of

75. Aristotle, *Metaphysics,* I Ch. vi.
76. Teresa of Avila, "Bookmark of St. Teresa," in *Selected Writings of St. Teresa of Avila,*
ed. Mons. William J. Doheny, C.S.C., (United States of America: William J. Doheny, C.S.C.,
J.U.D., 1950). Line from the prayer found in St. Teresa's breviary after her death.

others, and of the good constitutes the essence of one's personality, one's personal character.[77] One is born a human being but becomes someone, the person he is.[78] His "what" is given at birth; his "who" is formed by his beliefs and habits.

CONSCIOUSNESS, VALUES, AND THE SELF

With the disengagement of the thinking mind from the agent in the world there has been lost the sense of the self. Self seems to have to do with the mental, the conscious, but it is not clear how this is to be integrated with the physical. Descartes simply identified his self with the contents of his consciousness, without questioning carefully how this thinking substance should be related to the material being that was born of Mme. Descartes in 1596, was educated by the Jesuits in La Flèche, and so on. Locke saw the problem more acutely. If personal identity is rooted in one's consciousness, then once consciousness is lost—even in sleep—what becomes of personal identity?[79] We resist identifying ourselves simply with the organic body, but it is the only aspect of the human person that seems to endure reliably through time. Memories change and, as the phenomenon of Alzheimer's disease manifests, can be lost completely while the person is still alive. In common speech we say things like, "he's still there, but it's not him anymore." Or when the perpetrator of the crime a quarter-century ago is finally caught, living the exemplary life as a good citizen, she is still held accountable, her changed values and attitudes notwithstanding. Even if she has become "a new person," the law regards her as the same person. What, then, constitutes the self?

If the mind is a sign, as we showed at the end of chapter 4, and this sign is the person one becomes, then it is reasonable to identify this "sign" with the self. The relationship between values and consciousness sheds further

77. Generally by *personality* we mean the way one presents himself to others and the world as a whole. By *character* we mean the abiding habits that govern his activities and determine his goals. In this way, one may have a pleasant, engaging personality that masks a deeply pessimistic personal character. We may say in general that the terms *personality* and *personal character* refer to different levels of the same reality, the "who" that a person is.

78. Wojtyła, *The Acting Person*, 98 ff.

79. John Locke, *An Essay Concerning Human Understanding*, Book II, chap. I, §§11–12.

light on what this self is. As a sign, the human person ought to be logically consistent. To the extent that any sign fails to be logically consistent, it is to that extent incoherent—meaningless. It follows therefore that insofar as a human person is inconsistent, his life is incoherent and, indeed, meaningless. Where one's life is marked by contradiction his life lacks meaning. But is it not also true that a life dedicated primarily to logical consistency might well be pedantic, devoid of the deepest meaning? "Do I contradict myself? Very well then I contradict myself, (I am large, I contain multitudes)." Whitman was, evidently, not to be constrained by syllogisms and genus-species definitions. We note a certain hierarchical structure among beliefs, not in terms of relationships of direct implication but in virtue of relative importance. A man may be humble and modest, professing vanity to be a vice; yet, he takes care to comb his thinning hair over the growing bald spot. Although his friends may be mildly amused at his sensitivity, they judge this inconsistency to be of no real consequence. Not so, however, is Criseyde's betrayal of her promises to Troilus in Chaucer's poem. Her alliance with Diomede, after having given her word and her body to Troilus, reveals her as faithless and opportunistic, as one who takes her most solemn professions lightly. We take this to be a much more serious contradiction than a middle-aged man's comb-over. Values govern behavior, and because they are hierarchical, some govern broader areas of one's life. The practical dialectic forces choices of values and in doing so brings one's fundamental values to awareness. Criseyde pledged herself and her love to Troilus alone and lived according to that pledge for a time. A conflict arose among her values, however, when her father bargained for her deliverance from doomed Troy into the hands of the conquering Greeks. With the Greeks she gave herself to a man less noble and less attractive than Troilus, but who could offer this: that she would be safe and well. Through the conflicts and events of her life, Criseyde revealed herself ultimately as faithful only to herself and her own welfare. It is worthwhile contrasting Criseyde's behavior with Sophocles' Antigone, who faithfully served her blind father Oedipus until his death and then forsook the comfortable life of a queen and, indeed, life itself to bury her brother. As Criseyde's life is characterized by shrewd self-interest, Antigone's is defined by piety toward her family and the gods. The self is revealed as these more fundamental governing values are revealed.

What, then, determines the choice? Here it is tempting to delve beneath the rational structure into a pre-rational or materialistic explanation, to find the cause that impelled the choice of one value over another. Othello was insecure in his status as a black man married to the pearl of white society. Captain Ahab was blinded by rage at the white whale's mutilation of his body. To be sure, insult to the body, family and social factors, upbringing, and one's treatment by others can significantly affect a person's dispositions to act. Every day of his life, Ahab's stump reminds him directly of his first encounter with Moby Dick. However, it is no more possible to assign such factors a determining role than it is to deny the reality of suicide because every system in the body is ordered toward life. As a reasoning being, Othello could have recognized that an ambitious man passed over for promotion may not be the most reliable informant and faithful friend. Ahab knew better than most landlubbers that whales were ordinary, if dangerous, beasts and not endowed with malevolent wills. The body and its orientations, the crush of events, a person's history and relationships can all dispose him to act in different ways. If one of these could be decisive, however, we would then know the causal key to human life, the determinant of human behavior. As rational beings, we can conceive of alternative goods and evils to those already present to sense and imagination. More to the point, we can elect which good to pursue of those offered to us, and by such election realize what we desire most. Here Aristotle's dictum that choice is always of the means and not of the end[80] comes into play. Underlying our acts is a vision of the highest good, a vision that may lie inchoate in the heart and remain unexpressed by the mind, but which guides our acts and is developed by them. The free choice of the act takes place not in a vacuum, but in the context of an inner criterion, this vision of or attraction to some overarching good. In this context, one may even feel compelled. Jeremiah complains to God:

> O Lord, thou hast deceived me, and I was deceived; Thou art stronger than I, and thou hast prevailed. . . .
> If I say, "I will not mention him, or speak any more in his name," there is in my heart as it were a burning fire shut up in my bones, and I am weary with holding it in, and I cannot. (Jeremiah 20:7, 9 RSV)

80. Aristotle, *Nicomachean Ethics*, III, 3.

Jeremiah is free. Like Elijah, he can run off into the wilderness, or he can take to the sea like Jonah. Yet, even though nothing physical compels him, he continues to prophesy precisely because of his relationship with God. He has let the vision of God's goodness into his life and he cannot turn from it, even though it interferes with other goods that he desires (such as the esteem of his fellow Israelites). By contrast, the decent and intellectual Raskolnikov[81] conceives a plan to murder and rob the pawnbroker woman to benefit the suffering masses, but when he comes to act, his cool rationality almost completely deserts him. He murders from intellectual choice alone and botches the job rather badly, killing an innocent simpleton in the process. Not a true murderer or zealous revolutionary, he forces himself by sheer willpower and in doing so does violence to himself. In principle, he is free and exercises that freedom, but this exercise was not elicited by his love for some good to which he was drawn. We must note that this restraint of freedom is not determinism. Indeed, as the expression of a freely adopted love, it is the basis of freedom. For one, that love may have degenerated to self-pampering, for another it may be for himself as a god, and for a third it may be for the Creator. As one chooses the means to realize the good, his conception of the good is more clearly recognized and developed intellectually. But the governing factor is the good desired.

The self is what has chosen to form itself by the hypothesis represented by concrete acts. Existentially, the living hypothesis is a leap toward the good that is discerned, even if only vaguely. As intellectually determined, this hypothesis is to be embraced reasonably; one is morally bound to obey the principles of rational inference. Because this hypothesis—this value—is general, one has determined himself universally, that is, in his relationship toward the whole of reality. Let us note that precisely here appears the danger of relativizing values, for no one regards himself as an evil. Therefore, it is very difficult to recognize as evil the governing values of one's life, along with the decisive choice that established them. Furthermore, this choice of values is not always or necessarily explicit. Indeed, one may very well remain blind to his own fundamental values. We may suspect, for example, that Criseyde continued to think of herself as a noble and devoted Trojan woman, but one who had been forced to make some regrettable choices

81. In Fyodor Dostoevsky's *Crime and Punishment.*

during war. The implications of this fly in the face of what seems obvious, especially to a personalist philosopher, because we deny that the self is given in consciousness. The "contents of consciousness" are certainly relevant to one's sense of who he is, as is his memory of what he experienced, but these are not his self. The self is defined by the relationship one establishes with the good.

Because it is oriented to the future, the self is real but not fully determined. The structure of the self is rational, indeed (as we have shown) syllogistic, and its "engine" is the good as known and desired. This entails that the human self—the human person—cannot be reduced to a material entity whose behavior is (in principle at least) explicable by physical laws. Rather the human being is also spiritual, in the sense explained in chapter 3. The current chapter has addressed the question of the interrelation between the physical and the spiritual in human action. Our task now is to consider the ontological basis for this twofold character of the human person, that he is both material and spiritual. Our thesis is that this basis is the soul.

PART FOUR METAPHYSICAL

CONCLUSIONS

CHAPTER 6

Reality and Nature of the Soul

Having characterized the material and the spiritual and how they interrelate, we turn now to the question of the root of human rationality, of this material being's spiritual characteristics. If the human being cannot be reduced to a material structure alone but responds in love for the good experienced as beautiful, then he is also a spiritual being and this spiritual character requires an account. Other beings, such as machines and animals, do not evidence this spiritual character we find in human beings. Therefore we turn our attention to determining that factor in virtue of which the material being that is human is also spiritual.

It is common to speak of human beings as constituted of body and soul, as though made of two different parts, the animal body and its inhabiting and governing spirit—the body being what moves about the world and is seen by others, while the soul is inside containing the most important parts of the personality. Under the common conception, the soul is a kind of ghostly, ethereal entity, in a way similar to the body, but not constrained by physical barriers and laws. Upon one's death, this soul leaves and passes consciously into another world. Some believe that angels are the souls of good dead persons (for instance, Clarence in the movie *It's a Wonderful Life*). This common, "man-on-the-street" conception has parallels in the philosophical literature. Plato makes the soul an independent entity, so much so that it is ultimately not clear why it should be united to the body at all, and his myths describe it as traveling about the realms of the dead.[1] Bonaventure argued that the soul was a composite of form and a kind of spiritual matter.[2] Later, Descartes's conception of the thinking substance in association with the extended substance was characterized as the "ghost in the machine." What is significant about such notions is the conceptual image they suggest, a suggestion made explicit by Bonaventure, treating the soul as a peculiar kind of material entity formed of a kind of spiritual stuff that passes through walls and which can survive outside the physical body.

If the human soul is such an entity, then its relationship with the physical world and the body it animates is indeed problematic. We understand how the man in the gorilla suit makes the "gorilla" move, but how does the soul inside the body make it move? How does it fire the neurons in the brain or communicate feeling to the fingers? How can it, as something with neither matter nor physical energy, do the work of moving the body without thereby violating the fundamental principle of conservation of mass-energy?[3] If this were the only possible account of the human soul, then the task of accounting for its reality and of the spiritual component of human nature would indeed be difficult, perhaps impossible. It is not necessary, however, to embrace the ghost model. Indeed, the notion of a kind of spiritual entity consisting of ethereal matter does not of itself account for the existence and behavior of mind, of reason, of consciousness. Instead, it transfers the same questions into a new kind of material entity constituted of a different kind of matter—but matter nonetheless.

MATERIALITY AND MATERIALISM

Chapter 2 of this work identified materiality with reactivity. More significant, however, is that this reactivity is discovered originally through

1. Plato, *The Republic,* Book X; Plato, *The Phaedo* 107a–115a.

2. Bonaventura, *In 2dum Librum Sententiarum Magistri Petri Lombardi* (Ad Claras Aquas, Quaracchi: Ex Typographia Collegii S. Bonaventurae, 1882–1902), dist. 18, Art. 2, q. 1: "intellectus non dependet a corpore, igitur ab eo non potest individuari; . . . non tamen ejus individuatio est a corpore, sed a propriis principiis, *material scilicet et forma sua,* quas in se habet, sicut in se subsistit . . ." [emphasis added]

3. Daniel Dennett, *Consciousness Explained,* 33 ff.

bodily experience. Ultimately we know that matter is real because of the resistance of things to our wills, because we must exert an effort to get from here to there and to change ourselves and what lies around us. We know and encounter the world and, necessarily, ourselves as material. Materiality, however, does not of itself determine a thing to any specific kind of behavior. Furthermore, the notion of materiality does not necessarily entail the scientific-philosophical doctrine of materialism, which holds that every real thing is material and strictly governed by invariant laws (habits), which ultimately admit of mathematical expression; therefore the behavior of every existing thing can in principle be fully and adequately explained in terms of those laws. We recall Armstrong's statement of the materialist position: "It seems increasingly likely that biology is completely reducible to chemistry which is, in its turn, completely reducible to physics. That is to say, it seems increasingly likely that all chemical and biological happenings are explicable in principle as particular applications of the laws of physics that govern nonchemical and nonbiological phenomena."[4] When we turn to human nature, we face Searle's problem: "We think of ourselves as *conscious, free, mindful, rational* agents in a world that science tells us consists entirely of mindless, meaningless physical particles."[5] In actuality, such materialism is reductionist, reducing the behavior of the complex to the behaviors of its constituent parts. Therefore the behavior of the animal or the human being is strictly determined. Such a reductionism, however, is not required by the materiality of things or by the relatively determinate natures of very small material things (such as atoms and molecules). Furthermore, although we find no proof of strict determinism in large, complex natural things such as animals, we find nevertheless that we are able to understand their behaviors remarkably well.[6]

4. D. M. Armstrong, op. cit., 49. We ought to note that not every materialist will agree with Armstrong's formulation, in particular with his claim that all the physical sciences may be reduced to physics. Nonetheless, the general conception that the behavior of all material entities admits of description in terms of invariant laws a formulaic expression remains characteristic of materialism. We might say that the possibility of such description is essential to the definition of materialism.

5. Searle, *Minds, Brains and Science*, 13.

6. See David Braine, *The Human Person*, chap. 9, on the interpretation of animal behavior and its significance.

Freedom

A direct consequence of the arguments proposed in the preceding chapter is that human beings are free, and, indeed, these arguments presuppose a particular conception of freedom. It is neither a special kind of feeling (as Hume holds) nor a simple independence from physical laws (as Kant suggests). Rather, freedom is rooted in the capacity for self-determination,[7] in the human person's ability to form his own habits according to values he has recognized and adopted for himself. As a rational animal, whose behavior is self-determined by the logic of the practical syllogism, the human person can try to adopt any value whatsoever to govern his behavior (and thereby his existence in the world). As we look about, we see that people form their lives according to all sorts of different ideals—commercial, artistic, religious, familial, emotional. Their lives are different from those of their neighbors because of these ideals. According to our account, the ideal is not predetermined. In principle anything that can be recognized as a sufficiently general good can serve as a value by which a human being forms his life. This is the basis for human freedom.

On the other hand, because of the materiality of the body, and the dynamics of its animal structure, it has natural desires that impel the human being in certain particular directions. Inspired by the birds, Icarus desired to fly, but the exigencies of physical laws brought him ignominiously to earth. For the sake of the Kingdom of God, a young person takes a vow of celibacy. The ideal of total commitment to a religious ideal notwithstanding, the biological dynamics of the human reproductive system continue to insist on their own satisfaction. Some who have made such a vow fail to keep it, yielding eventually to nature's insistent demands. Reason's government of one's own nature seems to be limited. Hume held it to be no government at all: "Reason is, and ought only to be the slave of the passions, and can never pretend to any other office than to serve and obey them."[8] The human being has a physical nature, a subjection to physical laws, that

7. Wojtyła, *Person and Community*, "The personal structure of self-determination," especially 190, and "Participation or Alienation," 199, and Wojtyła, *The Acting Person*, Part III, chap. 3, especially 115 ff.

8. Hume, *Treatise on Human Nature*, in A. MacIntyre, ed., *Hume's Ethical Writings* (New York: Collier Books, 1965), 179.

clearly restricts—if it does not utterly negate—the freedom of the human spirit. The issue here is often mistakenly framed in terms of "willpower," as though there is a kind of mental force that the will exercises, a force which can—under some circumstances, at least—override the inclinations of nature. (This seems to be the conception that Hume was rejecting.) The dieter before the refrigerator would have, therefore, no recourse but to summon up greater willpower to resist the cheesecake within. To be sure, the experience of exercising willpower is real; it seems to be related to activities such as paying attention and working up enthusiasm. Indeed, working up one's willpower is very like giving oneself a "pep talk": "I *will* lose ten pounds. I *will* ignore the cheesecake." However, this is not a matter of engaging a separate power within, as though the mental events characterized by a feeling of resolution and firmness of commitment actually constitute a power that can resist the urges of the reproductive or digestive system—or indeed the force of gravity (for it is ultimately no more unrealistic to expect willpower to move a table than to move one's arm contrary to its natural inclination). How then can we speak meaningfully of freedom and the will? For it would seem that freedom should be really free and not bound by material conditions and that furthermore, if the physical order is to retain its integrity, the intervention of mysterious mental forces should be excluded.

We experience limitations of our freedom from the resistance of matter to change, from the establishment of a kind of law in our body. St. Paul complained that he found one law in his mind and another in his members, that by his reason he affirmed God's law but in his body he denied it (Romans 7: 14–25 RSV). Although he had adopted a belief to live by, a belief with immediate and significant behavioral consequences, he found that his body resisted his behaving according to the norms of his belief. Is Paul therefore divided? Not really. By the very act of adopting a belief, one begins to transform himself according to the value governing it. The belief, which forms the understanding, begins immediately upon acceptance to exercise its logical effect on other ideas and beliefs. The symbolic expression of beliefs, being constructed, as it were, of malleable signs, is most easily changed. This is why the easiest part of a religious conversion is learning the basic doctrines and prayers. More difficult is the task of bringing muscles and organ systems into conformity with the good that has been embraced. Similarly, the tennis tyro can learn the geography of the court, the rules of the game, and the different basic strokes in an afternoon, but he requires the entire summer to develop a reliable serve or forehand. To transform oneself requires not the action of the mental upon the physical, but the transformation of the physical according to the idea of the mental. Who intends to become a pianist must find a teacher and set up a practice schedule. One who takes a vow of celibacy needs a context, a supportive lifestyle and friends who value this vow, if he is to maintain it. And although Icarus failed, others have applied scientific understanding to the question of flight and developed airplanes.

Because human beings are free, materialism is inadequate to account for human behavior and nature. Materialists, however, object that to assert the reality of freedom begs the question, that freedom of the will is a myth, an illusion created by the mind, or a sentiment generated by the (materially determined) activity of the brain. Searle writes:

> But if libertarianism, which is the thesis of free will, were true, it appears that we would have to make some really radical changes in our beliefs about the world. In order for us to have radical freedom, it looks as if we would have to postulate that inside each of us was a self that was capable of interfering with the order of nature. . . . And there is not the slightest evidence to suppose that we should abandon physical theory in favour of such a view.[9]

Frankly, this position is unwarranted. Without denying that the brain is a complex material entity whose operations can and will be better understood with the advance of biological research, we must nevertheless deny that human behavior can be reduced to the physically determined operations of the brain and nervous system. First of all, it is unscientific to ignore the manifest evidence of human freedom, not only as each of us experiences it subjectively, but also as a principle for understanding the behavior of others. Although biology and the other sciences can advance our understanding by investigating the constituents of things, it is not reasonable to insist that the manifest properties of human beings can only, as a matter of principle, be fully explained by the eventual accounting of those constituents. The existence of free human beings ought to count as

9. Searle, *Minds, Brains and Science*, 92.

evidence that the world is not simply the blind interaction of meaningless particles.

Kant's celebrated "Third Antinomy" poses the problem quite succinctly. The *thesis* posits the causality of freedom. The *antithesis,* however, states: "There is no freedom; everything in the world takes place solely according to the laws of nature."[10] In presenting the problem, Kant characterizes freedom as an alternative form of causality.

We must, then, assume a causality through which something takes place, the cause of which is not itself determined, in accordance with necessary laws, by another cause antecedent to it, that is to say, an *absolute spontaneity* of the cause, whereby a series of appearances, which proceeds in accordance with the laws of nature, begins *of itself.* [emphasis in original][11]

This is not what we mean by freedom. The conception upon which Kant's antinomy turns is that freedom is radically discontinuous with the laws of nature, which are necessary mechanical principles governing the succession of phenomenal events; freedom is a kind of cause completely independent of nature's causal laws and, in a way, opposed to them. Such a conception seriously misconstrues human freedom. Even the freedom presented in Kant's own ethical works is not such "absolute spontaneity." If construed as a separate kind of efficient or instrumental causality operating from outside the normal physical order, such freedom does indeed conflict with physical laws. This is exactly how Searle understands human freedom: "On the one hand we are inclined to say that since nature consists of particles and their relations with each other, and since everything can be accounted for in terms of those particles and their relations, there is simply no room for freedom of the will."[12] Before presenting what freedom is, however, let us examine the evidence for human freedom and against determinism.

First Refutation of Determinism: The Argument from Experience.   The first and most evident argument against the mechanistic determinism of human behavior and for human freedom is that of human experience. We

10. Kant, *Critique of Pure Reason,* A 444–5, B 472–3.

11. Ibid. A 446, B 474, from the *thesis.*

12. Searle, *Minds, Brains and Science,* 86.

all make choices, which we experience as free, based on our wants, needs, whims, and beliefs. The experience of freedom takes the characteristic form, "I may, but I need not."[13] As such, this experience is not simply a kind of *feeling,* as Hume suggests.[14] Rather it is a matter of the confrontation of the as yet undetermined future with the awareness that what will happen depends on what I choose to do, that what I will do is not given to me in advance but depends on my decision. We experience such freedom every day, not only in moments of great moral conflict but in ordinary practical decisions as well—whether to take the country road or the freeway, to prepare barbecued chicken or casserole for dinner, to register for the logic course or contemporary British literature. In such situations the human person faces the future as something open, as not determined but rather dependent on his decision.

It is argued that such experiences of freedom are illusory, that—for instance—the cook's choice of a casserole is simply the result of a nexus of occult determining factors—"mood," craving, heredity, upbringing, influence of advertising, and so on. Although he may *feel* free, in fact what he does can be predicted by anyone cognizant of all the factors influencing him. When we consider further the effectiveness of sophisticated techniques of influence and manipulation used by advertisers, propagandists, cult leaders, and confidence men, it is not hard to extrapolate and conclude that all freedom is illusory. And indeed, there is no denying that human freedom is heavily conditioned. Most of us are probably too confident of our personal immunity to external conditioning. The addictive and life-changing effects of many drugs are well known; addicts are often called "slaves" to their addictions. Devastating injuries to the brain or a disease like Alzheimer's Syndrome can bring about radical personality change. Other factors also significantly condition our behavior. In his study of Nazi Germany, William Shirer confesses to having been shocked by his own vulnerability to Nazi propaganda:

I myself was to experience how easily one is taken in by a lying and censored press and radio in a totalitarian state. . . . It was surprising and sometimes consternating to find that notwithstanding the opportunities I had to learn the

13. Wojtyła, *The Acting Person,* 115 ff.
14. Hume, *An Inquiry Concerning Human Understanding,* 103.

facts and despite one's inherent distrust of what one had learned from Nazi sources, a steady diet over the years of falsifications and distortions made a certain impression on one's mind and often misled it.[15]

In the light of the immense power of modern propaganda and mind control techniques to strip one's apparent freedom from within,[16] it is clear that external agents do have great power to condition and even determine an individual's behavior. It is paradoxical that, although the past 250 years have seen dramatic social and political developments of the notion of freedom—one thinks of the Bill of Rights in the U.S. Constitution, the French slogan "Liberté, fraternité, égalité," the Universal Declaration Human Rights, the expansion of democratic structures throughout the world—the reality of the individual human subject's freedom has been called increasingly into question by our intellectual and cultural elites.

Nevertheless, we must reject the strong determinist premise that such factors completely and necessarily determine human behavior. Without denying the truth that addictive drugs, propaganda, biological urges, brainwashing techniques, and so on can dramatically affect human behavior, the evidence remains that the human being is capable of significant free choice. We know that some have resisted such influences as described above. Furthermore, even those who have not still exercise freedom in many areas of their lives. A hungry drug addict can still choose between a hamburger and a hoagie. Citizens of Nazi Germany chose partners to marry, selected trades and professions; their military leaders projected Allied troop movements and planned their own maneuvers accordingly. Freedom of choice appears even in the most determined situations.

The strict determinist, however, will respond that such free acts are no more free than those directly determined by the factors mentioned, that many other compelling human experiences prove to be misleading. Just as the progress of an avalanche is the result of a large number of factors—and not simply of the law of gravity—so to might be a human being's behavior. And even if the vast multiplicity of factors at work makes the avalanche's

---

15. William Shirer, *The Rise and Fall of the Third Reich* (New York: Simon& Schuster, 1960), 247–248.

16. See Robert J. Lifton, *Thought Reform and the Psychology of Totalism* (New York: W. W. Norton & Co., 1961).

behavior unpredictable, we do not ascribe freedom to it. Can it not be argued that since human behavior is arguably subject to even more factors, its unpredictability is only matter of practical limitations? It may be argued then that the only reason we believe we are free is that we are unaware of the complex manifold of physical and biological factors that actually dictate our behavior. Nevertheless, we can assert that human choices are not, in fact, strictly determined by an occult nexus of factors and adduce three lines of argument to support this.

The first argument is that, except for very low-level reflex behavior (such as blinking), there has not been found any single cause that strictly determines some well-defined form of behavior in such a way that, absent any other directly impeding factor, the effect will always follow in the same way in every subject. Human beings can and do learn to control their "instincts"—to endure great pain without flinching, to forego food even while starving, and so on. Think of the British "Beefeaters," who have trained themselves to stand rigid and unresponsive before Buckingham Palace. It is not to the point to object that the training constitutes an impeding factor. Training and preparation interpose nothing between the stimulus and the response; rather they alter the response. But the hypothesis was that there are responses strictly determined by the structure of the organism and the stimulus. Neither has scientific investigation discovered an aggregate of causes whose combined effect on a human being unfailingly produces certain behaviors. Although we know many kinds of *conditioning* factors, *determining* factors of human behavior have not been identified. No one has yet successfully constructed a context in which all or almost all human beings can be completely controlled. In other words, the existence of a causally determinative manifold of factors producing the same response in all subjects simply has not been established. Such a manifold is simply a theoretical construct. At this point, we have neither the requisite strict laws of human behavior nor the laboratory evidence to support the proposition that human behavior can be, or is, determined by external factors. To be sure, the non-existence of such an account does not of itself constitute proof that no such theory can eventually be given. However, if human behavior can be described adequately in other terms—specifically in terms of the rational faculty—it becomes hard to justify rejecting freedom in terms of an elusive materialist account that runs so counter to human experience.

The second argument is that knowledge undercuts determinism. Had Iago's wife, Emelia, pieced together her husband's scheme earlier and informed Othello, Desdemona would have been saved. Iago's insinuations would have found no effect. To know the truth about the conditioning cause is to gain freedom with respect to it. Even if most subjects do knowingly submit to a determining cause (as is the case with addictive substances), others demonstrate—by doing so—that such conditioning can be broken. And if an absolutely occult cause, that is, one that cannot be known at all, be posited, then such a cause cannot be real. If it is unknowable, it can have no experiential effects nor yield any sign of its presence, for by such effects or sign it could be known. It must be nothing.

The third and most important argument is that such a theory of occult determinants still misses the point. It is fundamental to the very notion of law to be able to predict and explain. A scientific law proves its mettle not simply in summarizing data from the past but in predicting the future, as well. Therefore, if human behavior is truly determined, then *I* should (in principle, at least) be able to predict what I shall do at some future point, *irrespective of any decision-making activity I may undertake in the meantime*. In fact, such predictive knowledge would be futile. Even if one could prove that this afternoon I must play tennis, doing so remains subject to my decision. The prediction misses the point; knowing what the scientific laws predict is no help in making up my own mind.[17] To be sure, a particular individual may express a kind of fatalism concerning his or her future behavior. "It really doesn't matter what I decide. Come Saturday night, I'm going to be drunk." "I know that I should take charge of my own life, but I know I'll go back to him. I always do." Indeed, there are those whose lives are marked by an experience of enslavement to a habit, an addiction, or a relationship, and such people despair of gaining control over some aspect of their lives. The defining word here is *despair*. Fatalist predictions are not the fruit of careful analysis of initial conditions and scientific laws. Indeed, the role of the scientifically trained professional counselor is precisely to enable the subject to overcome this fatalism and replace it with a greater sense of self-governance and autonomy.

17. Alastair MacIntyre makes a similar argument in *After Virtue* (Notre Dame, Ind.: University of Notre Dame Press, 1984), 96–96.

Characteristically in this debate over freedom and determinism, the determinist always argues from the position of the objective observer judging *after* the fact.[18] Using details from the agent's personal history and physical constitution, the observer may very well offer a plausible explanation not only of the factors that led to the act, but also show why no other act was possible. There is, in one sense, no refuting the observer who attributes an act to specific pre-existing conditions. However, the agent himself lives *before* the fact and therefore experiences his life as one filled with options, among which he can choose some and reject others. From the agent's viewpoint, the determinist's explanation is irrelevant. To put it another way, the agent may very well complain to the determinist, "You tell me what I *will* do, but I need to know what I *should* do." The agent experiences freedom, not as a separate force or emotion, but as his own responsibility for his future. It is not sufficient to call this experience an illusion, for by its very nature, the decision cannot be replaced by a theory.[19]

Second refutation of determinism: Lack of proof.   Although virtually any human being could attest to concrete experiences of freedom, this ordinary belief in one's own freedom is labeled "naive." In fact, however, it is the belief in scientific determinism that is naive. The deterministic necessity of individual human behavior is without proof. Materialist determinism consists in the reduction of the individual's behavior to that of his constituent parts. It is tantamount to denying the reality of the acting person and replacing him with a complex of simpler, interacting constituent entities. Materialist determinism is founded on the speculative application of presuppositions and not on hard evidence. From the fact that the smaller constituents of the human organism closely follow certain laws, necessitarianism extrapolates to the conclusion that the entire human being is determined in all his behavior by the totality of these laws.

18. See Wojtyła, "The Separation of Experience from the Act in Ethics," in Wojtyła, *Person and Community*, 23–44.

19. Wojtyła makes a similar point in "The Personal Structure of Self-Determination," in Wojtyła, *Person and Community*, 189–190. See also Wojtyła, *Acting Person*, chap. 2. The rejection of freedom is based on disregarding the reality of "I act" (or "A man acts") and considering only "what happens in a man." From the perspective of "I act" it is impossible to predict scientifically what I will do, because I am the dynamism of my act.

Implicit in the foundations of determinism is the premise that only a very few distinct *kinds* of things exist.[20] These are the fundamental components of reality—electrons, mesons, electromagnetic fields, and the like. What we call stars, fungi, zebras, chairs, and human beings are simply highly structured complexes of these few fundamental entities. In virtue of their differing structures, these complexes acquire certain properties of their own (a spherical mass of rubber rolls; a cube of wood does not). Thus the basis for understanding any particular kind of thing is the understanding of these constituent parts and the knowledge of their arrangement. Thus the question of the origin of life must trace back to the mechanism by which amino acids first joined to form replicating RNA or proto-RNA,[21] for once such a molecule is given, then a self-replicating structure is present and therefore life. The interactions of such molecules, along with their chance variations, would give rise to more complex life-structures and eventually to living beings.

In reality, such a reduction of complex structures to their most elementary units is irrational and contrary to the evidence. It is irrational because, while the reality of every complex kind is seen as problematic and in need of explanation, that of the primitive is regarded as foundational and therefore in need of no account. That is to say, the nature and (apparently teleological) behavior of a lion or an orchid plant is to be explained in terms of the mechanical interactions of its ultimate constituents, but the law-like, regular behavior of those fundamental constituents seem to require no account. Why do electrons always have the same charge? Why is the velocity of light *in vacuo* constant? The problem is not that we require an account for lions and orchids, but that we posit a class of beings (perhaps electrons and electromagnetic fields or perhaps something yet to be discovered) for which no account can be expected—a fundamental and foundational structure for which no explanation is required or possible. I call this kind of reductionism irrational, because it divides physical reality into two radically different kinds of being: those for which an account is possible and those which simply are what they are. In Peirce's terms, this amounts to

---

20. See David Braine, *The Human Person*, chap. 8, especially 259–263.

21. Leslie E. Orgel, "The Origin of Life on the Earth," *Scientific American* 271, no. 4 (October 1994).

"blocking the road of inquiry," decreeing that a certain question cannot be answered, that the limit of understanding has been reached. But such an understanding of the situation is no understanding at all.[22] Furthermore, science is never satisfied that it has reached the ultimate and foundational. Particle physicists persist in building more powerful and ingenious machines to tear apart the known "elementary" particles (like the electron) to find their constituents. No known thing ever actually counts as foundational.

Such reductionism is also contrary to much of the evidence. Among living things the behavior of the constituent parts is actually modified by the needs and desires—the teleology—of the organism as a whole. For example, single-celled organisms ought normally to respond to like situations in a like manner. Like stimuli trigger like responses. Therefore NK killer cells, which attack cancerous cells in the body, ought always to attack cancer cells in the same way. However, among breast cancer victims, those who become angry with the disease and resist it show a much higher level of NK-cell activity than do those who passively accept their disease.[23] Similarly, perception would seem to depend simply on the stimulation of nerve cells by light or sound waves, surface textures, and so on, and upon the subsequent transmission of electrical signals to the brain. In fact, the subject's own attitudes, interests, and orientations heavily determine perceptions, regardless of the stimulus to which the nerve endings are subjected. We all verify this when we block out even fairly strong sense impressions while devoting intense attention to some one thing. The cells of the nervous system serve the interests of the person whose system it is. Thus, much of the evidence supports the position that the organism as a whole affects the behavior of the component parts, that the behavior of the organism cannot simply be reduced to the combined behaviors of its components. But can it not be argued that this "top down" governance of constituent parts by the needs of the whole is simply a matter of our interpreting it so, that the body has mechanisms which govern the changed behavior, such as the more aggressive response of the NK killer cells? And indeed there must be some sort of physical relationship. We do not posit a

22. Peirce, *Collected Papers*, 1.135–139.

23. Sandra M. Levy, *Behavior and Cancer Life-style and Psychosocial Factors in the Initiation and Progression of Cancer* (San Francisco: Jossey-Bass, 1985).

kind of magical response of the NK cells to mental events. But that is not quite the point. The angry woman is not simply having emotional states that we identify as anger, but she has made a choice for her whole self: She is going to beat this disease. Her anger is an engagement of her whole self to overcome this deadly threat. Just as the champion athlete can focus the nervous energy that leads a lesser competitor to "choke," the woman focuses her body's resources, even those she is not aware of (the NK cells) to attain her goal. Whether to be defiant and angry or to despair and acquiesce is her choice. This choice ultimately affects how the NK killer cells behave.

Materialist determinism is a metaphysical postulate, not a conclusion demanded by the evidence. As we search for the bases of determinism, we find that they are necessarily irrational and scientifically unacceptable. The evidence itself forces us to look at the person as a whole for an adequate account of human behavior.

Third refutation of determinism: Empirical failure. The theory of the mechanistic determinism of human beings suffers from this further flaw: it has failed empirically. History provides the most dramatic and compelling evidence of mechanistic determinism's failure. The experiences of the past two hundred years—and especially of the twentieth century—provide compelling evidence that the human person cannot be regarded as a machine and the mechanism is fundamentally inadequate to account for human behavior. In this respect, we can point to two kinds of experience: the assembly line and totalitarian governments.[24] The principle of the assembly line is that the worker is a part of the machine. The advantage of any machine, be it a drill press or a machine gun, is that it can precisely repeat one operation without tiring, producing perfectly interchangeable products. The cook may select the best onion, but one 6 × 3′ bolt is as good as another. The assembly line is essentially a large machine, some of whose parts are human. Like the products they produce, assembly line workers are interchangeable. One worker may be more diligent than another or more adept at correcting minor breakdowns, but these differences are marginal with respect to the operation of the whole line. The assembly line works on the basis of an integration of men and machines functioning mechanically.

24. On this, see also Alastair MacIntyre's analysis of "managerial expertise" in MacIntyre, *After Virtue*, chap. 7, 8.

Although assembly-line manufacture has succeeded dramatically in many respects, the human cost of this form of industrialization has become notorious and not only for the financial exploitation of the workers in days past. By its very nature the assembly line gives rise to alienation. The assembly line produces uniform products, which the worker is not ordinarily able, by dint of superior skill or diligence, to improve. Conversely, so long as he functions adequately, he will not adversely affect the product quality (normally, the effect of a poor worker will be to decrease quantity). The product results from the machine, of which the worker is a part, and not from the worker's personal contribution of intelligence and skill. His job requires him to interact only incidentally with other human beings on the line. Unless he happens to work at the end of the line, he may not even see the finished product. His incentive is not the work itself, but the pay he will receive (and indirectly the threat of being discharged, should his work prove inadequate). Thus, to protect himself from the employer and *to provide himself with something that is his own*,[25] he and his fellows form a labor union. The union is the social response to, and a manifestation of, the workers' alienation. The ultimate, decisive form of this alienation occurs when more sophisticated technology replaces workers completely; this development dramatically proves that the assembly line worker is and has always been himself little more than a part of the machine he serves.

The worker's alienation runs directly counter to the mechanistic view of human nature. That is, if the human being were fundamentally a highly complex mechanism, then it would be natural for him to fit comfortably into a properly designed machine. Under the mechanistic assumption, far from being alienating, assembly-line work should be the form of labor most congenial to human beings. Even granting that the original assembly lines may have been imperfect or badly flawed, we would expect that—given the amount of expertise dedicated to improving them—workers would, on the whole, find such work more and more congenial and well-suited to them.

If the assembly line has led to alienation, totalitarianism has proved genuinely destructive. The fundamental premise of the totalitarian state

25. It is noteworthy that most unionized workers identify much more closely with the union than with the company they work for. But ought not the company really be a community of service, pursuing a common good?

is that human beings are not free, that society can successfully be organized so that each member can be given a place and fit into it smoothly. Individuals are controlled through an effective system of rewards and punishments; indeed, almost every human good is controlled—and therefore allocated—by the state, which also enjoys the power to inflict the most severe punishments. The free individual has no place in such a state; to be free and creative is deviant and subversive (or "counterrevolutionary"). Besides the system of rewards and punishments, the totalitarian state employs an extensive propaganda apparatus, including the resources of pictorial, dramatic, and monumental art—as well as cradle-to-grave indoctrination programs—to form the citizenry to fit into the whole scheme. The Soviet Union, the Third Reich, and lesser totalitarian regimes have had every opportunity to eradicate the belief in and desire for freedom among their subjects. Nevertheless, the experiment has failed. Even under the absolute control Stalin exercised over every aspect of Russian life, many people actively or quietly resisted the regime's totalitarianism. Human beings cling to the idea that their lives are and ought to be their own and not the state's. If we were not created to be free and responsible, totalitarianism in some form should be expected to succeed. Instead, men and women resent and resist it.

Without doubt, a complex set of reasons could be adduced to explain the transformations in industrial labor practices and the fall of totalitarian states. Certainly, other factors have intervened. Nevertheless, the failure of these historical efforts to subvert or circumvent human freedom constitutes a serious challenge to the theory that the human being is fundamentally determined. If this theory were true, we would expect its implementation to enjoy some convincing successes. On the contrary, the most successful economic and political systems, those that enjoy the support of those living under them and that are most experienced as beneficial, are the systems founded on personal freedom understood precisely as the self-determination of intelligent agents. Despite the advances in psychology and sophisticated techniques of manipulation, no one has been able to overcome completely the very human love of freedom, that inner sense in each human being that his life is his own and that only he enjoys the ultimate right to rule it.

THAT HUMAN BEING CANNOT BE REDUCED TO, OR EXPLAINED AS, A PURELY PHYSICAL SYSTEM

That human persons are free is undeniable. No materialist or determinist account can eliminate this reality. The issue before us now is to account for it. How can the human being transcend the physical order, how is personal freedom possible?

Truth as a nonphysical relationship

The human person is essentially related to truth—that is, a rational being. Truth is a relationship, the conformity of the understanding and the thing. The understanding is true when it represents the thing as it is in reality and false when it does not. As such, truth is a nonmaterial relationship, one which is neither dependent on nor constituted by any physical relationship. True understanding is not physically caused in the mind of the understanding person. But let us consider this more closely.

A representation can be physically related to a thing in two ways: by resemblance and causally. A scale model airplane is physically related to a real one by resemblance; a one-to-one correspondence between their respective parts exists, in virtue of which the model is an icon of the original. On the basis of this kind of relationship we are able to deceive animals, setting decoys in the water to attract ducks, using moose-calls, and otherwise presenting them with images that they will take for real. Animals can appropriate the physical image and be deceived by it, for they cannot reason to the truth. Like animals, the human being has the power to image the world through perception. In perceiving, the person appropriates the physical appearance of the thing, in such a way that he can recognize it in the future and even replicate the image (say, with a drawing or some kind of mimicry) for others. This power enables the human being to make his way about the world rather well. We navigate through busy traffic, crowded markets, and primeval forests, relying on our sight, hearing, smell, and touch. But, as philosophers from ancient times to our own have repeatedly remarked, this power to perceive is subject to error. Furthermore, perception accesses only certain aspects of things, light and sound within narrow bands of frequencies, physical surfaces above a certain minimal size, and so on. We have developed the sciences precisely to gain knowledge of properties that are not given directly to the senses. In short, the human intellect can question the truth of perception and compensate for its limitations. One can say, "I see, but is that how it really is? Is that everything to be known about this thing?"

The second way that a representation can be related to something is as caused by it, that is, as an index. The weathervane and the thermometer respectively represent wind direction and temperature by the effects that these things have on them. We use such causal relationships frequently in the training of animals. The electrified fence, the sharp jerk on the lead, and the sound of the can opener followed by food all induce animals to change their behavior. The cow "knows" not to approach the neighboring field, the dog "knows" to heel, because they have been trained by physical causes. And, to be sure, human beings acquire such knowledge, too. The warmth of the room induces the man to take off his overcoat, and hunger pangs induce him to eat. One knows what to expect from repeated experience. As with perception, however, the experience does not have the final word, but the cognitions from experience are subject to the evaluations of reason. With his whip skillfully applied, the rider can train his horse to run and jump at his command. On the other hand, wise parents learn that the application of physical sanctions can lead to different results with different children. One child may defy discipline, while another is not only chastened but crushed. The horse responds to the whip, but the child *interprets* it. For the sake of framing the principal dancers, ballerinas in the cast accept training to hold awkward stationary poses for extended periods without flinching. Soldiers push toward the enemy in the face of murderous fire and the real threat of death, because they have accepted training. In these and many similar ways, we find that the human being does not constitute a direct index of his environment. What one thinks and believes cannot be attributed simply to the effect of causal factors acting on the body.

To represent the truth as truth we use symbols, conventional signs that signify, neither in virtue of their resemblance to anything nor because of some stimulus, but in virtue of their meaning, that is, in virtue of their logical relationships with other signs and their capacity to represent classes of things. The image represents a possibility that something may be the case, that things might stand in such a way, and the index indicates that an interaction took place. Only the symbol—not the icon or the index—can state that this is how things stand in truth. Therefore, its relationship with its object necessarily transcends the physical relationships of resemblance and causality. The symbol states, in meaningful (that is, general) terms, that this is how these things actually stand. Therefore, the intelligence that formulates the symbolic representation necessarily transcends the physical order.

The pragmatist objection: Giving William James his due

The status of truth is central to my account, and one might well object that such an account is metaphysically overloaded. This was essentially William James's position in his lectures on pragmatism, in which he held that truth is utility. To believe certain things to be true is useful because they lead us successfully to attainment of our needs and wants. Truth is, for James, something dynamic: "*True ideas are those we can assimilate, validate, corroborate and verify. False ideas are those we can not. That is the practical difference it makes to us to have true ideas; that, therefore, is the meaning of truth, for it is all that truth is known-as.*"[26] James does not care and, more to the point, he believes that none of us (except a few intellectualist philosophers) cares about an ultimate correspondence between symbol and thing, about a static relationship of conformity of intellect and its object. Truth is what we need to get through our present situation and to move on in the future. If what I believe today should prove false tomorrow, it is not so important, so long as my practices based on this "truth" work out. We see in James's account a wonderful consonance with contemporary reflections on science and scientific theory. Today's theory, accepted as true, guides us to the research that will prove it false, but at the same time will establish a new theory that is closer to truth. Further, James's account harmonizes well with, and indeed can be used to undergird, the theory that human rationality is nothing other than a sophisticated survival adaptation.

The first problem with the pragmatist account, as well as any other that attempts to confine truth to the realm of direct experience, is that it does

26. William James, "Pragmatism's Conception of Truth," Lecture Six in James, *Pragmatism*, 88–89.

not correspond with what we mean by truth nor with how we deal with it. It is essential to the notion of truth—what people intend by "truth"—that the symbol represent the thing as it is. Galileo, compelled by ecclesiastical authority to place the earth static at the center of the universe, allegedly muttered, "*Eppure, si muove.*" ("And yet, it moves.") Perhaps one might find here an oblique protestation that someday the scientific community would recognize Galileo's Copernican view as the most advantageous theory, but Galileo meant that the real earth, as it actually exists, moves. Lizzie Borden lives on in legend and rhyme as a murderess, and yet beyond the myth-making, we know there was a reality—one that may well remain unknown—to which the allegations either correspond or not. In many practical matters we do settle for what works, but not every truth is of pragmatic concern. It is important that one's spouse love in truth and not in pretense. To one who, after years of living happily confident in a husband's fidelity, learns that he has another wife and family in another state, those years of happy family life have become a lie, and the memory of those happier days have no power to console. The pragmatic objection that the belief in her husband's fidelity served her well, during that time, at least, will doubtless bring a bitter self-reproach from one who now thinks herself a gullible fool. Similarly, the truth of religious doctrines is of more than pragmatic concern. (We do well to remark that although William James was eager to defend religious belief, he was careful to evacuate it of substantive content.) Whether Jesus actually rose from the dead is all-important to the Christian, who lives in the hope of one day enjoying the presence of God face to face. The truth of this belief matters. Louis Menand's comment is apt: "Pragmatism explains everything about ideas except why a person would be willing to die for one."[27]

The second and equally serious problem is that intellect is actually formed by one's understanding, that is by the logically interrelated system of beliefs one holds. Belief is a kind of habit, and therefore understanding is not just data but a forming of the thinking and acting self. One wants the truth not simply in order to be successful in his undertakings but to have one's being in accord with reality. Underlying James' pragmatism, howev-

27. Louis Menand, *The Metaphysical Club: A Story of Ideas in America* (New York: Farrar, Straus, and Giroux, 2001), 375.

er, is the assumption that the good is given otherwise than as known in truth. If the truth is the useful and the useful true,[28] we must ask about the status of the "useful," about what good it is useful for. What good should be valued and striven for? To this one needs an answer that he can hold as true. So, for example, the truths of financial management may be useful for maximizing wealth and improving the comfort of one's life, but we may ask whether a wealthy, comfortable life is to be valued highly. To answer a similar question posed by Glaucon and Thrasymachus, Socrates[29] found it necessary to determine the truth about the human soul. That is, he had to determine whether that which Glaucon assumed to be the good desirable for every human being—wealth, honor, comfort, and pleasure—corresponded with the truth about human nature. Pragmatism falls short because it presumes—without argument—that the standards of truth and good must be empirical, matters of sensible experience. What the analysis in the previous two chapters shows, however, is that the person is formed by his habits, by the values he holds to be true goods. Whether, like Mother Teresa, I choose to serve Christ in the poorest of the poor or instead to pursue pleasure and wealth, or even choose to become a philosopher rather than a mathematician, I form myself. I form my *self*. But I want this self to agree with reality (or for reality to agree with it, if I think I have the power to make it so). Otherwise my life becomes painful, frustrating, and ultimately nonsensical.

Truth's logical demands

There is a variety of ways to evaluate a proposition: for its euphony, for its rhetorical effect on others, for its conformity with the expectation of authority. To evaluate it logically, however, is to evaluate it in the light of truth. The governing values in logic are truth and falsity. And the canons of logic are nonmaterial, nonphysical. Let us consider an oral proposition: "Bruno Hauptmann murdered the Lindberg baby." Besides being subject to the physical laws governing sound and hearing, this proposition was formed in the mind of a prosecuting attorney and communicated to the

---

28. William James, *Pragmatism*, 90.
29. In Plato, *The Republic*, Book II.

members of the jury, all of whom are animal organisms with brains, nervous systems, sense organs, and powers of imagination and memory. The
statement, at the time it was uttered, was also emotionally charged. Prosecutor and jury (and the public at large) had heard testimony and seen
photographs, and, in varying degrees, all were horrified at the kidnapping
and brutal murder of a small child. In the context of the trial, however, the
jury was charged to determine whether this proposition was true or false:
"Bruno Hauptmann murdered the Lindberg baby." To this end, the prosecutor brought forward evidence concerning the ladder used for the kidnapping, the kidnapper's note (with its distinctively German spellings and
usage), eyewitness testimony concerning the ransom, and other evidence.
He then proposed this thesis to the jury: If Bruno Hauptmann committed
the crime, all these facts are accounted for, and there is no other reasonable hypothesis to explain all these facts. Therefore, the jury must determine that the proposition is true. That is, they are asked by the prosecution
to perform a public act of uttering "guilty."

In this historical case, many factors were at work on the jury. American
public opinion wanted someone to pay for the crime, and there was great
pressure to convict. It is likely that many jurors experienced psychological
pressure to bring forth the socially expected verdict. Indeed, some jurors
may well have gone into the courtroom with their minds made up, and others might have voted what they knew friends, family, and neighbors wanted. Nevertheless, they were charged under the law to decide on the basis of
the truth. The prosecutor presented them with an argument in the form of
a hypothetical explanation; the only reasonable way to account for all the
facts put forward in evidence is to recognize Hauptmann as the murderer.
This is a good form of argumentation, the only kind ordinarily available
to prosecuting attorneys, but also common among scientists. According
to this argument, the indictment against Bruno Hauptmann, thoroughly
understood, can explain all the facts in evidence, and no other reasonable
proposition can. (Another reasonable explanation would, of course, constitute "reasonable doubt.") This argument was intended to guide the future behavior of that jury, that in their deliberations they would severally
and jointly agree to state, "Bruno Hauptmann committed this kidnapping
and murder." The judge's charge to the jury was to allow rational argument
to determine their decision. We know full well, of course, that in crimi-

nal trials, especially high-profile ones, emotion, fear, and the pressures of public opinion can powerfully influence how a jury acts. We expect and believe, however, that rational argument can be and generally is decisive in most cases. We believe that reasonable persons, despite motivations of sympathy, fear, prejudice, and public opinion, are capable of the act of rendering a judgment on the basis of truth.

What is decisive for our point here is not the social-psychological question of the extent to which juries are capable of unbiased judgments, but of the relationship between premises and conclusions of arguments. The premises do not physically cause the conclusion of an argument. The statement, "The kidnapper's ladder was made of wood from the accused's attic," evokes images in the minds of its hearers. The prosecutor weaves this image with others evoked by testimony concerning ransom notes, overheard conversations, and so on, creating a narrative, or encompassing image, for the jurors. This image may well make strong emotional impact. This image does not of itself cause the decision. What causes the decision is the juror's determination that what the image represents is true. The relationship between premises and conclusion of an argument are logical, not physical. "That Socrates is mortal" follows from the premises that "Socrates is a man" and that "all men are mortal," because to deny it would be to make one term meaningless. The requirement to assert Socrates' mortality or Hauptmann's guilt arises not from the sounds of words nor from the reactions triggered by the premises but from the meanings of the terms, from the logical relationships among the propositions.

The example of the juror's decision is misleading in one way. What we have said so far suggests that the jurors have two options: to act according to logic and respond to the arguments or to act impulsively, that is, to react nonrationally to the triggers in the courtroom and broader environments. In one sense this is true, but in the broader sense, the jurors—like every other human being—respond rationally to the task laid before them by the court. The jurors are *expected* to respond to the arguments of the prosecuting and defense attorneys; they may respond to other factors, but even these factors are rational. One who "has no choice," who feels compelled by external forces, acts rationally. The practical syllogism governs *all* human behavior. Let us suppose that one juror concludes from his understanding of the evidence and his own analysis of the arguments based on it that the accused was innocent. He then realizes that he is supposed to utter the conclusion, "Not guilty." However, he knows also that the other eleven are convinced of the accused's guilt and furthermore that he will have to face a firestorm of media questioning and public hostility if he sticks to his evaluation as "not guilty." He votes "Guilty," with the rest of the jury,[30] and his opinion is indeed illogical *in relation to beliefs that he professes to hold concerning the evidence.* In relation to other beliefs and values, however, he is quite reasonable. Pressed hard by a logician, he might admit that he values his own comfortable life more than the strict rule of law and impartial justice, or he may plead that, although he is not convinced by the prosecution, others whom he judges to be cleverer are convinced, and he chooses to follow their views. That human behavior is always rational does not mean that human beings always behave according to the beliefs and arguments that they express verbally; it means that their behavior can be so represented and that it is in accord with beliefs and values.

The human person acts according to a vision of himself and his place in the overall order of things. This is evident from the fact that one can train and rehearse to control one's responses to future circumstances. Soldiers, firefighters, emergency workers all form themselves according to a vision or ideal, according to which they behave. The trainee marches, shoots, and obeys commands in Basic Training in order to conform future behaviors to those of a soldier. That is to say, the human person acts so to realize the good for himself as he envisions and understands it. The juror who succumbs to public opinion simply has chosen the evident truth that to vote a particular way will induce others to like him. His actions are directed toward a vision he has of himself, a vision that can be expressed in language and whose implications can be worked out in logical arguments and which are worked out in his actions. We could say that the human person wants an admirable life, a life formed by an ideal of beauty, and his behavior is governed by that ideal. Forming his habits in the light of the admired beauty, he conforms his life—even if he has no explicit intention of doing so—to that ideal. This is as much the case when one pursues wealth for the sake of enjoying "the finer things" as when one pursues nobility by imitat-

---

30. I should note here that this example is not, in this respect, historical. None of the Lindbergh jurors, to my knowledge, voted in bad faith for conviction. In other cases, however, this sort of dynamic was certainly at work.

ing or modeling a hero. Integrating the admired beauty into his own life, he conforms himself and, indeed, perfects himself according to the standard of goodness that the beauty in question manifests. In every case, the person has an ideal governing his life, and the relationship of that ideal to his behavior is nonphysical.

THE IMMATERIAL BASIS FOR HUMAN ACTION

Ideas as governing principles

Aristotle wrote, "the soul is in a way all existing things."[31] The account developed here, especially in chapter 4, is a kind of reflection on this saying. By intellectually grasping the essences of things according to its ideas, the reasoning human being ideally conforms himself according to the nature of that thing. The physicist puts on, as it were, the habits of physical entities, and the zoologist puts on the habits of animals. They are intellectually formed by the objects of their study. This is why a good scientist or, indeed, anyone who truly understands something knows almost instinctively what to expect of that kind of thing. The intellectual habits of the knower parallel the regular behavior of the object of his knowledge. As a consequence of this, human intelligence transcends all physical reality. It is not predetermined to understand only certain limited aspects of the physical world; whatever there is in the physical world is accessible to the inquiries of human intelligence. Whatever can be discovered can also be named, classified, and then related theoretically with other things. We are not limited in our knowledge to what can be seen or otherwise sensed nor even to what can be imagined. The discoveries especially of fundamental particles in contemporary physics carry us far beyond what can be pictured or imagined by even the most creative imagination. Nonetheless, by means of advanced mathematics, scientists characterize these entities and devise experiments concerning them. In virtue of the ideas forming his understanding, the knower internalizes the natures of things. What he understands exists, in a way, within his understanding. His understanding is, in a way, all things.

31. Aristotle, *On the Soul*, III, 8 431b 21.

This power to be "in a way all existing things" cannot be a material power, because it is ideal. Vision is a material power. The healthy eye can see only those things that reflect light of particular frequencies, and light must be available. Vision cannot transcend itself to be able to see sounds or smells—or, indeed, even to see ultraviolet light, X-rays, and radio signals. The intelligence, on the other hand, can understand anything. It can form concepts of any material thing and indeed even of immaterial things. (Whether one believes they exist or not, we have a concept of angels.) Ideas become the factors by which the person is formed as *this* person. The idea, adopted intellectually and integrated through intellectual work (from doing the exercises at the end of the chapter to the work of perfecting and developing one's proficiency in a science) and the fostering of habits in conformity with the idea, forms the person. It becomes a real factor in his life, unifying his actions, thoughts, values and beliefs according to a common principle. (We stress again that the idea is not the term that expresses it, nor is it the mental image.) The idea is the form or the basis of one's habitual behavior. Writing about Aquinas's moral theory, Dario Composta puts this point especially well: "The human subject, therefore, faced with an emergent situation, is already fortified with a strong armor of ethical principles. . . . he is not like one who has a head full of moral principles and wanders into the world to verify them, nor to test their validity or evidence."[32] One acts on the basis of already accepted ethical principles, without necessarily running a mental check, just as the scientist "naturally" follows scientific methods and protocols, and the accomplished musician uses appropriate technique and plays Mozart differently from Copland.

This ideal factor cannot be reduced a priori to a material factor or concatenation of such factors. One may, for example, account for religious beliefs in terms of an idealization of human virtues and perfections (as Hume did),[33] as a projection of the relationship with the father figure (as did Freud),[34] or as an elaborated expression, mythical or otherwise, of and response to the unknown monstrous fears that human beings have experi-

---

32. Dario Composta, "Riflessioni sull'Enciclica Veritatis Splendor," in Composta, *S. Tommaso Filosofo: Ricerche in occasione dei due centenari accademici* (Vatican City: Libreria Editrice Vaticana, 1995), 139.

33. Hume, *An Inquiry Concerning Human Understanding*, Section II.

34. Sigmund Freud, *The Future of an Illusion* (Garden City: Doubleday Anchor, 1964), III.

enced since ancient times.[35] Plausible as such ideas seem at first, they make a common error; such approaches assume that the idealization, projection, or mythology is adequately accounted for by natural forces and conditions. There is no evidence, however, that this is true. Other animals live as precariously as early humans did, but they do not evidence that peculiarly human dread of death and disintegration. The animal is watchful and flees; human beings suffer Angst, fearing a death that may be years in the future. Only humans can imagine a "fate worse than death." The adult males of several animal species kill their own offspring and compete with the males among them when they reach adulthood. Yet no lion or wolf worships a Mighty Father. Intergenerational conflict seems to be very much a normal thing in the animal world. The human idea of *god* cannot be reduced to a simple response to a complex nexus of stimuli. This idea—like every idea—is a principle of unity by which a variety of experiences can be drawn into unity. (Indeed, the Christian conception of God as Creator and End of all things draws everything into unity.) A god is an ideal or exemplar, a protector (but in his wrath also a danger), a ruler, an unpredictable power, to whom appropriate human responses must be made. In many cases these human responses may well be counter to one's physical best interests, understanding these naturalistically. Believers have sacrificed wealth, livestock, and even their own children to appease the gods. In Christianity, there are those who abstain from sexual contact and, consequently, reproduction of offspring. Christians, Jews, and Moslems all fast on occasion, even though eating is a fundamental human need. As a natural response to natural conditions, the idea of *god* is an overreaction and in some ways even counterproductive. Furthermore, not only is this idea accepted despite its questionable relationship with natural needs, but it is subjected to logical constraints. The idea of *god* has to meet logical and conceptual demands. The ancients told stories about the gods. Plato criticized the mythmakers on rational grounds, arguing on the basis of what a superior being must be like to be real and worthy of human homage.[36] In his *City of God*, Augustine is scathing in his logical dissection of Rome's pagan gods. The book's polemical edge would be lost, however, if requirements of rational-

---

35. See Walter Burkert, *Creation of the Sacred: Tracks of Biology in Early Religions* (Cambridge, London: Harvard University Press, 1996).

36. Plato, *The Republic*, Book II.

ity (conceptual clarity, logical consistency, well defined relationships with other beings, and so on) had nothing to do with the ideas of religion. The idea of *god*, one of the most powerful ideas in the formation of human life and behavior, cannot be reduced to an environmental response, to a naturalistic adaptation to a concatenation of causes. It is, rather, a principle for the formation of individual and social life, a principle that admits of analysis, comparison, and study, a principle that can be rejected or accepted or changed.

The origin of ideas in the person

It may well be objected that in real life the ideas that individuals and societies accept are conditioned by physical factors. Some very intelligent scholars have no sense for mathematics, while others find it congenial. Some persons are seriously deficient of intellectual capability, unable to understand any but the simplest ideas. A mark of a good teacher is the ability to recognize the particular talents that a student may have and to encourage the development of those. Furthermore, entire societies share dispositions toward certain ideas or families of ideas. The Japanese, like the British (who also live on small islands), have a keenly developed sense of politeness that Americans and Australians (whose countries offer vast stretches of sparsely inhabited land) do not share. Italian artistic traditions are richer than the Swedish and different from the Indian. Spanish composers tend not to write music on the grand scale, unlike their German and Italian counterparts with their symphonies and operas. If genetic, physical, environmental and cultural factors so strongly determine what ideas a person can even grasp, how can ideas be anything but physical principles?

Ideas are not physical principles, but they are principles of physical things, specifically of the operation of the thinking human being. The idea forming the human intelligence is never separated from matter, not even if it is the idea of something immaterial, such as an angel or God. The idea is that by which physical things are meaningfully related, by which one thing represents or interprets another. The *things* we are referring to here are the experiences, feelings, actions, and responses of the person's body. In virtue of one's own body, then, as well as his history, one may well have a certain affinity for some kinds of ideas and antipathy for others, because his physical nature is predisposed towards certain other natures in certain ways. We know that Mozart was especially sensitive to sound[37] and that, since his father was a court musician, Wolfgang was surrounded by music from his infancy. Mickey Mantle, the great baseball player of the 1950s, was physically gifted with strength and coordination, and his father trained him from early youth to play baseball well. My argument is that such prodigies owe their excellence not simply to their physical constitutions. Rather they need the right kinds of ideas to pull themselves together, as it were, to make sense of the world and themselves as they experience them.

Ideas and the body's characteristics.   By ideas the person governs his own body, bringing its behaviors into a unity. This body, however, has its own nature as an organic, living being. We have already noted the various dynamisms inherent in the human body—the respiratory, digestive, reproductive, and other systems. The body, as an organism, has a nature; it is subject to physical laws and has its characteristic behaviors. If you prick us we will bleed, and if we fall we will accelerate downward at the rate of 9.8 meters per second per second. If one's body is male, the pubescent flow of testosterone will incline him toward aggression and exhibition. The female will discover her maternal and "nesting" instincts as estrogen begins to flow. The man and the woman experience their bodies respectively as male and female, with the desires and potencies that masculinity and femininity bring with them. Further, each human body has its own more or less distinctive combination properties, such as height, build, state of health, sensitivity, physical strength and coordination, mental acuity, and so on. Through the body one experiences what it is possible to do. The body is that by which the person is present as an agent in the world, by which he interprets and manipulates the world. The body is also, in virtue of its limitations, an obstacle to attaining everything one wants. The requirements of the respiratory system and the limitations of the human frame prevent one from diving to the Titanic; it is necessary to build a special submarine. These various characteristics mean that the first nature to be discovered is one's own as a bodily organism. A kind of dialogue takes place between the

---

37. Milton Cross, *Encyclopedia of the Great Composers and their Music* (Garden City, NY: Doubleday, 1953), 513.

nature and the ideal interpretation. For one receives a nature but interprets and forms it according to his ideas. Through his body the person experiences materiality, space and time, and causality. The body's own nature suggests, as it were, ideas to the intelligence, for the human body, as a living organism, is already an integral whole. Its unity suggests or proposes principles of unity to the understanding.

In the light of this we may understand Aquinas's insistence that, even in the case of the human being, the form (in this case, the soul) is individuated by matter. The problem for the medieval philosophers was that if the soul can survive separation from the body in death, then how can different souls be distinguished one from another? If souls are spirits, then the only ways they can be distinguished is either by constituting different species or by being themselves composites of form and a special kind of matter, a spiritual kind.[38] Aquinas's response is that, although it is incorrect to say that the soul is individuated entirely by the body, it is a partial cause in that it pertains to this soul to be joined to this body.[39] This becomes clear if we realize that those characters by which one person becomes spiritually different from another—what he knows, loves, strives for, and molds his life according to—are defined and determined through bodily experience.

Language and communication with others.   Human persons communicate ideas to each other—and develop them for themselves—through their acts and symbolic communication. Infants learn how to understand the

38. Aquinas, *Summa Theologiae,* Ia q. 75, a. 5; *Quaestio Disputata de Anima,* downloaded from http://sophia.unav.es/alarcon/amicis/qdao0.html, articles 6–7.

39. Aquinas, *Opuscula 32: Responsio de 108 articulis ad magistrum Ioannem de Vercellis,* downloaded from http://www.unav.es/filosofia/alarcon/amicis/os4.html, 108: "Quod vero centesimo octavo ponitur, *animae individuantur per individuationem et materias corporum, quamvis ab eis separatae retineant individuationem, sicut cera in impressione sigilli,* potest et bene et male intelligi: si enim intelligatur quod animae individuentur per corpora, quasi corpora sint causa totalis individuationis animarum, falsum est; si vero intelligatur esse aliqualiter corpora causa individuationis animarum, verum est: unumquodque enim secundum quod habet esse, habet unitatem et individuationem. Sicut igitur corpus non est tota causa animae, sed anima secundum suam rationem aliquem ordinem ad corpus habet, cum de ratione animae sit, quod sit unibilis corpori, ita corpus non est tota causa individuationis huius animae; sed de ratione huius animae est quod sit unibilis huic corpori, et haec remanet in anima etiam corpore destructo." [emphasis added]

world around them from parents, brothers, and sisters. Students learn how to think about history, literature, mathematics, and science from teachers. And we all transmit ideas in our workplaces and seminar rooms, churches and living rooms. Through language and action we communicate to each other how we understand things.

The linguistic utterance is a series of signs, ordered according to ideas, that is, in logically coherent and meaningful array. In human communications, these are presented to the listener in a way that makes clear that this is indeed a communication, intended for him and in a context intelligible to him. The utterance is an artificial construct whose meaning the listener must decipher or interpret. Through this construct, the speaker communicates his understanding to the listener, transferring what he has in his mind to that of the listener. This process can be quick and clear ("Where do you want this plant?" "Just put it in that corner by the table.") or tedious and difficult. The reader of a challenging scholarly piece may have to parse sentences and look up words in the dictionary, cross-referencing similar passages to trace the author's argument. It is a matter of common experience, in other words, that the listener (or reader) must work with the utterance to determine its meaning. The utterance is a series of signs bearing meaning, conveying understanding that the listener can grasp by finding the meaning in the signs.

When philosophers reflect on the capacity of physical signs to convey meaning, we marvel at the mystery of this and try to account for the paradoxical fact that physical things can carry mental properties or entities. When we turn our attention to the way human beings of all ages and conditions behave in relation to the propositions we utter, we discover that our processes of interpretation are quite sophisticated. By examining them we can illuminate our subject significantly. In the previous paragraph we already pointed out some of the logical tools that we commonly use to clarify meaning: parsing sentences, referring to dictionaries, asking questions, and cross referencing. No sentence, no utterance bears its meaning in a vacuum, for meaning consists in the logical relationships that a symbol has with other symbols and things. Therefore, other sentences shed light on what this sentence means. (Thus in the sales meeting, an agent may ask, "But Harry, I thought you said earlier that this new feature supplements the old. Are you saying now that it replaces it?") The meaning of the sentence is clarified by how it interprets and is interpreted by other sentences. Terms explain other terms; for instance, students beginning physics hear repeatedly from their teacher that *mass* is not the same as *weight*. The communication of ideas is seldom simply a matter of conveying words alone. Most commonly, communication is accompanied by or accompanies actions relating to the communications. To teach colors and names of things to an infant, parents show, tell, and explain. Science teachers know well that to teach from the textbook alone is inadequate. If they are to grasp new ideas, students need to see classroom demonstrations and then run through experiments on their own in the laboratory. This is why it is particularly difficult completely to grasp the ideas of someone whose only presence is in writing. This present book is an Aristotelian analysis of the soul—Aristotelian because the author believes that such an explanation comes closest to reality. But what did Aristotle say about the soul's immortality? Thomas Aquinas interpreted him to argue clearly that the rational soul is immortal. Others, however, read him quite differently, arguing that the Stagirite never intended such a thesis. All we now have of Aristotle are his texts and a few testimonies by his contemporaries. We cannot pose questions of him or ask him to show us what he meant, perhaps by citing some helpful examples. As a result, it is more difficult to grasp the entirety of his ideas *as he held them*. Our understanding of how Aristotle actually thought is therefore limited. We may note that this reveals the problem with such thought experiments as the Turing Test and John Searle's "Chinese Room."[40] All that the questioner and subject have to go on in the Turing Test are symbolic representations, not interactions with each other or a common environment. The Chinese Room interacts with nothing; it does not explain what it is doing and is not aware of what its interlocutor is doing.

What makes communication possible at all is the listener's ability to use ideas, to grasp the ideas forming the speaker's utterances and to relate them to other experiences of his own. That is to say, listening (or reading) is not the passive reception of signals. Nor is it simply a kind of causal impression or training, although these have their place in learning. However, the

---

40. *The Internet Encyclopedia of Philosophy*, "The Chinese Room Argument," which further cites Searle, "Minds, Brains, and Programs," *Behavioral and Brain Sciences* 3 (1980): 417–424. Accessed from http://www.utm.edu/research/iep/c/chineser.htm#source.

learner who is trained by the drill sergeant to march in time or by the Latin teacher to identify *agricola* with *farmer* does not, by that fact alone, understand an idea. To be a soldier is to know how to conduct oneself combatively during warfare, not simply to obey direct commands promptly, and to know Latin is more than to have memorized vocabulary lists. To understand a communication requires thinking of one's own. More precisely, it demands the effort to grasp an idea, to understand the communication according to its central, organizing principles. Unlike the situation where one discerns ideas as they are in the world, one who is communicating can actually address his interlocutor to help gain understanding. He can rephrase and reinterpret the idea as he understands it, and by doing so may clarify his own as well as his interlocutor's understanding.

The principles of idea formation

Ideas govern the mind and are formed in the mind. We have attempted to indicate what are the "raw materials" of idea formation, which suggest these ideas. The question remains, however, by what principles ideas themselves are formed. What governs the development and discovery of ideas? The human intellect, unlike animal powers of cognition, is directed toward the thing as it is in itself, and not simply inasmuch as it is of use to human needs or wants. That is to say, human intelligence is directed toward knowledge of the governing principles of the thing as it is in its own being. Earlier we cited Thomas Aquinas's principle from *De Veritate* 1, 1: "*illud quod primo intellectus concipit quasi notissimum et in quo omnes conceptiones resolvit est ens.*" That which the human intelligence knows first is being, and it is into this conception that all other conceptions are resolved. That is to say, the human intellect thinks first of beings; it looks for beings to hang its thoughts onto.[41] It is of beings that it seeks predicates, and predicates express ideas. Or more precisely, predicates express how things are understood to be according to ideas. In the course of the first article in his *De Veritate,* Aquinas presents and explains the universal or transcendental predicates of being, predicates that must apply to every being inasmuch

41. See Joseph Bobik, *Aquinas on Being and Essence* (Notre Dame, IN: University of Notre Dame Press, 1965), 3–5.

as it is being.[42] These transcendental predicates guide the intellect in the discernment or grasp of ideas; they constitute, as it were, the primitive or foundational ideas, by which our rational power works.

Thing of a particular kind.   The first of these transcendental predicates is *thing* (*res*), by which is expressed the essence, or more precisely, that the thing has an essence. *Thing* is, as it were, the first term to identify a being, and constitutes the preliminary answer to the person's first question: "What is it?" In its encounter with reality, there can be no question of the mind's dismissing any being, any reality as meaningless. Everything has its nature or essence that can be known. This does not mean that every human person immediately knows the essence of every thing he encounters. One can certainly be in error, as well as in confusion. Even when one despairs of such knowledge, he knows that it is a something and, indeed, that it possesses certain properties or ways of behaving. He can identify it in broad, general terms. Every being one encounters presents itself as perceptible (and if so, by sight or hearing or touch or some combination), or perhaps intellectual or emotional. The rational power encounters it knowing that it has an essence and expecting to be able to discern that essence, to identify it by a general term governed by an idea. We might say that an idea "fits" to a *res*.

It is an oft unnoticed, but actually remarkable fact of our minds that we so confidently raise the question "What is it?" In chapter 2 we noted that the material interaction does not of itself explain what the material thing is or enable us to predict how it will behave in the future. The physical encounter itself gives us no grounds to say that the cause of the interaction or resistance is a something, that is an enduring entity with an essence. Nevertheless, the human person expects that ideas will apply to experience, that experiences can be ordered by the intellect at work in order to grasp what things are.

One: the unity of a thing.   If, as Aquinas argues, *thing* is what one can predicate positively of every being, considered in itself, *one* is the negative

---

42. See Adrian J. Reimers, "St. Thomas's Intentions at *De Veritate* 1, 1," for a more detailed account and interpretation of this deduction.

predicate, for *one* means *undivided being*. One can recognize as a being only that which is in some way *one*. The human intellect is ordered toward things as integral wholes, to find the unity in virtue of which a common predicate can be applied. The logical structure for interpreting another person's utterance is the hypothesis, which unites a series of disparate predicates under some common predicate. The same hypothetical approach is at work when students try to understand what the teacher was getting at in class and, indeed, when the infant learns to respond to the mother's words and movements as she offers the breast and encourages her child to suck. Instinctively the child sucks, but he must be taught where to turn and how to recognize the source of nourishment. Being is accessible first to the intellect precisely because it is the intellectual power that can unite the various presentations of a thing to conceive it as one thing. Similarly, the mind interpreting experiences in the real world constantly seeks unity. To ask what is the cause or the explanation is to find a unifying principle in virtue of which the experience can be explained.

We have noted several times in the course of this study that the "effect" of an idea is to bring unity to multiplicity. Conversely, where there is not unity, there is no governing or ordering idea. An episode of the television crime series *Law and Order* presents a nice example. The young violinist was found murdered and her rare and valuable violin was missing. Police rather quickly discovered that the janitor had stolen the instrument. Other clues subsequently revealed, however, that the janitor could not have killed the victim. There was not one crime that night—a killing in the course of robbery. There were two entirely unrelated crimes against the same victim on the same day. Police could not find one principle to unify all the events. However, two ideas did work. "Theft conspiracy" explained one set of facts, and "jealous lover" explained the other. So it goes in our lives and thought every day. Confronted with the multiplicity of facts, stimuli, and experiences, we human beings cast about to find what draws them together into unity. If the homeowner finds mice in his basement, might that be related to the plowing of the field nearby? Of course, not every hypothetical principle of unity is true. Think of crop circles, flashing lights, and mysterious events in Roswell. Are these unrelated, or is earth being visited by aliens? The point is simply that by seeking the unity of the beings in our experience, we discover the ideas that are the principles of unity.

Something: different from the others.   Because the being under consideration is different from other beings, Aquinas says that we call it *aliquid*, (something), for although it is undivided considered in itself, with respect to other things, it is divided from them. The intellect recognizes a being as standing (potentially, at least) in some kinds of relationships to other things that are not it. Recall that in chapter 2 we determined that a thing's behaviors are known in virtue of its relationships with other things. Indeed, the materiality of material things is discovered only in this way, and its material nature is determined according to its interactions with other things. The notion of *aliquid*, however, is broader than that of material substance. Every being is a *something*, an *aliquid*, in that it is divided or distinct from other beings. The significance of this point will become apparent when we consider Aquinas's position that the soul is "*hoc aliquid*— this something."

These first three predicates manifest the inherent realism of the human intellect. That is, it looks for and expects to find really existing unities having their own intrinsic natures that govern their behavior and interactions with things. Each being can be distinguished from and related to other things, which also have their own essence and unity. The experience of chaos is invariably experienced as a challenge, as something to make sense of, and that "making sense of" is the discernment of the essence and the unity of the being in question.

Good: Fitting into the order of things.   "'Good' expresses the correspondence of being to the appetitive power" of the rational soul.[43] Although Aquinas makes clear in other texts (such as *De Veritate* q. 22 and *Summa Theologiae* Ia, q. 5) good is intrinsic to the thing itself, rooted in its form, this text has been frequently misunderstood to mean that good consists in what someone wants.[44] The "correspondence to" the appetitive power is not necessarily a straightforward desire. Thomas's point is that every being

43. "Convenientiam ergo entis ad appetitum exprimit hoc nomen bonum." Aquinas, *De Veritate* q. 1, a. 1 Reply.

44. See, for example, John Crosby, "Are Being and Good Really Convertible?" *The New Scholasticism* 57, no. 4 (Autumn 1983), and Douglas Flippen, "On Two Meanings of Good and the Foundations of Ethics in Aristotle and St. Thomas," *Proceedings of the American Catholic Philosophical Association* 57 (1984).

stands in relation to the appetitive power, that by which we value. We have traced the relationship of values, especially governing values, with behavior. In principle, any situation (Z) can relate to a value, and therefore the components of that situation stand in relation to that value. Furthermore, this correspondence need not be to an actual desire, for it can pertain to a possible or conceivable desire. Nothing is value neutral. The person, as a rational being, encounters the world alert to the values—the goods—that he will find there. The rational mind recognizes how things impact upon others to enhance or destroy them, to serve their growth or functioning, or to hinder them. The idea of a thing is that by which one can determine its corresponding appropriate goods and evils.

In contemporary thought, both philosophical and scientific, such a conception is not at all so clear as it was to Aquinas and his contemporaries. As we have already noted, the concept *good*, along with the related conceptions of end and purpose, has been excluded from scientific thought. *Good*, so regarded, would be a predicate that arises simply from human intentionality, from our peculiar form of consciousness, and not from things as they are in themselves. The contemporary theorist would, in a way, agree with Aquinas's analysis in *De veritate*, but in doing so would deny any ontological status to the good that is predicated. One might object that if *good* expresses the *convenientia* between a being and the appetite, this proves nothing about the being itself but only about the subjective appetite. Underlying this objection is the notion that we have no warrant to affirm human subjectivity's direct connection with or relationship to the objective realm. That we cannot help thinking of things as good or bad does not mean that there is an order of good and evil in nature.

In fact, this objection enables us to understand Thomas's point more sharply, for his analysis does not reduce simply to human subjective desires or quirks of human subjectivity. There is no doubt that to his premodern mindset there was no reason to question the reality and validity of the conception *good*. But this does not mean that the medieval conception was naive. Aquinas is seeking the predicates that express one being's order to another. Insofar as it is different from or over against another it is *aliquid*. In what sense does it agree accord with another? Thomas's answer is that such an agreement cannot be expressed unless there is some being that agrees with other beings (*et hoc quidem non potest esse nisi accipiatur aliquid quod natum sit convenire cum omni ente*), and this being is the soul, which is, in a way, all things (*autem est anima, quae quodammodo est omnia*).[45] What we may note here is that Thomas gives to the moderns their objection. The agreement—*convenientia*—which constitutes goodness is not to be found simply in beings as they stand in relation to each other as beings. The good is found in relation to the human appetite (which for Aquinas includes the will as well as the sense urges) because the soul is "in a way, all things." The human being's rational appetite, therefore, is not simply a kind of subjective urge but rather an orientation toward goods that inanimate being cannot recognize. This same point is reflected in the Fifth Way and in related discussions of the end-directedness of things in nature, where he notes that things without intelligence are directed to their ends by another, as the arrow is directed by the archer.[46] For Aquinas the evidence that things act for an end is evidenced by their acting always or for the most part in the same way. But the operation of a thing comes from its form. Therefore the form of the thing is the foundation of its goodness.[47] As concerns our present study, the point of all this is that to recognize the thing as formed, that is, as having a nature, is to recognize it as having a good. Unless writing formally, the most disciplined scientist will speak of the "purpose" of a biological adaptation, of what is "wrong" with the behavior of the object of the experiment, and so on. Aquinas's points are, first, that the human intellect is capable of recognizing an order that another intelligence has established and, second, that the human appetite is therefore capable of desiring what is good appropriate to the kind of being a thing is.

This notion of *good* turns out, in fact, to be one of the most powerful factors in the formation of ideas. If a thing is good because it is ordered to something as its perfection or fulfillment, then to determine the good of a thing is to go a long way toward understanding it, toward grasping the idea of that thing. In virtue of the conception of *good* we can ask whether something is missing from an account or a conception. We can project additional relationships that things governed by an idea might enter into. The notion of good renders the human intellect particularly fertile.

45. Aquinas, *De Veritate*, q. 1, a. 1, corpus of the article.
46. Aquinas, *Summa Theologiae*, Ia q. 2, a. 3; q. 59, a. 3; q. 103, a. 1 and 8; IIa-IIae, q. 90, a. 3, etc.; *De Veritate* q. 22, a. 1.
47. Aquinas, *Summa Theologiae*, Ia q. 5, a. 5; Aquinas, *De Veritate* q. 21, a. 6.

True: the understandability of being.   C. S. Peirce's first rule of reason was "Do not block the way of inquiry."[48] The obstacles Peirce finds to the way of inquiry are those that philosophers and other scholars erect, saying that this cannot be known or that cannot be explained. Peirce notes that science invariably proves them wrong who insist that something cannot be known or that something that is known is known perfectly. Indeed, the practice of science depends on the confidence that inquiry can gain understanding of things, that everything real can be understood and everything known can be understood more thoroughly. Truth is the correspondence of the understanding with the thing; it is the intellectual grasp of the thing's essence in relation to other things. Whatever is real can, therefore, be known through ideas.

As with the good, the notion of the true is fertile for the discovery and development of ideas. If the intellect is "in a way, all things," then its structure and the relationships among its notions can be expected to reflect things and how they really are. If the human mind is adapted to the reality of things, then we can expect it to be insightful. Indeed, Peirce himself marveled at the human ability to guess right about things, to come up with fruitful hypotheses. "And in regard to any preference for one kind of theory over another, it is well to remember that every single truth of science is due to the affinity of the human soul to the soul of the universe, imperfect as that affinity no doubt is."[49] What we know from the history of science and thought in general is that this is borne out. Logical principles suggest (but do not establish) metaphysical truths. Mathematical patterns suggest physical structures. Although anthropomorphism may sometimes be misleading, an anthropomorphic view of reality—properly corrected by experience and rigorous analysis—proves fruitful.

Ideas and the structure of the thinking mind

These transcendental predicates of being reveal the fundamental structure of human ideas. These transcendental predicates are abstract, general in the extreme, for they apply to everything that can be said, in any sense

---

48. Peirce, "Notes on Scientific Philosophy," in *Collected Papers*, 1.135.
49. Peirce, *Collected Papers*, 5.47. See also 1.316, 2.750, and especially 5.173–174.

whatever, to be. From these transcendental predicates we cannot directly deduce further, more specific predicates. From *good* we cannot immediately infer "helpful for me" or "pleasing to God," nor can we derive from *thing* (*res*) the essence of this thing here before us. Indeed, it may not really have an essence of its own. (The mirage lacks the essence of an oasis and has the essence of an illusion, in common with the apparent pools of water on a hot highway.) The specific predicates that apply can be determined only through the various ways we have of investigating things. The very generality of the transcendental predicates, however, indicates the breadth of the human intellectual scope. Perception is limited to the perceptible, to those properties of things that can affect the senses. Work can affect only material entities, for to work is precisely to interact with the material world. The intellect is not so limited, however, for the transcendental predicates of being do not specify materiality. That a thing has an essence means that it has a "whatness," a "what-it-is," but not necessarily that it has a physical nature. The goodness of a thing does not necessarily consist in its physically interacting with the human subject in a favorable way, and the truth of it does not necessarily reduce to its physical relationship with human perception or brain states. In short, by its ideal structure, the human mind is, in principle, open to understanding not only the material and perceptible realms, but the immaterial as well, if such exist. It is this scope that allows the imaginative creation of alternate realities, whether Middle Earth, the Elysian Fields, or the faraway galaxy of *Star Wars*. More significant, however, is that the human intellect can investigate the nature of nature's laws and the possibility that they are authored and administered by nonmaterial entities. Furthermore, because ideas structure not only human symbolic representations (in the form of myths, philosophical speculations, and religious statements) but also human habits, the human person can structure his life according to nonmaterial principles, that is, according to values whose realization is to be outside the physical realm.

THE SOUL: REAL AND IMMATERIAL

We are now in position to show that the soul is real and immaterial. By this I mean that the soul is not simply a kind of useful fiction or a term we use to express that the body behaves in certain ways. I argue that the soul is something and that it is—must be—immaterial. The argument proceeds as follows:

(1) *Something material is rational.*   Specifically, human beings are rational. I could argue that it is indeed the human being as a whole which is rational, that we are rational to the tips of our fingers, but that is not necessary here. Even if someone were to locate our rationality in a part of the body, such as the brain, that would be a material thing. What we have established by means of argument and examples is that these material things—human beings—are capable of acting according to principles of meaning and inference, which is to say rationally. In fact, all their acts are imbued with rationality. Human beings act according to their understanding of the truth of things.

(2) *Reason does not reduce to a mechanical operation.*   A mechanical operation is one that flows from the physical natures of the interacting entities and is determined by them. The mechanical operation is essentially dyadic or—more properly—the result of dyadic interactions, determined by the essence of the thing (or its components) and of the environment with which it interacts. To the extent that the material interaction is intelligible, it is so according to unchanging (or *perhaps* very slowly changing) laws of nature. The material interaction is one of effort and resistance and is governed only by the natures of things making the effort and resisting.

If to be material is to interact, the relationship of truth is not a material one. The sign represents its object in virtue not of any physical interaction but of an interpretive relationship, which is to say that the sign represents because of an interpretive rule or principle used by the mind to understand the sign. Absent this interpretive principle, the sign does not represent. Therefore the relationship of representation is not purely material. Consequently, if the sign truly represents its object, this relationship of truth is not material. Indeed we may even say that truth is less material than is signification, for a sign may signify in virtue of a resemblance (for instance, a portrait) or a causal connection (such as a tire pressure gauge). The proper subject of truth, however, is not the representative symbol (such as the proposition) as such, but the mind or intellect of the person who holds it to be true. This mind functions in relation to the truth according to principles of logic. That is to say, the thinking mind evaluates (and sometimes corrects) its creation and use of signs according to the laws governing significance. This is the point of the extended discussion of the practical syllogism and the practical dialectic.

(3) Therefore the reasoning being cannot be purely mechanical.   If the human being can reform itself by developing its own habits on the basis of values held to be truly good, then we must ask on what basis it is able to do this. Materialism holds that this can be the result of physical processes. Stephen Weinberg, for example, writes: "In principle, no obstacle stands in the way of explaining the behavior of other people in terms of neurology and physiology and, ultimately, in terms of physics and history. When we have succeeded in this endeavor, we should find that part of the explanation is a program of neural activity that we will recognize as corresponding to our own consciousness."[50] There is such an obstacle, however. Insofar as it is physical, an entity is incapable of developing a new form according to a new idea and therefore of forming new habits. What we have shown is that the human person can adopt new hypotheses and in doing so develop new ideas. By hypothetical reasoning the person is able to posit that a thing exists and that it conforms to a particular idea. Of the three fundamental forms of reasoning, hypothesis is that which has no physical counterpart. Hypothesis has the character of a leap, an intellectual connection of what was previously unconnected. The mechanical process cannot accomplish this logical operation.

Further, the reasoning person can reform his mind by adopting ideas, in order to be able habitually to grasp some hitherto unknown aspect of reality. In this way, the intellect is creative, enabling the human being to change the order of nature itself: Descendants of a primordial primate, we routinely fly. Our civilizations were born in the valleys of great rivers, and now underground rivers of our own creation carry waste from our cities. From understanding the mysteries of lightning and lodestone we have penetrated into the exotic secrets of the atom and its constituents. Impressive

50. Stephen Weinberg, "Life in the Universe," 47.

as these achievements are, even more impressive—and this is the essential point here—is the freedom of intellect that has given rise to the conceptions underlying these discoveries and inventions. What is "obvious" to us now in the twenty-first century is so because our minds and world have been formed by our intellectual forebears.

What guides this development is not a mechanical or physical law, but the inclination of the mind to truth and the desire for good. The hypothesis is the adoption of an idea by which experience may be unified in some respect so as to be understood and its value to be disclosed. In virtue of its capacity to predicate of any being an essence, unity, and relationship with other things, and to regard it as conceivably an object of desire and knowledge, the human intellect can grasp whatever has been, is, or might in some sense be real. The human intellect so surpasses the physical order that it can know that order and even conceive of a different one.

(4) An immaterial principle is needed. To account for this ability human beings have to behave rationally, it is necessary to posit an immaterial principle. A strictly materialist account of human rationality falls into incoherence. Artificial intelligence researchers may seek to mimic some aspects of human reasoning by complex mechanisms, but such mechanical mimicry does not answer the question of the roots of our rationality. In the first place, the logic of hypothesis (in Peirce's terms, abduction) defies mechanical reproduction. Researchers speak hopefully of parallel processing, but this, in itself, is insufficient to account for the development of new ideas. What the human thinker does in coming up with ideas is not to survey vast numbers of facts, checking and cross-checking for correlations. The process is much simpler. While the truly creative mind has a great deal of knowledge and experience, the moment of creative insight is precisely that—an insight, a moment of simple understanding. Further, this moment is not one of having successfully summarized the data in a new way, but rather of having grasped a new relationship among things formerly not seen to be related, in order to understand something better. Indeed, the step *after* gaining such an insight is to check to see if it corresponds with some of the known facts. Hypothetical insight is simply not a mechanical process. It is not adequate, therefore, to hold that the mind is nothing more than the body (or its brain) in motion.

The second characteristic modern approach (after materialism) is dualism. The classical representative of this, of course, is Descartes, who was certain that he was "A thing that thinks. What is that? A thing that doubts, understands, affirms, denies, wills, refuses, and that also imagines and senses."[51] This thinking thing is thus a center of consciousness, and according to Descartes it was completely distinct from and independent of the body. Descartes wanted to defend the distinction of the soul from the body and show that the former is immortal. His contemporary heirs have retained the notion of the center of consciousness independent of the body, while denying it the ontological status Descartes sought for it. The contemporary account locates feelings, intentions, reasons, desires, thoughts, and arguments in the conscious self, that locus of the colorful inner life with its illusions of freedom and self-governance, but it denies this self any real influence over the behavior of the human organism.[52] This is precisely the point. What we need to explain is not how we have thoughts (or mental events) but how we behave rationally. The dualist position suffers the serious difficulty that it thoroughly severs thought from action. But many important kinds of behavior deliberately and directly express thought. Further, as we have seen, all our acts express beliefs. The conscious self as the center of reason disconnected from the physical is an irrelevant self.

Therefore we must posit that the human being as a whole is formed by an immaterial principle by which he is oriented toward and adapted to the spiritual, which is to say towards the good and the true. This is not a mechanical principle, as we have shown, but an intellectual one. I say that it is a principle in virtue of which the human being is *formed,* because, as we have seen, the human person's habits are fundamentally rational, developing according to the laws of inference. Even when being irrational, there is rational method to the apparently irrational madness. Although this principle may be separable insofar as it can survive the death of the person (as we shall show below), it does not exist as a separate thing inside or somehow associated with the body. It is the rational principle, that by which the person can behave rationally, and it is that which is capable of forming or

51. Descartes, *Meditations on First Philosophy,* Meditation Two, p. 20.
52. See Searle, *Minds, Brains, and Science,* especially chap.6, "Freedom of the Will."

adopting ideas by which the mind can know any other real thing and by which the body can adapt to it.

We call this principle the soul.

THE SOUL'S MODE OF BEING

Thomas Aquinas begins his *Disputed Question on the Soul* with the question, "whether the human soul can be both a form and 'this something.'"[53] Following Aristotle, Aquinas understands the *form* to be the principle in virtue of which a substance is the kind of thing it is, and therefore the soul is that in virtue of which the human being is human, or "rational animal." He then goes on to ask whether this form can be a *this something* (*hoc aliquid*). This is a tricky phrase, for one is tempted to interpret 'this something' to refer to a particular substance, which would entail that the human being is a composite of two distinct substances, that is, not a true unity. We recall, however, that Aquinas introduces this Latin term, *aliquid*, as one of the transcendental predicates of being. Any being whatever—a cat, the blue of Frank Sinatra's eyes, democracy in Asia, quantum mechanics—is not only one and a good and true, but also something, *aliquid*, by which we mean that it can be distinguished from other things. Thus, by referring to the soul as *this something* Aquinas intends that it can be distinguished from and considered in relation to the body and the human being as a whole, while admitting that "properly speaking, 'this something' is said of the individual in the genus of substance."[54] This distinction, however, is not merely conceptual. Aquinas argues that because the soul has its own operation—the power to abstract from material conditions—it is independent of any bodily substance and capable of subsisting separately from the body, even though it is not itself a complete substance.

We now face the same question. Having established that the human person is distinguished from other physical beings by his rationality, we concluded that he has a rational principle, which we may call the soul. We further concluded that this soul is, in a fundamental way, nonmaterial, for it

---

53. Aquinas, *Quaestio disputata de anima*, a. 1.
54. Aquinas, *Quaestio disputata de anima*, a. 1, corpus.

forms the behavior of the human being in a way that cannot be reduced to any physical principle. Every action that a human being performs is physical, but the habits by which human actions are regulated are themselves governed by an immaterial principle according to the laws of reason. We must now inquire about the status of this rational principle—this *hoc aliquid* that is not a substance.

Limited dominion over and dependence on matter

The soul has a kind of dominion over matter in that it is the principle of a material being's behavior. Yet, as we have noted, that dominion is limited. The dynamisms of nature—the appetites and operations of the body's systems—will insist on having their way. Furthermore, the soul does not exist in the world as a causal agent, as an existing being with a behavior of its own by which it interacts with other things. The only way that the soul acts in the world is as the rational principle of the body. Further, only the body can be said to act physically. As we have reiterated frequently, the soul is not inside the body moving it or causally pushing it to act. The body, like any material thing, behaves according to the principles of its nature. The difference of the human body is that these principles are not given to it in the same way as are those of other material things. The human being forms his own principles of action according to rational criteria. The soul is therefore not simply a principle of behavior, but rather a *principle of principles of behavior.* In virtue of this soul, the human being is a different kind of entity than any other physical being that we know of. No other physical being is rationally governed in the way that the human being is.

The power by which the soul operates is spiritual, which is to say that it is ideal. The soul has the power to discern meanings of things and bring meanings into unity. In the first place it brings into unity the behaviors of the body according to a meaning that it determines or discerns. The human being brings his own person into unity with other human beings through the sharing of good with them. Then, as the person engages the world bodily, he brings things in the world into unity in various sorts of ways through his artistry. The human being behaves rationally according to the soul's understandings of things and love for its ideals. This is why perception and basic human responses are rational, serving the needs of the rational being and not functioning automatically or mechanically. Although the systems of the body have biological dynamisms of their own and therefore can be said to have their own agendas, these are not entirely independent of rational governance, as we have seen. Indeed the ongoing project of every human life is to gain control over one's body and surroundings in such a way that they serve one's ideals of life.

Since every act that a human being performs is a bodily act—the soul has no existence of its own in the world—the soul without its body is unable to act. A direct consequence of this is that the soul without its body cannot be conscious, since, as we have seen, consciousness is nothing but the application of knowledge to the act. If the possibility of acting is removed, then evidently so is consciousness. This point is especially important to philosophical psychology, for it means that we simply cannot identify the soul and consciousness. Consciousness itself is not direct experience of the spiritual in human nature, nor does it provide privileged access to one's own soul. The soul is not an object of consciousness, nor is consciousness an immediate manifestation of the soul. Consciousness is as much as consequence of our being bodily beings as of our spiritual nature. To identify the soul with consciousness or as the seat of consciousness is wrong and will invariably lead to confusion.

Independence from matter

The previous section notwithstanding, the soul also enjoys a certain independence from matter, as is clear from the freedom the will enjoys in relation to physical determinants. The scope of human reason is universal, extending in principle over the entire physical universe and every kind of being in it. The human soul is capable of recognizing every kind of being and giving an account (more or less accurately) of its principles. In doing so, the soul discerns and identifies (perhaps provisionally and not infallibly) principles by which the universe is governed. It identifies being *as being* as a subject of inquiry. Whether or not one acknowledges the existence of a Creator or Author of the universe, he must recognize that the question has come up. The human intellect can reasonably ask about the reality of general characters of reality and of an author of them. In other words, the human soul can raise questions about immaterial things and attempt to answer them.

In its work of governance of the person, the soul impresses its ideas on the body and life of the person. The human intelligence and life are formed by what the soul has grasped intellectually. The idea has real being in the life, and therefore in the soul, of one who adopts it. The pianist becomes musical and the scientist in a way becomes physical or chemical. This adoption of the idea is reflected in the affinity one has for the object to which that form is naturally fitted. This idea, which is at the foundation of beauty, thus abides as an ongoing inspiration to the person in his activity. In this respect, work is a kind of outgrowth of contemplation. (We may remark that when it ceases to be such, one typically experiences "burnout," dryness, or loss of direction. The work becomes drudgery.) More important, it is the basis of leisurely creativity, that ability one has who knows a thing well to turn it over in his mind and by doing so to come to know and appreciate it more thoroughly—what Peirce calls "Musement."[55]

Soul as this something

On the principle that the operation of a thing depends on and flows from its nature, Aquinas argues that since the soul has an immaterial operation of its own, it must subsist immaterially, at least in its intellectual part.[56] We have seen that the human intellect can indeed perform operations that cannot be fully accounted for by physical principles. The principle of human reason is immaterial. In other words, it is impossible to hold that this rational principle, that in virtue of which the human person is capable of acting rationally, is nothing more than an aspect or manifestation of the brain's physical structure. Furthermore, the rationality of human nature is evidenced outside the brain; the responses of the senses and the behavior of the organs admit of governance by human reason. They serve reason. This rational principle, which acts most evidently and in perhaps a privileged way through the brain, forms the behavior of the entire body, the entire life of the person. Therefore it is independent of the body.

The spirit's independence of the body is evident even in those cases

---

55. Peirce, "A Neglected Argument for the Reality of God," in *Collected Papers,* 6.452 ff.

56. Aquinas, *Summa Theologiae* Ia, q. 75, a. 2; Aquinas, *In De Anima,* III, §743; Aquinas, *Quaestio disputata de anima,* a. 1.

where the body is incapable of expressing rationality in a full, satisfactory, mature way. We have already discussed the rationality of infant behavior in some detail. Although one cannot say that infants think explicitly—that is, verbally—they most certainly do manifest rational operations, learning language, imitating and improvising, and generalizing about their environment. This is why adults, especially the mother, talk to them in a tone of voice that seems particularly suited to infantile comprehension. The infant enjoys peek-a-boo, a game based on spatial and temporal continuity. The game over, his parents put him to bed and watch the conjurer on television making people and things disappear. The game is the same, albeit more sophisticated. And it turns on the rational intellect's need to make sense of space and time. Although one might find close similarities between the behavior of human infants and that of other animals, especially the apes, the peculiar development of the human infant manifests the rationality at work from the earliest days. So I deny that a specifically human consciousness does not appear until later to differentiate the human infant from the non-human. Such consciousness is secondary, in any case. Rather, in the human we see a progressive unfolding of rationality already present, as the infant learns from others and from his own efforts to understand a rapidly growing experiential environment by means of his developing body. As this rationality develops, so does his self-consciousness. The soul, inasmuch as it is spirit, guides and forms the development of the imma-ture human being. Comparably, even when the human person is deprived of the ability to think clearly and "behave rationally," whether by injury or illness (such as Alzheimer's syndrome), his fundamental rationality is not lost. This is evident from the fact that (except in the most extreme cases)[57] such persons can continue to use language, remember facts and principles, make needs known, and function in at least some tasks. Memory and the powers of cogitation, requiring as they do developed neural connections in the brain, can be impaired by damage to the brain, and this hinders much rational activity from reaching full expression. The human being, even when the body falls short of full mature functioning, is rational. Its

---

57. By "most extreme" I mean catastrophic injury that so damages the brain and nervous system that only vegetative and the most limited motor functions remain. In such circum-stances, the victim's fundamental rationality can hardly be in evidence.

rational principle remains, even when the body and its systems are damaged and its powers compromised.

The fundamental reason we can say that the human soul is a *this something*, a reality, is that to understand human being and behavior requires their governance by a nonmaterial principle, a principle that transcends the physical aspects of human being and can coordinate these according to the idea which the spirit alone is able to discern, identify, and incorporate in behavior. In other words, the human being, which is undeniably material, is just as undeniably spiritual. We are material spirits. If the body is the material part of us, the soul is the spiritual.

Epilogue

God, the Person, and the Afterlife

What happens to the soul when a person dies? At the end of this very theoretical book, we address the very real and concrete question of our own destiny and hope. The philosophical discussion, abstruse though it may be, addresses a matter of intense personal concern to every human being. Early human beings, dwelling in the caves of France, ceremonially buried their dead. Religions and myths, folkways, and even legal practices in various ways reflect the belief that one who has died continues in some way to live on, whether in the realm of the ancestors, in Hades among the shades, or in heaven with God. In this section, we turn our attention to the question of personal survival after death. What (if anything) survives and how? If the soul, which is a spiritual principle, survives the death of the body, what manner of existence can it have? For a purely physical being, there is no such question, for the thing's essence—at least as particularized in that thing—is gone. When the tree falls, its internal organizing principles cease to exist. Its leaves stop growing and it begins to decay. The human being, however, has a soul that enjoys a certain superiority to or transcendence with regard to the material. It is not unreasonable to grant that this soul can survive the dissolution of the body. Given the understanding developed here, as well as the results of the various sciences, can such a survival be construed as a personal survival? If the soul continues to persist after death, does this mean the person lives on?

If the soul is the spiritual principle of the body, it is also true that without the body the soul is helpless. Strictly speaking it seems not to exist, for it is only insofar as a thing can interact with other things that we say it exists. Two facts are clear: First, such a soul has no existence in the realm of material things. If some of the dead should be able to appear as ghosts, it is because their souls stand in a new relationship to matter, not because the souls themselves can appear. The soul is not of itself capable of perception and interaction with other things. Second, as incapable of action in the world, the soul cannot be conscious. Consciousness is a state of the embodied person in action, not of the soul by itself. Therefore we must reject the popular images of an ethereal self departing the body and translating to another realm where it will perceive the shades of its deceased friends and relatives. On this we may remark that whatever account science may give of near-death experiences, it cannot be that the soul itself floats out of the body.

THE SOUL AND GOD

The book of Genesis tells us that God created human beings in his own image (Genesis 1:26 RSV), an image that Christian philosophers and theologians have located in the rational soul. This notion that the human soul reflects something of the divine is not, however, peculiar to biblical religion. Plato saw the human soul as having a spark of the divine.[1] Aristotle characterized the highest form of life as the contemplative because it is the most like the life of the god.[2] Prometheus was punished by Zeus, not simply for giving fire to the men, but for providing them with the sciences and arts to elevate themselves above animal life.[3] The very fact that the human person transcends the physical order, able to represent the world as a whole and know the things in it, capable of judging any existing thing to be good or bad, suggests the existence of a God. That the world is so intricately ordered is marvelous, but perhaps more amazing is that the human mind can come to know that order, that our intelligence is in harmony with the unifying principles of the cosmos. That we—frail, subject to pain,

---

1. Plato, *Phaedo* 80 a–b.
2. Aristotle, *Nicomachean Ethics* X, vii, especially 1177b 30.
3. At least according to Aeschylus in *Prometheus Bound.*

and mortal—can survey the world and all within it suggests that there is an Author, a Designer who, like us, stands outside that order, but, unlike us, enjoys full power to realize that order. These reflections do not so much constitute an argument for God's existence, as they offer an account of the origins of the idea, of the hypothesis that a Supreme Being exists. The human experience of the world as a realm of truth and goodness, even if also infected with evil and falsity, has invariably led humans to belief in some kind of supreme being.

As Author of the world and its order, whether as Creator, Ruler, or Demiurge, God is spirit, that is, an intelligent and purposeful immaterial being capable of carrying out his plans. Indeed, we get our idea of spirit, not so much from looking at ourselves as by reflecting on what a divine being must be like. Because we have a kind of share of the divine perspective, human persons are themselves spiritual. This perspective has religious significance, of course, but that is not the significance I am referring to here. Rather I am talking about the inevitable confrontation of every reflective person with the fact that the universe reveals itself to us as the product of mind, of intelligence. So it is we hear physicists speak of their science as knowing the "mind of God."[4] Indeed, if the knowledge we have is real, it is founded on the possibility that the ideas which form human thinking, the ideas that we discover as we reflect on the world and our lives in it, can accurately reflect the ideas by which nature itself is formed. That is, our ideas intend so to order our understanding as to duplicate logically and in action the principles by which things in the world are structured and exist, the principles underlying their regular behavior. If these ideas can really do this, then they reflect what can only be described as the effects of mind in the order of the world, in its structure and existence.

The normal and usual way that we develop our ideas is in interaction with others. Children neglected by their parents grow stunted intellectually, while those whose parents converse with them advance. John Henry Newman suggests that a decisive element of higher education—perhaps more important than professorial lectures and books—is the interaction of the students among themselves.[5] Our explorations of the world are guided

4. See Paul Davies, *God and the New Physics* (New York: Simon & Schuster, 1983), 229.
5. John Henry Newman, *The Idea of a University,* Discourse VI, §9, 111.

by others until we are able to undertake them on our own, and even then we generally work best with others. When we turn to nature and reflect on her principles, however, we find that she responds in a way not unlike that of our friends, colleagues, and teachers. Nature poses us problems and reveals possible approaches to their solution. To put it more directly, nature is present to us as a language representing the Mind of its Author. We relate personally to our world and in doing so—even if some may resist the implications of this notion—we relate to the mind that nature represents. As reasoning, acting persons, therefore, we experience ourselves as beings in the image of God. This experience does not, to be sure, of itself convey all that is implied by Genesis 1:26. It does, however, suggest that human beings are by nature in relationship to God.

LIGHT AND THE POWERS OF THE SOUL

Lurking beneath the surface of the discussion in chapters 4 and 6 of this work is the question: Where do the ideas come from? How does the soul (or intellect) generate or discern the ideas by which it operates? Whence the soul's spiritual power? This is the central mystery of human intelligence. We can explain deduction in terms of class membership and the scope of general predicates, and we can explain induction by the force of repetition, of association, and the "school of hard knocks." Students can be trained to memorize and apply rules, but not—strictly speaking—how to recognize or come up with new ideas. There is no mechanism similar to memorization, repetition, or diagramming that will enable one forthwith to form an hypothesis, which is to identify and apply an idea. Every technique falls short, whether in teaching or in thinking for oneself. To recognize a new idea, one should know as much as possible, not only about the subject at hand, but about others, too. One can brainstorm, imagine permutations, and fantasize. One can run experiments and work out different scenarios. None of these techniques, however, will take one the final step to the idea. Indeed, it is a common enough experience that what proves intractable one day may suddenly become clear the next or after the weekend. Further, what is immediately clear to one person may be grasped only with difficulty by someone else equally intelligent. When asked, 'how did you come up with that?' one can only answer in terms of having come finally to see it, that at a certain point, something occurred and the subject became clear.

It is precisely to answer this question that Aquinas appeals to the notion of illumination by the divine intellect, arguing that since "the human soul is called intellectual by reason of a participation in intellectual power... there must needs be some higher intellect, by which the soul is helped to understand." "Therefore," he continues, "in the soul is some power derived from a higher intellect, whereby it is able to illumine the phantasms. *And we know this by experience, since we perceive that we abstract universal forms from their particular conditions.*"[6] He then cites Aristotle, who calls this participation a kind of light, and Plato's metaphor of the sun from Book VII of *The Republic*. Only after citing these philosophical authorities does he appeal to the teaching of the Christian faith, identifying that higher intellect with that of the Creator. The argument is philosophical, not theological. How the human intellect grasps new ideas, where it comes up with them appears mysterious, because ideas—unlike the symbols and models by which we represent them—are not perceptible. The mind is not directly aware of its ideas or of their origins. (So, there comes occasionally that happy moment when the teacher can congratulate the student for having discovered on his own some important idea, which the teacher then identifies by its right name.) Ideas come, but not *directly* as the result of our efforts. They cannot come from a material source; their origin must be spiritual. Deliberately using the Platonic metaphor, Aquinas speaks of a "participation" in a higher intelligence. To account for this relationship we must use metaphors, because direct description with our concepts, rooted as they are in the material and perceptual, is not possible. Our experience with ideas is always mediated by the physical and perceptual. Let us note, too, that Aquinas does not immediately identify that higher intellect as God's. In principle, it could be some other pure intelligence, that is, intelligent spirit.

This notion of illumination by a higher intellect intends to provide an account for what is otherwise inexplicable, namely, that we can grasp ideas. Recall that Aquinas says that we can know "by experience" that the

6. Aquinas, *Summa Theologiae*, Ia, q. 79, a. 4. [Emphasis added.]

soul is derived from a higher intellect, because we have the power to abstract forms (or species) from phantasms. While this notion of illumination by higher intellect may seem mysterious, it is not entirely without parallel to other experiences. Indeed, we all can identify kinds of higher intellect in our ordinary experience. I refer to the cultural and intellectual milieus that we find ourselves in, as well as to mentoring and other educational relationships. A particular milieu—be it a research center, a political party, a nation, or a clan—is formed by specific, characteristic ideas in terms of which its members interpret the reality they move within. The guiding ideas are, as it were, available and "ready to hand" for those in the milieu, and the neophyte picks them up by living them. This is most evident in advanced educational situations, where the student learns not just new facts and techniques but also that scientific community's way of approaching the subject matter, its criteria for identifying pertinent issues, and its values. Similarly, when a great artist breaks new ground, his successors develop his ideas, taking the art in a new direction. In such ways, therefore, we do experience a kind of illumination, whether by the "great mind" of a master or by the collective ideas and values of our milieu. Were such the only possible illumination, however, then no individual could rise above or presume to question what he had received from others. Tradition would not simply be normative (as it usually is and ought to some extent to be), but it would be definitive. One could not transcend his own teachers and heritage. But it is a matter of common experience that individual persons do so transcend what they have received. They do interpret things anew according to ideas that have not been expressed or accepted by others. Such experiences indicate an illumination beyond that from one's culture and social context.

We must ask, however, about the root of this participation in the higher intellect, about its "point of contact" with such an intellect. Aquinas certainly does not want to claim that each human being needs divine grace or revelation just to think scientifically. Further, although he says that we "know by experience" that we so participate in a higher intellect, this is not a direct experience of that higher intellect as such. What does this mean, then, that the thinker participates in the higher intellect? The answer lies precisely in the metaphysical orientation of the human mind. Because the human intellect can conceive of being *qua* being or being in general, its scope is, in a sense, equal to that of the Author of the universe. Alejandro Ribas identifies this with the truth of *common being* (or being as such).[7] This sharing in the higher intellect consists in the human mind's power inquire into and form conceptions concerning reality in any form, that is to say, in its power intellectually to reconstruct reality according to its own principles. If the world is indeed created—as Aquinas believed—by a God who is himself subsistent being and Author of all being, then this participation is the capacity to recognize God's own principles of creation. The human person participates in the higher intelligence in this: He can regard the order he sees about him and speculate, "Were this *my* creation how could I have brought it about that this state of things (that is, that now before me) should obtain? And why would I have done that?"

THE SOUL'S EXPERIENCE POSTMORTEM

This trace of the divine and relationship with a superior intelligence suggests an answer to the question of the status of the separated soul. The soul is never a pure spirit; in its survival after the death, it does not continue on as a kind of unattached reasoning power with no object to think of. During the course of the person's life, the soul is formed by the ideas he understands and the values he lives for, all of which are influenced by the disposition and characteristics of the body, as well as by the various environmental and social factors in one's life. One is formed by what he knows and loves. Through the course of one's life, his soul acquires definition: Mozart's soul must have a musicality to it, where Marie Curie's has a scientific character. Furthermore, the soul must have a kind of experience of this. The natural response to the discovery of an idea is admiration at its beauty and complacency in the contemplation of it. What is noteworthy about this admiration is that after the initial astonishment, the glow of admiration recedes. From astonishment at the elegance of the calculus, one undertakes a rigorous study of mathematics. The admiration of a young man's or woman's beauty leads to a lifelong commitment in marriage. The

7. Alejandro Verdés Ribas, "El desocultamiento de la luz del alma en Santo Tomás," *Studium*, vol. 42, no. 1, (2002), 37.

most important effect of encounter with beauty is not the immediate experience of admiration but the incorporation of the beauty into the form of one's life. The husband and wife get up every morning and tend to their domestic life, the children, and their work. The musician practices her phrasing and the rhythm of her triplets. The scientist sets up his apparatus or runs data through the computer. And every now and then, in the midst of the activities formed by the beautiful ideal, the couple or musician or scientist can step back in a moment of leisure and reflect on what the ideal has meant. (This is why we have scheduled celebrations of anniversaries and birthdays, and why we give awards in the arts and sciences. The beauty of the form of life is not a matter of daily direct experience.) It is reasonable to expect that this fundamental complacency in contemplating some beauty can continue on in the soul, even after separation from the body. Further, if (as seems reasonable) the soul stands in some kind of direct relationship with that superior intelligence by which it was illuminated in life, then this ideal interaction could constitute a kind of experience.

We cannot say that the soul separated from the body is conscious, for it has no body and no interactions with the world. On the other hand, neither can we deny it all awareness, for it is informed by ideas and oriented to its lifetime values, which it continues to value. The natural state of the separated soul thus appears to be rather unsatisfying, not far removed from the mythical image of shades in Hades. At this point, Christian theology can point to Revelation's assurances of an encounter with God and a communion with at least some of those who have predeceased one. Such an afterlife could then constitute a rewarding (or devastating) state for the soul. The account we have developed here can do no more than provide the basis for formulating theological speculations on the afterlife.

CONCLUSION

If we cast off the strictures of mechanistic materialism, we can discover a theory of the human being as an embodied spirit, as a "sign, developing according to the laws of inference," as rational to the tips of his fingers. The basis for our conception of the material is in human experience. That same experience, however, is the basis for the conception of the spiritual, which, along with the material, constitutes a fundamental aspect of our experience. If the material is that in virtue of which the human subject interacts with the environment, the spiritual is that in virtue of which the human relates to reality under its aspects of good and true. The spiritual is as real as the material. The spiritual in human nature is realized in rationality, that is in the human capacity to represent things according to ideas, in symbols which are governed by logical principles. One's rationality is not simply a skill, something acquired as one ages or that can be lost through illness, injury, or old age. It is a fundamentally distinct way of being in the world, irreducible to the laws governing inert matter or nonrational living things. The rational principle governs the body, doing the best it can, as it were, with the biological tools at its disposal. We may also conclude that the spiritual aspect of the human person—what we ordinarily call the soul—does survive the death of the body. The manner of its existence *postmortem* is beyond our experience and therefore beyond our imagining. The philosopher, relying on analysis of the spiritual powers of the human person, is not in a position to say what this existence is like. What the philosopher can affirm is that in this afterlife the soul retains and continues to experience the reality of the ideas that have formed it. It is only by Revelation that we can go beyond this. If the souls of the dead suffer punishment or enjoy rewards, if the just can intercede before the Throne of God, if the deceased share a kind of communion among themselves, we cannot know these on the basis of our experience in this life. Before these questions the philosopher must defer to the prophet and the apostle.

Bibliography

Books

Aquinas, Thomas. *Aristotle's "De Anima" in the version of William of Moerbeke and the Commentary of St. Thomas Aquinas*. Translated by K. Foster, O.P., and S. Humphries, O.P. New Haven: Yale University Press, 1951.

———. *The Disputed Questions on Truth*. Translated by Robert W. Mulligan, S.J. Chicago: Regnery Co., 1952.

———. *Commentary on the "Nicomachean Ethics."* Translated by C. I. Litzinger, O.P. Chicago: Henry Regnery Co., 1964.

———. *Opusculum VIII: Explanatio Dubiorum de Dictis Cujusam Edita*, Quaestio CVIII. In Aquinas, *Opera Omnia*, vol 27. Paris: Bibliopolam Editores, 1875.

———. *Quaestio Disputata de Anima*. In Aquinas, *Quaestiones Disputatae*, vol. II. Edited by P. Bazzi, et al. Editio VIII revisa, Rome: Marietta,1949.

———. *On Evil*. Translated by John A. Oesterle and Jean T. Oesterle. Notre Dame, IN: University of Notre Dame Press, 1995. Latin text accessed at http://www.unav.es/filosofia/alarcon/amicis/qdmo2.html.

———. *Summa Theologiae*. Vol. 1, *The Existence of God*. General Editor, Thomas Gilby. Garden City, NY: Image Books, 1969.

———. *Summa Theologiae*. English translation by Fathers of the English Dominican Province. In *Great Books of the Western World*, vols. 19–20. Chicago, London, Toronto: Encyclopedia Britannica, 1952.

Aristotle. *Metaphysics*. Edited and translated by W. D. Ross. In *Great Books of the Western World*, vol. 8. Chicago, London, Toronto: Encyclopedia Britannica, 1952.

———. *Nicomachean Ethics*. Translated by David Ross. Oxford: Oxford University Press, 1998.

———. *On the Soul*. Translated by J. A. Smith. In *Great Books of the Western World*, vol. 8. Chicago, London, Toronto: Encyclopedia Britannica, 1952.

———. *Physics*. Translated by R. P. Hardie and R. K. Gaye. In *Great Books of the Western World*, vol. 8. Chicago, London, Toronto: Encyclopedia Britannica, 1952.

Armstrong, D. M. *A Materialist Theory of the Mind*. New York: Routledge & Kegan Paul, 1968.

Augustine. *The City of God*. Translated by Marcus Dods. In *Great Books of the Western World*, vol. 18. Chicago, Toronto, London: Encyclopedia Britannica, 1952.

Ayer, Alfred Jules. *Language, Truth, and Logic*. London: Victor Gollancz Ltd., 1938.

Bacon, Francis. *Novum Organum*. In *Great Books of the Western World*, vol. 30. Chicago, London, Toronto: Encyclopedia Britannica, 1952.

Belmans, Theo G. *Le sens objectif de l'agir humain: Pour relire l'amour conjugale de saint Thomas*. Vatican City: Libreria Editrice Vaticana, 1980.

Bergmann, Frithjof. *On Being Free*. Notre Dame, London: University of Notre Dame Press, 1977.

Bernstein, Leonard. *The Joy of Music*. New York: Simon & Schuster, 1959.

Bloom, Floyd E., Arlyne Lazerson, and Laura Hofstadter. *Brain, Mind, and Behavior*. New York: W. H. Freeman & Co., 1985.

Bobik, Joseph. *Aquinas on Being and Essence: A Translation and Interpretation*. Notre Dame, IN: University of Notre Dame Press, 1965.

Bolt, Robert. *A Man for All Seasons*. New York: Vintage Books, 1962.

Bonaventura. *Commentaria in quatuor libros Sententiarum Magistri Petri Lombardi*. Ad Claras Aquas (Quaracchi): Ex Typographia Collegii S. Bonaventurae, 1882–1902.

Braine, David. *The Human Person: Animal and Spirit*. Notre Dame, IN: University of Notre Dame Press, 1992.

Burkert, Walter. *Creation of the Sacred: Tracks of Biology in Early Religions*. Cambridge, London: Harvard University Press, 1996.

Burtt, E. A. *The Metaphysical Foundations of Modern Science*. Garden City: Doubleday, 1954.

Crick, Francis. *The Astonishing Hypothesis: The Scientific Search for the Soul*. New York: Charles Scribner & Sons, 1994.

Cross, Milton, and David Ewen. *Encyclopedia of the Great Composers and Their Music*. Garden City, NY: Doubleday, 1953.

Darwin, Charles. *The Descent of Man*. Edited by Robert M. Hutchins. *Great Books of the Western World*, vol. 49. Chicago: Encyclopedia Britannica, 1952.

Davies, Paul. *God and the New Physics*. New York: Simon & Schuster, 1983.

Dennett, Daniel. *Consciousness Explained*. Boston, Toronto, London: Little, Brown & Co., 1991.

Descartes, René. *Meditations on First Philosophy*. 3rd ed. Translated from the Latin by Donald A. Cress. Indianapolis, Cambridge: Hackett Publishing Company, 1993.

Di Blasi, Fulvio. *God and the Natural Law: A Rereading of Thomas Aquinas*. South Bend, IN: St. Augustine's Press, 2003.

Doyle, Arthur Conan. *The Complete Adventures and Memoirs of Sherlock Holmes*. New York: Bramhall House, 1975.

Edie, James M. *Edmund Husserl's Phenomenology: A Critical Commentary*. Indianapolis-Bloomington: Indiana University Press, 1987.

Edwards, Robert. *Life before Birth: Reflections on the Embryo Debate*. New York: Basic Books, 1989.

Freud, Sigmund. *The Future of an Illusion*. Garden City: Doubleday Anchor, 1964.

Frith, Uta. *Autism: Explaining the Enigma*. Malden, MA: Blackwell, 2003.

Hannay, Alastair. *Human Consciousness*. London, New York: Routledge, 1990.

Hume, David. *An Inquiry Concerning Human Understanding*. Indianapolis, New York: Bobbs Merrill, 1955.

———. *Treatise on Human Nature*. In *Hume's Ethical Writings*, edited by A. MacIntyre. New York: Collier Books, 1965.

Hyde, Janet Shibley and John D. DeLamater. *Understanding Human Sexuality*, 7th Edition. Boston, New York, San Francisco: McGraw Hill, 2000.

James, William. *Pragmatism*. Buffalo: Prometheus Books, 1991.

———. *The "Will to Believe" . . . and Other Essays in Popular Philosophy*. New York: Dover Publications, 1956.

John Paul II [Karol Wojtyła]. *The Theology of the Body: Human Love in the Divine Plan*. Boston: Pauline Books & Media, 1997.

———. *Crossing the Threshold of Hope*. Edited by Vittorio Messori. New York: Alfred Knopf, 1994.

———. *Letter to Artists*. Chicago: Liturgy Training Publications, 1999.

———. *Veritatis splendor*. Encyclical Letter, October 5, 1993. Boston: Pauline Books and Media, 1993.

(Publications as Karol Wojtyła)

———. *Love and Responsibility*. Translated by H. T. Willetts. New York: Farrar, Straus, Giroux, 1981.

———. *Osoba i Czyn*. Cracow, 1969.

———. *The Acting Person*. Dordrecht, Boston, London: D. Riedel, 1979. Wojtyła, *Person und Tat*. Freiburg i. Br., Basel, Vienna: Herder, 1981. (Respectively, the English and German translations of the *Osoba i Czyn*).

———. *Person and Community: Selected Essays*. Translated by Theresa Sandock, O.S.M. New York, San Francisco: Peter Lang, 1993.

Kant, Immanuel. *Critique of Pure Reason*. Translated by Norman Kemp Smith. New York: St. Martin's Press, 1965.

———. *Grounding for the Metaphysics of Morals*. 3rd ed. Translated by James W. Ellington. Indianapolis, Cambridge: Hackett Publishing, 1993.

Kaufmann, Walter. *Existentialism from Dostoevsky to Sartre*. New York: Meridian, 1975.

Kierkegaard, Søren. *Concluding Unscientific Postscript*. Translated by David F. Swenson and Walter Lowrie. Princeton, NJ: Princeton University Press, 1941.

———. *Either/Or*. Translated by David F. Swenson and Lillian Marvin Swenson. Garden City, NY: Anchor Books, 1959.

LeDoux, Joseph. *Synaptic Self: How Our Brains Become Who We Are*. New York: Viking, 2002.

Levy, Sandra M. *Behavior and Cancer Life-style and Psychosocial Factors in the Initiation and Progression of Cancer*. San Francisco: Jossey-Bass, 1985.

Lifton, Robert J. *Thought Reform and the Psychology of Totalism*. New York: W. W. Norton & Co., 1961.

Lincoln, Abraham. *The Collected Works of Abraham Lincoln, (1853–1855)*, vol. 7. Edited by Roy P. Basler.

Locke, John. *An Essay Concerning Human Understanding*. Indianapolis: Hackett, 1996.

MacIntyre, Alasdair. *After Virtue: A Study in Moral Theory.* 2nd ed. Notre Dame, IN: University of Notre Dame, 1984.

Margaris, Angelo. *First Order Mathematical Logic.* Waltham MA,Toronto, London: Ginn & Co., 1967.

Marx, Karl. *The Portable Karl Marx.* Edited and translated by Eugene Kamenka. New York: Penguin Books, 1983.

Marx, Karl. *Thesen über Feuerbach.* In Marx u. Engels, *Werke,* Bd. 3, Berlin, 1978. Available from Marxists' Internet Archive http://www.marxists.org/deutsch/archiv/marx-engels/1845/thesen/thesfeue.htm.

Menand, Louis. *The Metaphysical Club: A Story of Ideas in America.* New York: Farrar, Straus, & Giroux, 2001.

Merleau-Ponty, Maurice. *Phenomenology of Perception.* New York: Humanities Press, 1962.

Mill, John Stuart. *Utilitarianism.* Edited by Robert M. Hutchins. *Great Books of the Western World,* vol. 43. Chicago: Encyclopedia Britannica, 1952.

Newman, John Henry. *The Idea of a University.* Notre Dame: University of Notre Dame Press, 1982.

Patterson, Colin. *Evolution.* Ithaca: Cornell University Press, 1978.

Peirce, Charles Sanders. *Collected Papers.* Vols. 1, 2, 5, and 6. Edited by Charles Hartshore and Paul Weiss. Cambridge: Harvard University Press, 1965.

Penrose, Roger. *The Emperor's New Mind.* New York, Oxford: Oxford University Press, 1989.

Pieper, Josef. *Glück und Kontemplation.* Munich, 1979.

——. "Wahrheit des Dinges — Wahrheit des Seins." Lectures given at the Internationale Akademie für Philosophie, Liechtenstein, Winter 1986.

Plato. *The Collected Dialogues of Plato.* Edited by Edith Hamilton and Huntington Cairns. Princeton: Princeton University Press, 1961.

Popper, Karl. *The Logic of Scientific Discovery.* New York, Evanston: Harper & Row, 1968.

Reimers, Adrian J. *An Analysis of the Concepts of Self-Fulfillment and Self-Realization in the Thought of Karol Wojtyła/John Paul II.* Lewiston, NY: The Mellen Press, 2001.

Rorty, Richard. *Contingency, Irony, and Solidarity.* Cambridge, New York: Cambridge University Press, 1989.

Rousselot, Pierre, S.J. *L'intellectualism de St. Thomas.* Paris: Gabriel Beauchesne, Éditeur, 1936.

Searle, John R. *Minds, Brains, and Science.* Cambridge: Harvard University Press, 1984.

——. *The Rediscovery of the Mind.* Cambridge MA, London: MIT Press, 1992.

Shakespeare, William. *The Oxford Shakespeare.* Edited by W. J. Craig. New York: Oxford University Press.

Shirer, William. *The Rise and Fall of the Third Reich.* New York: Simon & Schuster, 1960.

Singer, Peter. *Practical Ethics.* 2nd ed. New York: Cambridge University Press, 1993.

——. *Rethinking Life and Death: The Collapse of Our Traditional Ethics.* New York: St. Martin's Press, 1994.

Stanford, Craig. *Significant Others: The Ape-Human Continuum and the Quest for Human Nature.* New York: Basic Books, 2001.

Weigel, George. *Witness to Hope: The Biography of Pope John Paul II.* New York: Harper Collins Books, 1999.

Whitman, Walt. *Leaves of Grass: The First (1855) Edition.* Edited by Malcolm Cowley. New York: Penguin Books, 1959.

Wittgenstein, Ludwig. *Tractatus Logico-Philosophicus.* New York: Routledge & Kegan Paul, 1961.

Articles

Arnett, Bill. "Other Planetary Systems?" Students for the Exploration and Development of Space. Accessed from http://seds.lpl.arizona.edu/nineplanets/nineplanets/other.html.

Bower, Bruce. "Consciousness Raising—Part I." *Science News* 142, no. 15 (October 10, 1992): 232.

Burrell, David, C.S.C. "Freedom and Creation in the Abrahamic Tradition." *International Philosophical Quarterly* 40, no. 2 (2000): 161–172.

Chalmers, David. "The Puzzle of Conscious Experience." *Scientific American* (December 1995): 80–86.

Churchland, Patricia Smith. "Can Neurobiology Teach Us Anything about Consciousness?" Presidential Address to the Pacific Division Meeting of the American Philosophical Association. *Proceedings and Addresses of the American Philosophical Association* 67, no. 4 (January 1994): 23–40.

Composta, Dario. "Riflessioni sull'Enciclica Veritatis Splendor." *S. Tommaso Filosofo: Ricerche in occasione dei due centenari accademici.* Vatican City: Libreria Editrice Vaticana,1995, 129–153.

Crick, Francis, and Christof Koch. "The Problem of Consciousness." *Scientific American* (September 1992): 152–159.

Crosby, John. "Are Being and Good Really Convertible?" *The New Scholasticism* 57, no. 4 (Autumn 1983): 465–500.

Damasio, Antonio. "How the Brain Creates the Mind." *Scientific American,* (December 1999): 112–117.

Danielou, Cardinal Jean. "Y a-t-il une nature humaine?" In *De Homine: Studia hodiernae anthropologiae,* vol. 2. Officium Libri Catholici: Rome, 1972, 5–12.

Dawkins, Richard. "God's Utility Function." *Scientific American* (November 1995): 80–85.

Dennett, Daniel. "Consciousness." In *The Oxford Companion to the Mind.* Oxford, New York: Oxford University Press, 1987, 160–164.

Di Blasi, Fulvio. "Practical Syllogism, *Proairesis,* and the Virtues: Interpreting the *Nicomachean Ethics.*" *Nova et Vetera* 2, no. 1 (2004): 21–42.

Flippen, Douglas. "On Two Meanings of Good and the Foundations of Ethics in Aristotle and St. Thomas." *Proceedings of the American Catholic Philosophical Association* 57 (1984): 56–74.

Gilby, Thomas, O.P. "The Five Ways." In Thomas Aquinas, *The Existence of God.* Aquinas, *Summa Theologiae*, vol. 1. General Editor, Thomas Gilby, O.P. Garden City, NY: Image Books, 1969, 267–292.

Gould, Stephen Jay. "The Evolution of Life on Earth." *Scientific American* (Oct. 1994): 84–91.

Horgan, John. "The New Social Darwinists." *Scientific American* (October 1995).

Fieser, James, editor. "The Chinese Room Argument." In *The Internet Encyclopedia of Philosophy*. Bradley Dowden, General Editor. University of Tennessee at Martin. Accessed from http://www.utm.edu/research/iep/c/chineser.htm#source.

Koch, Christof. "Towards the Neuronal Substrate of Visual Consciousness." Koch Laboratory, Division of Biology, California Institute of Technology. Accessed from http://www.klab.caltech.edu/~koch/tuscon-94.html This article is adapted from the chapter by Christof Koch, "Towards the neuronal substrate of visual consciousness," In *Towards a Science of Consciousness: The First Tucson Discussions and Debates*. Edited by S.R. Hameroff, A.W. Kaszniak, and A.C. Scott. Cambridge, MA: MIT Press, 1996.

Lucas, John. "Minds, Machines and Gödel." In *The Modeling of Mind: Computers and Intelligence*, edited by K. Sayre and F. Crosson. New York: Simon & Schuster, 1963, 255–261.

Nagel, Earnest, and James R. Newman. "Goedel's Proof." In *The World of Mathematics*, edited by James R. Newman. New York: Simon & Schuster, 1956, 1668–1695.

O'Callaghan, John P. "The Problem of Language and Mental Representation in Aristotle and St. Thomas." *Review of Metaphysics* 50, no. 3 (March 1997): 499–545.

———. "Abandoning or Modifying a Tradition: Interpreting Aristotle's *De interpretatione*." Unpublished.

Orgel, Leslie E. "The Origin of Life on the Earth." *Scientific American* (October 1994): 77–83.

Posner, Michael I. "Seeing the Mind." *Science* 262 (October 29, 1993): 673–674.

Reimers, Adrian J. "A Definition of Consciousness." *Gregorianum* 76, no. 3 (1995): 535–554.

———. "St. Thomas's Intentions at *De Veritate* 1, 1." *Doctor Communis* 42, no. 2 (Maggio–Agosto 1989): 175–183.

———. "Truth and the Open-Endedness of the Natural Order." In *The Concept of Nature in Science and Theology*, Part I. edited by N. H. Gregersen and W. Parsons. Geneva: Labor et Fides, 1995, 193–199.

Ribas, Alejandro Verdés. "El desocultamiento de la luz del alma en Santo Tomás." *Studium* vol.42, no. 1, 2002, Madrid, 31–73.

Sartre, Jean Paul. "Existentialism Is a Humanism." In Walter Kaufmann, *Existentialism from Dostoevsky to Sartre*. New York, London, Scarborough Ontario: New American Library, 1975, 345–369.

Sen, Amartya. "Human Rights and Asian Values: What Lee Kuan Yew and Le Peng Don't Understand about Asia," http://www.brainsnchips.org/hr/sen.htm. Article extracted from *The New Republic*, 217, no. 2-3 (July 14, 1997).

Sperry, Roger Wolcoll. "Consciousness and Causality." In *The Oxford Companion to the Mind*, edited by R. L. Gregory. Oxford, New York: Oxford University Press, 1987, 164.

Teresa, of Avila. "Bookmark of St. Teresa." In: *Selected Writings of St. Teresa of Avila.* Edited by William J. Doheny, C.S.C. United States of America: William J. Doheny, C.S.C., J.U.D., 1950.

Turing, Alan M. "Can a Machine Think?" *Mind* (1950). Reprinted in *The World of Mathematics,* edited by J. R. Newman. New York: Simon & Schuster, 1956, 2099–2123.

Voll, Daniel. "Soul Searching with Francis Crick." *Omni* 16, no. 5 (February 1994): 46-82.

Weinberg, Stephen. "Life in the Universe." *Scientific American* (October 1994).

Wertheim, Margaret. "After the Double Helix: Unraveling the Mysteries of the State of Being." *New York Times,* April 13, 2004.

Index

abstraction, 43, 191, 193

act, action, xii, 9, 24, 29, 30–35, 37, 46, 59, 64–66, 68–71, 81, 86, 93–97, 100, 102–5, 107, 109–10, 112–13, 115, 122–23, 125–28, 132, 135, 137–38, 140, 148–50, 153–55, 159, 162–83, 185–90, 194, 197, 199–200, 208–10, 212, 215–16, 220–22, 229–30, 233, 236, 247–49, 251, 253, 255–57, 263, 266, 269, 271–73, 278–79

Aeschylus, 278

afterlife, 38, 167, 284–85

aliquid, 261–62, 270–71

animal, xii, xiv, 6–7, 11, 18, 23, 25, 27–9, 26, 49–50, 53, 55, 60, 61, 62, 71, 79, 84–5, 91, 105–7, 109, 118, 125, 128, 131, 136, 140–42, 145, 147–48, 153, 155–59, 165, 168, 179–80, 184, 186, 190–91, 198, 200, 210–16, 225, 227–28, 242–43, 247, 250, 252, 258, 270, 274, 278

Aquinas, Thomas, ix, xv, 10–11, 22–25, 28, 30, 38, 49, 58–59, 66–67, 72–73, 81, 97–98, 133, 137–38, 140, 144, 146, 151, 156, 159–60, 166, 168–69, 172–74, 186, 193, 196, 213, 251, 255, 257–59, 261–63, 270–73, 281–83

Aristotle, ix, 19, 22–25, 29–30, 43, 50, 57–58, 69, 77, 84, 94, 97–99, 115, 124, 142, 144–45, 158, 164, 166, 169–70, 188, 193–94, 196, 210, 213, 217, 220, 250, 257, 261, 270, 278, 281

Armstrong, D. M., 10–11, 52, 143, 159, 227

art, artist, 7, 12, 18, 79–84, 92

Augustine of Hippo, ix, 4, 252

autism, x, 105, 129, 205–6

Ayer, Alfred Jules, 75

Bacon, Francis, 58, 72, 154

beauty, 79–85, 105, 138, 158, 189, 212–13, 215, 225, 249–50, 273, 283–84

behavior, 3, 8–11, 24, 27, 29, 33, 35–37, 43, 45–47, 49–53, 55–62, 64, 66–67, 77–79, 86–87, 91, 93–94, 96, 98, 100–101, 110, 113, 115, 117, 128, 131–32, 135, 140–41, 144, 150, 153–55, 158, 161–69, 171, 173–74, 176, 179–80, 182, 184–88, 198, 200, 202–6, 211, 216–17, 219–20, 222, 226–39, 243, 247–51, 253–54, 257, 261–63, 267, 269, 271, 273–75, 279

being, xiii, xv, 4, 10, 14, 18, 25, 28, 31, 34, 36, 42, 44, 46–49, 58, 62–63, 66, 72, 76, 78–81, 85, 87, 97–98, 100, 104, 118–19, 128, 133, 136–37, 141–42, 145–47, 151–52, 160, 164, 173, 191–92, 208, 210, 213, 218, 220, 225, 237, 242, 245, 252, 255, 258–65, 267–68, 270–73, 277, 279, 282–83, 285

belief, xi–xii, xiv, 7, 42, 52, 75, 92–97, 99, 112

Belmans, Theo, 16

Bergmann, Frithjof, 12

Bernstein, Leonard, 132

Bobik, Joseph, 258

body, xv, 3–4, 10–11, 13–17, 23, 28, 30–33,

The Soul of the Person: A Contemporary Philosophical Psychology was designed and typeset in Minion by Kachergis Book Design of Pittsboro, North Carolina.

Printed in the USA
CPSIA information can be obtained
at www.ICGtesting.com
JSHW020718031223
52717JS00022B/24